MAN DISCOVERS GOD

MAN
DISCOVERS
GOD

By

George

SHERWOOD EDDY

Essay Index Reprint Series

BOOKS FOR LIBRARIES PRESS
FREEPORT, NEW YORK

LIBRARY OF CONGRESS CATALOG CARD NUMBER:

68-24849

PRINTED IN THE UNITED STATES OF AMERICA

CONTENTS

CHRONOLOGICAL TABLE

Hebraic and Hellenic Civilizations

B.C.

Before 1000	Pre-monarchic period. Oral accounts of Abraham and Moses
1000–900	The time of David, Solomon, the Book of the Covenant, Exod. 20:23—23:19
c. 850	The Yahwist history, "J," the first Hebrew historian, who calls God Yahweh, or Jehovah, beginning with the story of creation
c. 750	The Elohist history, "E," a prophetic writer who uses "Elohim" for God, with advanced theological and ethical views
c. 750	Amos, first literary prophet of social righteousness
c. 745–735	Hosea, prophet of the mercy and love of God
738–700	Isaiah and Micah
721	Fall of Northern Kingdom of Israel
621	Deuteronomy published, written by an anonymous mastermind, uniting prophetic and priestly views of ethical monotheism
626–c. 585	Jeremiah prophet of personal religion
605	Defeat of Pharaoh Necho by Nebuchadrezzar at Charchemish
586	Destruction of Jerusalem, and Babylonian captivity
546–539	Deutero-Isaiah, the Prophet of the Exile
539	Capture of Babylon by Cyrus, 538 return of the exiles
c. 460	Malachi
165–164	Daniel

B.C.	GREEK CHRONOLOGY
c. 940–850	Homer. The Iliad and the Odyssey
c. 600–500	Thales, first Greek philosopher, and the Milesian school
582–c. 507	Pythagoras
469–399	Socrates
431–351	Plato
384–322	Aristotle
356–323	Alexander the Great
c. 20 B.C.– c. 50 A.D.	} Philo of Alexandria

THE CHRISTIAN ERA

A.D.	
c. 6 B.C	Birth of Jesus; c. 30 the crucifixion
c. 30–60	The Apostle Paul
70	The Fall of Jerusalem. The Gospel of Mark
c. 80–90	The Gospel of Matthew, Luke and the Acts
c. 110	The Gospel of John
c. 205–270	Plotinus
354–430	St. Augustine
410	Rome pillaged by the Goths; 476 End of the Roman Empire
1182–1226	St. Francis of Assisi
1379–1471	Thomas à Kempis
1483–1546	Martin Luther
1611–1691	Brother Lawrence
1623–1662	Blaise Pascal
1624–1691	George Fox
1628–1688	John Bunyan
1703–1791	John Wesley
1703–1758	Jonathan Edwards
1642–1727	Sir Isaac Newton

1822–1895	Louis Pasteur
1858–1935	Michael Pupin
1828–1910	Count Leo Tolstoy
1856–1906	William Rainey Harper
1858–1915	Booker Washington
1892–	Arthur Compton
1892–	Reinhold Niebuhr
1869–	Mahatma Gandhi
1875–	Albert Schweitzer

PREFACE

T HIS book seemed almost to force itself upon the writer. However inadequate the treatment, he makes no apology for the more than thirty personalities—common men yet great characters all of them—chosen to exemplify the theme, *Man Discovers God*. From many lands and various religions, Hebrews, Hellenists, Europeans, Orientals, mystics, rationalists and scientists, through the span of three thousand years of history, these men discovered God. If there is a God—a God adequate to the universe as it is—then the discovery of this Reality must be the supreme issue in life. If there are moral conditions to be fulfilled, if it is the pure in heart who see him rather than the erudite, then we shall not need to give space to a labored argument to prove the existence of God, because God cannot be rationally proved, and such rational proof, moreover, would not discover God, nor find him in experience. As between science, art and religion, if religion represents reality at all, then its place is central. In so far as it is real, religion becomes the throbbing heart of life.

Twenty-six centuries ago a rugged peasant, Amos, made a discovery of God with revolutionary consequences. He saw the *righteous judgment* of Jehovah and proclaimed the swift doom of the northern kingdom of Israel—complacent, smug and prosperous though the people were. Shortly afterward, Hosea in the tragedy of his own heart and home, discovered the *mercy and love* of God, but confirmed the doom of unrepentant Israel, which fell in 721 B.C. Since that time, aided by these great spiritual pathfinders or prophets of the race, a growing multitude of men have shared in this great heritage.

Across nearly three millennia of history, we have selected more than thirty men who seem, undeniably, to have made the discovery of God, each for himself, in a way most helpful to us.

xi

Probably no two would select exactly the same persons. Others were greater saints than almost any in our list, but their circumstances, or experiences, or language were so far removed from our own that they are not so practically helpful. We have found it more useful to begin with Plato and the Platonists rather than the prophets of Israel who preceded them.

The prophets are so well-known and so accessible to all that we have only dealt briefly with five typical ones: Amos, Hosea, Micah, Jeremiah, and the great Prophet of the Exile. In studying the New Testament discovery of God, we have confined ourselves to the first three Synoptic Gospels, where the Son of Man is still a mystery or a theologically unsolved problem, the supplementary portrait given in the Fourth Gospel, and the interpretation of Paul which unites the two views.

In our quest of the discovery of God, we must study the two chief sources from which the modern world has derived its life: Hellenism and Hebraism, Plato and the prophets of Israel, culture and character, the aesthetic and the ascetic sides of life, humanism and rigorism, self-realization and self-sacrifice. We begin our study with the Greeks. We find this strain appearing and reappearing in the rich culture of Greece and Rome, in the Renaissance, the Enlightenment of the eighteenth century, in romanticism, in modern science, in Western culture and civilization, and in contemporary humanism, noting the influence of Platonism through the centuries and in the philosophy, literature and life of our own day. Humanism believes that God's whole creation is "good" and that we should not flee the world but conquer and capture it.

In contrast to humanism, rigorism or asceticism was derived not only from Jewish but from Greek and pagan life, from philosophers like Plotinus, as well as from ascetics like John the Baptist. To attain their spiritual goal, rigorists taught the discipline of character by self-denial and self-mortification. We find this side of life emphasized in Stoicism, ascetic Hinduism, throughout the best of Judaism, in monasticism, medieval mysticism, the Reformation, Puritanism, Jansenism, Mohammedism,

especially of the mystic Sufis, and very real but often unseen
today, hidden in a thousand monasteries and lonely mission
fields, and among a multitude of obscure saints and humble
Christians all over the earth. If either humanism or rigorism is
developed alone to the extreme it becomes a danger and results
in a one-sided life. We shall find, however, that both humanism
and rigorism are necessary elements that must be held in dialectic tension for the highest realization of the divine fellowship,
of individual character and of social well-being.

When we come to the scientists' discovery of God, it may
seem at first sight that spiritually none of these men made such
a remarkable discovery that he should be included with these
mountain-peak prophets and saints of old. But in our skeptical
and materialistic age, many of our contemporaries who have
little faith or experience of their own, may find these kindred
souls, men who have faced our world, the most helpful of all.
The same is true in the case of President William Rainey
Harper. He did not claim to be a saint, but out of the depths
of doubt and of modern skepticism he made the discovery of
God for himself. He so embodies the scientific spirit and the
principle of historical criticism in the application of reason to
faith and of critical scholarship to the Scriptures, that he and
other higher critics enable a multitude of modernists and liberals
to make the discovery of God for themselves, under conditions
of intellectual self-respect which are for them imperative. For
anyone who finds a stumbling block in the word "revelation"
in the title of the first chapter, as we raise the question whether
our human search for the divine meets any answering response
of self-revelation on the part of God, we would urge that he
read first the life and teaching of the four scientists and of
President Harper. Each of these men believed he had discovered
an aspect of God, but that the vast ocean of God's unfathomable truth and of the inner reality of his divine nature lay beyond the few pebbles he had found upon the shore of life—the
illustration used by the great Newton.

Happily forced to consult more than a hundred volumes in

the preparation of this obviously inadequate work, and levying heavy tribute upon all, the author lays no claim to originality. He has borrowed literally from a hundred sources. The one practical object in writing has been that declared by the writer of the Fourth Gospel (John 20:31), that others may make for themselves the discovery of God as did these thirty pioneers.

The writer is indebted to several critics who have each generously read several chapters of the manuscript and made valuable suggestions, including Professor Roland Bainton of Yale, Professor Justin Nixon of Rochester, Professor Charles N. Cochrane of Toronto for his suggestions on Plato and St. Augustine, and Clifford Stanley.

We are grateful to the University of Chicago Press and to Edgar J. Goodspeed for permission to quote occasionally from *An American Translation of the New Testament*.

The method followed by William James in his *Varieties of Religious Experience* soon appeared imperative in quoting from the various writers. In almost every case, long quotations are abbreviated and printed in smaller type without quotation marks. Practical exigencies did not permit quotations in full and the patience of the reader would scarcely tolerate incessant ellipses, breaks in the context, and endless meticulous footnotes and references, for our aim is not academic but practical. As in the Authorized and Revised versions of the Bible, pronouns for God and Christ are not capitalized, but when we quote a St. Augustine or Luther we follow their capitalization.

SHERWOOD EDDY

New York, September 1, 1942

MAN DISCOVERS GOD

CHAPTER I

HUMAN DISCOVERY AND DIVINE REVELATION

AT THE outset the agnostic must face this difficult, or to him meaningless word, revelation. Many admit that humanity has made a long and agonizing search for God and that some of the mountain-peak characters in this book had found the comfort, the motivation, and dynamic of a vital religious faith. But the modernist shrinks from the word "revelation." Both historical relativism and historical criticism have so emasculated former orthodox views of the Bible, of Jesus of Nazareth, and of God, that many are no longer sure of the divine in life. Is there a God adequate to the universe, to its immensity, to the world's unsolved moral problems, to its abysmal human need? Have we a God who has both power and purpose, who both can and will reveal himself, and who has entered history to meet every need of man? Here is man's ultimate problem. It is not a question of an inspired Book, or of what is our estimate of Jesus and what honor we would do him. The one final question is: Have we an adequate God? If we have, all our problems, individual and social, will be solved in time. If we have no adequate God, able and willing to reveal himself, able and willing to meet man's every need, then we are of all men most to be pitied. Most of the characters in this book did worship him whom they considered the God and Father of their Lord, Jesus Christ, and their lives were transfigured by their faith in God. On the other hand, as Browning said: "The loving worm within its clod, were diviner than a loveless God." Even if mistaken, a Jesus willingly crucified on Golgotha would be infinitely superior morally to a God who could not or would not reveal himself, who could not or would not meet man's desperate need.

Within the terms of our own experience, we can most rationally approach this difficult word, revelation, from the analogy of human friendship. The analogy is not perfect for there is no question of the existence but only of the character of the human friend. Nevertheless friendship is not made possible by a rational demonstration of the existence and character of our friend, but only by the co-ordinate activities of self-revelation and discovery. The process is not one of logic but of love, that is, the desire of persons for one another, leading finally or ideally to the full sharing of life. The relation of husband and wife, or that of an ideal friendship, is based upon common interest, common trust and the common sharing of life. An ideal friendship will depend upon mutual integrity, breadth and depth of personality, and upon mutual self-revelation and answering trust. Only upon these conditions can we discover a human friend—or God. In our relation to God, revelation means divine self-disclosure, rather than the communication of information or of truths about God.

Throughout this volume we hold a certain *Principle of Revelation*. It is, that divine revelation and human discovery are not contradictory or independent functions, but rather supplementary and correlative. This can perhaps best be illustrated by the relationship of parent and child. The parent has begotten the child and, motivated by love, is progressively educating and developing his offspring. The method is the self-revelation of the parent calling forth the progressive discovery and response of the child. The child in making its seemingly original and independent discovery is seldom aware of the initiative of the wise parent's self-disclosure, which induces the child to make its own discovery. The realization and appreciation of the character of the parent, and of his love, providence, and sacrifice are a very late development of maturity. The parent has many things to say and much of himself to reveal which the child cannot bear at any given stage of immaturity. The initiative is always with the wise parent; the relative progress and discovery belong to the child, who is inevitably self-conscious, self-centered, limited and fallible. It is the same with the human in relation to the divine.

The divine self-disclosure is not unrelated to the impact of history on the minds of men and their seemingly independent discoveries in the spheres of science, art, and religion; in things both human and divine. Thus progressive revelation is a combination of divine self-disclosure as well as of human insights and achievements in experience. It is a dialectic process like the interplay of divine sovereignty and human freedom, a part of the mystery of life. We are vividly aware of our human discoveries but seldom of any revelation. The latter is only apprehended "piecemeal, and incoherently, in separate times and places."

We wish to make an even wider application of this principle of revelation from the individual to the race, and from personal experience to history. We are familiar with Professor Hocking's principle of alternation in individual life, holding that there is a rhythm in experience as we necessarily alternate between worship and work, contact with God and the world, receiving and giving out, introversion and extroversion, solitude and society. Work exhausts us and we are driven to spiritual renewal in worship. But we shall find in tracing the discovery of God through three millenniums that there is a racial rhythm, a social principle of alternation, a dialectic preservation of opposite tendencies in a state of tension in the various periods of history, as well as in individual life. We shall discover a causal alternation between the antecedent revelation of God and the halting human discovery of the divine on the one hand, and of the secular activities of men in the various periods of history on the other. The divine revelation and human discovery of God do not pertain merely to a watertight compartment of life called religion. Rather the infinite life of God calls out the multiform activity of man in economics, politics, science, art, philosophy and religion. For man is made in the image of God. There should be no false division between the so-called sacred and secular; no man-made separation of the divine and the human.

These activities of self-centered man, however, are not self-sustaining. They are catabolic, spirit-spending, disintegrative. Man's materialistic, worldly life results in skepticism in intellectual matters; in greed, sensuality and selfishness in material things; in formalism, ecclesiasticism and the Pharisaism of self-righteous good works in religion. This brings social decay, decline and crisis at the end of an age, when chaos, anarchy or revolution impend. Then a discoverer of God appears, renewing man's vision, calling the world back to its Source. The hidden

God, the wise Father, who has been there all the time, reveals himself afresh and we have the correlative processes of divine revelation, usually hidden or disclosed only to the prepared prophet or community, and the bold, seemingly original and fresh discovery of God.

Thus among our thirty pathfinders we shall find that, over a vast span of history, Plato discovers God after the skeptic Sophists had dissolved Greek religion with their relativity and hedonism, and their egocentric doctrine that man, not God, is the measure of all things. Amos and the early prophets are seeming iconoclasts after a period of idolatry, conventional temple religion and prosperity. Jeremiah follows the downfall of Jerusalem and the end of the old covenant with the proclamation of the new. The Suffering Servant could only arise at the end of an age after the judgment of the Exile.

Jesus and Paul appear after the failure of legalism, Pharisaism and a secular form of a religion of law: "The law and the prophets were until John: from that time the good news of the Kingdom of God is preached, and every man entereth violently into it." Augustine arises in the skepticism at the downfall of Rome so well described by Gibbon, calmly writing his *City of God*, and receiving a kingdom which could not be shaken. Luther and the Reformers revolt from the papal system of religious good works and its corruptions. John Wesley sought to save decadent England from a French revolution. Jonathan Edwards arises after the failure of New England theocracy. The scientists lead the revolt against medieval superstition and enslavement to the Inquisition. Tolstoy leads the spiritual revolution against Czarism and Russian Orthodoxy in state and church. President Harper pioneers in the revolutionary application of science to religion and of higher criticism to orthodox fundamentalism. Booker Washington seeks to lead his people from slavery to freedom. We shall find that our contemporary modern discoverers of God assail the skepticism, materialism, imperialism and other evils of our unjust social order, which seem to be breaking down at the end of an age when God's judgments are abroad in the earth. Thus most of our prophets appear when most needed in periods of crisis and transition in the dialectic progress of history. Divine revelation and human discovery are correlative though not clearly apprehended processes.

Indeed, our adventurers not only illustrate our thesis that man discovers God, but that he does so especially at every crisis in history when men have forgotten God and need to be called to repent and return to him. Almost without exception they were rebels or prophets who in their defiance and denunciation were accused of "pessimism." They insisted that man has sinned and that he cannot save himself, and they called for faith in the saving grace of God, individual and social, both in the so-called religious and in the secular spheres. Always the discoverers of God appear when God has been forgotten. God reveals himself just when men have concluded there is no revelation. "Man's extremity is God's opportunity." God's cosmos appears in the midst of man's chaos. The hidden divine revelation stimulates and challenges man's open discovery. Never was the discovery of God more needed than in the present unprecedented world crisis.

With this view of the correlative relation of divine revelation and human discovery and without asking for any blind faith in the former until it reaches us with its own self-evidencing conviction, let us go forward to see how these men discovered God. For those who are not yet convinced of revelation, who are in the sphere of what has been traditionally called "natural religion," who feel they must depend upon their own reason, let us begin with an intelligent self in a kindred, intelligible universe. Then let us go forward to see whether or not we can discover God in the great areas of life where, perchance, God has revealed himself and where others have found God—in nature, in man, in a world of values, in persons of spiritual genius, and finally in our own personal experience.

Surely multitudes of men are convinced that they have discovered something of God in nature. The husbandman, the artist, the poet, the scientist and the philosopher have often found God there. One writes, "I have never seen a high mountain or the ocean or any other vast and beautiful sight, without a strengthening of my belief in God." The solid fact of the universe challenges us for an adequate explanation of it. From the infinitely minute mathematical orbits of the electrons within the atom, to those of the infinitely distant heavenly bodies, all move with apparent rationality and universality in one system of law.

The late Professor Henderson of Harvard has pointed out in "the fitness of the environment" the apparent definite and minute preadaptation of the physical world as the dwelling place of life. He shows that there was not literally one chance in a billion that a blind, material universe would be fit to sustain life and produce an ordered and progressive evolution upon the planet. Charles Darwin reverently states his conviction, "If we consider the whole universe the mind refuses to look upon it as the outcome of chance—that is, without purpose or design . . . The theory of evolution is quite compatible with the belief in God."

A higher clue to the character of God may be discovered in man. If, according to our hypothesis, there is a God who is revealed in nature, we would expect him to be most adequately known not by the lowest but by the highest in nature, which is man. Indeed there is no possible way to interpret God save by the analogy of one of the two aspects of our experience, its highest aspect, mind, or its lowest, matter. Was it not the method of Jesus to see God in his own experience and then reveal him to men so that they could themselves discover God in man's best? "If ye then, being evil give good gifts to your children, how much more will your heavenly Father give the best to you?" If a shepherd seeks his lost sheep, if a woman seeks her lost coin, if a father receives back his lost son, how much more will a heavenly Father seek and receive his own. Jesus discovered God in himself and then saw his goodness everywhere in humanity and in nature. That is one reason why his message is so human and so true. The great Spanish mystic Unamuno says:

How do you know that the man you see before you possesses a consciousness like you . . . because the man acts toward you like a man. And in the same way I believe that the Universe possesses a certain consciousness like myself, because its action toward me is a human action, and I feel that it is a personality that environs me . . . It is the Universe, living, suffering, loving, and asking for love.[1]

[1] M. de Unamuno, *The Tragic Sense of Life in Men and Peoples*, pp. 194, 195.

Man is forced to face not only an outer world of fact but an inner world of value. All sensation forces upon man the outer fact; all thinking involves value. Explain it as we may, the experience of the race has gathered around man's threefold quest in his hunger for the true, his sense of obligation to the good, and his longing to realize the beautiful, in the harmonious exercise of function and the joy of satisfaction in the effort to make life whole. To discover with Kant not only the fact of the starry heavens above but the evidence of value of the moral law within, leads many to the wonder of worship and to the indomitable hope of spiritual achievement. Man does not create subjective values so much as he discovers what is already there in the heart of the universe, as the external stimulus of his own response. The universe discloses itself to the man who is obedient to its ultimate values. The key fits the lock. If the ultimate fact of the universe is not mechanism but purpose, then the recognition of value will get the best response from reality. Somehow for men of faith, hope and love the universe not only confirms these values, it commands them. In so far as we are true to our best and realize the values of life, we do not merely infer that there is a God, but we are thereby discovering God himself. In this we agree with John Robinson the pastor of the Plymouth Pilgrims: "Whatsoever truth is in the world, it is from God, by what hand soever it be reached to us," and, "There is yet more truth to break forth from God's Word."

Perhaps the reader already knows something of God but does not recognize him as Father. If God is not an object of perception, you need not expect to come suddenly upon him, as you might catch a workman at his task. You will not find him as a residuum in your test tubes nor at the end of your microscope or telescope, nor at the conclusion of an argument. For God is not so much the conclusion of one argument as the necessary ground of all. He is like the sun. He is the one object in the world at which we cannot steadfastly gaze, yet in the light of which we see everything else. You may never suddenly come upon God—nor upon yourself. You will find no objective proofs of either the self or its Source, apart from the body and nature. God and the self are both too intimately near to be seen or objectively experienced, like the eye that cannot see itself save in some material reflection that interrupts its vision. Practically all the means of life are mechanistic and material; all its ends and higher values are spiritual.

We may also discover God in persons of spiritual genius. Has not the chief method of human progress in all branches of knowledge been the discovery of new truth by a leader, and the sharing of the discovery in personal experience by others? Plato became a pathfinder in philosophy, Aristotle in the sciences, Phidias in the plastic art, Bach incorporated much of what was best in music and made possible Beethoven and all who have followed him. Few are great creative geniuses in science, art or religion, but the normal man can respond to truth, goodness, and beauty—or to God when a spiritual genius makes a new discovery and shares it with his fellow men. That is why we have selected these thirty representative men in their discovery of God. All were men of like passions with us. Each had his problems, his doubts, his unexplained sufferings. Each had his periods of depression, or his "dark night of the soul," but each fought his doubts and gathered strength. As far as space has permitted, and wherever it was possible, we have tried to show something of the life and character, the service and teaching of these representative men, where and why they succeeded and where and why they failed. For the discovery or revelation of God was in their character as well as in their teaching. We believe that all these were instruments of divine revelation and that revelation and discovery are the same act seen from two sides, the divine and the human.

The modernist need not then start with the difficult word *revelation*, but the more human word *discovery*. God is not revealed as an abrupt Matterhorn, stark and bare above the plane of nature and human life. Rather we make the spiritual ascent of life gradually over a thousand foothills and lower shoulders of the mountain, as part of the solid earth of natural human experience. And we believe in God, not as a word, or doctrine, but as the basic reality of our lives, bound up with all the other verities and primary facts of our experience. We start from our most universal human experiences. Confidence in God begins with the child's trust in its parents, then with the confidence we have in ourselves, in our senses, our rational faculties, our moral powers, our spiritual aspirations. It includes confidence in the world as a real world and in a universe of reality and truth. It is bound up with our faith in the goodness of the good and the moral evil of the bad, in the eternal reason and the moral order, in the normal assumption of rational minds that life has been fairly and honestly given us, as a blessing and not as a curse. And it is a faith validated by our best experience through the years.

We need start with no theological presuppositions. We need not fear our doubts, for doubt is one of our ways of knowing, or rather of learning. We start just where we are. The dogmatic atheist, the thoroughgoing materialist, or the complete skeptic are rare indeed. Almost all have something to live by, however inadequate their faith may be. Indeed all living implies some faith. When Jesus called the first four disciples to follow him, he asked them for no theological commitment, but the record shows that thus simply they began to make a fuller discovery of the God whom they had known dimly in the law and the prophets. We refuse to accept either the fatal alternative of an unscientific belief or an unbelieving science, of religious dogmatism or scientific skepticism. We do not grudgingly accept the scientific method of historical and biblical criticism, and the bringing to bear of reason upon our religious faith; we glory in them.

From start to finish throughout human history, in every human life including our own and the life of Jesus, in every book including the Bible, we find a divine and a human element. Whatever the changing human metaphor, the divine is always apprehended under such symbols as light, life, spirit; it partakes of the true, the good, the beautiful. *But always when it passes through our murky human atmosphere, the divine light is refracted, it is colored and discolored in the human spectrum of sin.* There are chasms and dark depths of human sin and resulting misery wherever life is without God. There are temporary hells of human experience as long as God is willfully excluded. There are demonic and malignant forces in life. There is a mystery of evil. And in the tension between the good and the evil, the divine and the human, there is in each and every man this root of evil.

Once we find this ever-refracted and imperfect revelation of

God in history then all our common life and all history become intelligible, for we have found the key to the lock of human existence. We are no longer without hope and without God in the world. Dr. H. Richard Niebuhr shows in his *Meaning of Revelation* that where a godless life once seemed anarchy or chaos, a "tale told by an idiot, full of sound and fury, signifying nothing," when it discovers God, it becomes, with all its imperfections, a grand epic; and every line, stanza and canto falls into its proper place. The Scriptures then become not an inerrant history of revelation, but the history of the sinful Jewish people understood and unified in the light of the revelation of God's purpose for all humanity. Then we see both the martyrdom of Socrates and of Jeremiah, the wanderings of the Greeks as well as of the Hebrews, as instances of a general principle of creative love and judgment in one inclusive process in all history. Then we see not only man's discovery but God's revelation in all realms "sacred and secular."

As we have already observed, the unobtrusive God is bound up with the central certainties and the deepest realities of our lives. When we say revelation we point to something more fundamental and more certain than the Bible, or than Jesus, or than self: "Revelation means God, God who discloses himself to us through our history as our knower, our author, our judge and our only Savior." And Professor Herrman writes: "All revelation is the self-revelation of God. We can call any sort of communication revelation only when he so incontestably touches and seizes us that we wholly yield ourselves to him . . . God reveals himself in that he forces us to trust him wholly."

As illustrative of our progressive discovery of God, to what extent had Columbus discovered America? He had never set foot upon our soil, he never dreamed of a vast continent beside which "the wealth of Ind" was poverty, he had no conception of the coming centuries of American history, but only thought of a primeval forest, of Spanish gold and slaves, the latter converted and baptized by his "gospel" of the Inquisition. And yet he had found a new world which even we have not yet exhausted and whose boundless possibilities we have not yet completely discovered. It is thus in our progressive discovery of God.

The revelation of God is progressively discovered in history—e.g., as from the moral barbarism at the time of the Judges to the beauty of the Galilean gospels. There is ever a painful moral lag in our halting failure to respond in climbing to the highest peak in sight, and this peak is never the final summit or ultimate goal. Our plodding relativisms never scale the Everest of the Absolute. In the meantime, though we know little of philosophy, or of God as Absolute, those who have it prize the humble language of religious experience: "The Lord is my Shepherd" and "My sheep hear my voice."

Gradually there is built within us a central core of certainty in verifiable experience. This becomes our touchstone to test new truth. This core is a moral certainty, irrespective of unverifiable historic facts, of philosophic speculation, or dogmatic creedal formulation. And it is not incompatible with historical relativism and historical criticism. With endless patient scientific experiment, with plodding and ever-doubting advance from Newton to Einstein, we are undismayed that the cloud-capped summits of the Absolute are forever hidden to the gaze of our humble relativities. Meantime in intimate experience though we know and ask to know only in part, we can still say, "He maketh me to lie down in green pastures. He leadeth me beside still waters."

To repeat, we may gradually discover an inner core of truth in the revelation of God in Christ by which we test and try every contradictory or irrelevant conception. It is always the revelation not of abstract truth nor of correct creedal dogmas but of *God himself*, and a revelation which implies the character of God. We find ourselves on bedrock when we share Amos' discovery of the righteousness, holiness, or justice of God. We are not at first so sure of the higher idealism of Hosea which maintains that God is love, even when learned in the tragedy of the prophet's own home, until this revelation is confirmed in Christ. For those who attain this priceless gift in experience the assurance of the righteous love of God becomes a kind of gravitational force in the moral world; as certain but as unseen and unobtrusive as gravity, often known by faith but not by sight.

Once sure of the righteous love of God, nothing can be revela-

tion that contradicts this truth. It cannot be divine revelation but contradicts it when we read the hatred of the awful imprecatory Psalms, or the more terrible tortures of helpless victims depicted in an endlessly burning hell, which would be morally worse than Hitler's and Himmler's *Gestapo*. Such horrible images resemble the dark shadows in Plato's cave, which are so true to realistic human experience. These immoralities are not the revelation of an always loving, righteous God, who is the same yesterday, today and forever. These are the distorted pictures, upside down, or dimly seen in a mirror, of God's revelation in the life of the ever-limited prophet, and the ever-fallible scribe or writer. John Locke, the great empiricist philosopher and devout Christian, writes:

> No proposition can be received for divine revelation if it be contradictory to our clear intuitive knowledge . . . Wherein the proposition supposed revealed contradicts our knowledge or reason (it) must overturn all the principles and foundations of knowledge He has given us, render all our faculties useless . . . Whatever God hath revealed certainly is true . . . Such a submission as this, of reason to faith, shakes not the foundations of reason but leaves us that use of our faculties for which they were given us . . . Reason is natural revelation . . . Revelation is natural religion enlarged by a new set of disclosures communicated by God immediately which reason vouches the truth of.[2]

The revelation of God for the Christian, and his touchstone of truth, is not the Bible or the church. It is *God revealed in Christ*. It is the self-revealing God who at last reaches us at our most fathomless depths, who convicts us, converts us to himself, captures us and give us this central core of truth, this moral certainty within. It is this sovereign and effective God, adequate to man's every need, even to his failure and sin, who finds us. The writer of course does not claim that God's only revelation is in Christianity. All revelations are true and there is much truth in all the higher religions. But in the light of his own experience and after thirty years in Asia in that great arena of religions, the writer believes that all religions find their climax and completion in Christ. Though there are always "other sheep" and other folds they are really his. All can say "The Lord is my shepherd."

[2] *Essay Concerning Human Understanding,* IV:XVIII, pp. 3, 11.

Calvin was the unconscious father of fundamentalism with his virtually infallible Bible. Luther was more liberal, revolutionary and critical with regard to the Old Testament, to James and every portion of the Bible which was not for him the gospel of the forgiving love of God that had found and redeemed him. That alone was the Word of God for him. For Luther and for the modern Christian God-in-Christ, or the God and Father of Jesus, is normative, central, final. He is at once our touchstone of truth and our frame of reference by which we test or judge the Bible and all its self-contradictory portions, the church, Catholic and Protestant, and all its failures, as well as human character and conduct, human history and destiny. We thus part company at this point both with the fundamentalist and the modern nontheistic humanist. It is therefore irrelevant for us that the Bible, the church, the human life of Jesus of Nazareth and human reason itself are always limited, relative and fallible. Our kingdom which cannot be shaken lies within, where our halting discovery of God has met God's prevenient revelation of himself.

In the light of the revelation of a God-centered life and universe, a fearless disinterested science and an emergent evolution may be evidence of faith to a mind now freed from defending the folklore of creation stories of an ancient book and man's place in an earth-centered solar system. The revelation of God in Christ does not include infallible information regarding a natural miracle of birth or a miracle of authorship, the inerrant record of events or the times and seasons of catastrophic history or prophecy. "The revelation of God is not a possession but an event, which happens over and over again when we remember the illuminating center of our history."

It is not "the flight of the alone to the Alone," or of one beyond the many, but as One who acts in and through all things, who is the conditioner, and the ground of our own familiar life, expressing himself in every pulse beat, meeting us in every event. He is nearer than breathing, he is in our own inner integrity, our singleness of mind, the purifier of our hearts, the ever-present Judge before the bar of our innermost consciousness; "a Presence that is not to be put by," who has discovered us and revealed us to ourselves. That which has neither intelligence, power nor sympathy cannot reveal itself nor command our worship or even respect. Let the gods of Valhalla fall! We welcome not only their twilight but the death of every fantasy and idol and man-made creation of this powerless and pitiful pantheon. Day has broken and it is high noon in the self-revelation of God to the pure and lowly in heart.

All that we need is found in the Father of Jesus, what he was to Jesus and what he did for him and for us. Just this is what we mean by God and revelation; nothing less and nothing more. "We sought a good to love and were found by a good that loved us." It will not be Plato's abstract Form of the Good, nor a heartless Unmoved Mover who finds us but a God who so loved that he gave—himself.

Revelation is not the development and not the elimination of our natural religion; it is the revolution of the religious life . . . God requires of us the sacrifice of all we would conserve and grants us gifts we had not dreamed of—the forgiveness of our sins rather than our justification, repentance and sorrow for our transgressions rather than forgetfulness, faith in him rather than confidence in ourselves, instead of rest an ever-recurrent torment that will not let us be content . . . This conversion and permanent revolution of our human religion through Jesus Christ is what we mean by revelation.[3]

Here human discovery and divine revelation meet.

[3] Richard Niebuhr, *The Meaning of Revelation*, p. 190.

CHAPTER II

PLATO AND THE PLATONISTS

PLATO, 431-351 B.C.

W E KNOW even less of Plato's life than of Shakespeare's, but his soul is revealed in his writings. His family was one of the most distinguished in Athens in the age of Pericles. He had known Socrates from childhood and from about the age of eighteen to twenty-two he belonged to the inner group of his disciples. It was, in fact, the life—and death—of Socrates that converted Plato from his early ambition to enter politics to the study of philosophy as a lover of wisdom. Leaving Athens after the martyrdom of his master, he traveled widely and at about the age of forty he returned and founded the Academy for Philosophical and Scientific Research, as the first university in Europe. He was able to test some of his ideas in the attempted education of a philosopher-king, the young reigning "tyrant" of Syracuse, but failed to reform him. Plato returned to the academy for his remaining years, dying at the age of eighty-one. The span of his long life saw the end of the great Hellenic city-state civilization, lasting almost until Philip of Macedon secured the hegemony of Greece and Alexander began to extend his conquests over the world.

Together with Aristotle as the greatest of all philosophical writers, Plato explored the major problems of the mind. His seminal thought germinated and fructified throughout the succeeding centuries as a liberator of the human spirit, the inspirer of philosophers, prophets and poets of all time. As he himself had learned from Socrates, he was the guide of his younger pupil, Aristotle, from the age of seventeen to thirty-seven. The latter referred to his character as one "whom it is blasphemy in the base even to praise." After these two men, as Coleridge remarked, everyone born into the world had to be either Platonist or Aristotelian, an idealist or a realist. Philosophy for Plato was a passion, the apprehension of truth, goodness and beauty in a persistent faith in spiritual realities and eternal ideas.

Plato's inevitable shortcomings were due to his background. He was driven to philosophy in reaction to the Sophists and the behavior of the Athenian democracy in putting Socrates to death. The Sophists taught that all knowledge is relative and they ended by dissolving Greek religion in skepticism. Man not God was the measure of all things and life was reduced to relativity and hedonism. Plato's aim was to refute these skeptics, and the revelation of God for him meant the possibility of genuine knowledge. As his interests were chiefly restricted to the intellectual, the God he discovered was seen in a narrow range. The defects of Plato were those of Greek society, for the intellect is only a part of the human spirit. Righteousness and holiness in the Hebrew sense were concepts unknown in Athens, hence Plato's God was without these attributes. He found the God whom he was looking for and whom he first needed. God revealed himself within the limits of the capacities of Plato and the Greeks.

Plato does not spring full-panoplied from the mind of Zeus. He makes a synthesis of pre-Socratic and Socratic thought and, like all his successors, he stands upon giant shoulders. Plato derived much from Pythagoras a century and a half before him, accepting and developing the doctrine of the antithesis between soul and body, mind and matter, the one and the many, permanence and change, universal and particular, knowledge and experience. Plato believed that it is the function of the mind to bring order out of chaos, that it must be trained to "turn away" from the flux of particulars and to focus on the unity and harmony that lie behind them. In the *ascent* of the soul from appearance to reality, it must turn from the murky twilight and the shadows in the realm of change to the pure light of the eternal, changeless world above. Much of his language suggests religious conversion and the sacred quest of the light of truth. There is a strain of the mystic in him, as in Pythagoras and Plotinus.

Plato probably realized that he could not reach God by the reason through philosophy alone and so was driven to Orphism as a mystery religion of salvation. In the sharp dualism between the evil of matter and pure spirit, Orpheus uses, not the usual bath in the blood of a bull, but music as a means of purification, thus opening the door to salvation through ecstasy. Orphic salvation seeks to achieve immortality by the attainment of divinity through ascetic purification. The missionary zeal of Orphism, as one of the purest of the reformed mystery religions, made an individualistic appeal to personal experience. Plato though affecting to despise the system was much influenced by it as when he considers the body the prison of the soul, and, like Orphism, he emphasizes reincarnation. Orphic disciples sought to escape rebirth in the evil world as do Buddhists and Hindus today. They "ate the flesh" of their god in a communion service whereby God and man became one, and also taught personal purity. Orphism influenced early Christianity as when Irenaeus says, "God became man in order that man might become God." Through the Lord's Supper the believer, after the method of Orphism, was supposed to partake of Christ's divinity and immortality. Plato's stooping to Orphism shows his spiritual need which could so much more eagerly have welcomed the Christian way of life.

Plato identifies the "soul" with the "vital principle" of the universe. A man ought therefore to live in perfect holiness. God and man are so widely separated that it is impossible for human beings to render service to God, or to make any return for the good which they receive from him. Therefore to try to influence deity by sacrifices or vows or formulas has no meaning. In the *Laws*, Plato says that we may consider ourselves as a marvelous form produced by the hands of the gods, made either as their plaything or formed for a serious purpose. We are the slaves of the gods, without rights or claims before them. But we have our divinely willed calling, the fulfillment of which ennobles us and brings us happiness. We must do the good just as God does the good. We cannot do good to God or for God, for we are not his fellow workers, but we can only aid our neighbors. In the social order, we must fight every evil that is contrary to the divine nature. In the *Apology*, religion consists in self-giving love for one's neighbor, by giving up every comfort, in spite of bringing enmity and ingratitude upon oneself. Such piety is counted pleasing to God and brings his help and protection.

Plato values and urges prayer as the simplest means to approach the Deity. The worshiper should seek God with sincere reverence and purify his heart of all haughtiness and arrogance. God is asked to forgive and to be gracious. Public religious fes-

tivals should arouse joyous devotion to God. Songs should praise
the power and goodness of God and the joy of piety.

However waveringly and with whatever inconsistencies and
contradictions, Plato seeks to find ultimate reality by every possible approach—through the Ideas, through the concept of the
Good, and from the analogy of the human soul to the divine. Beyond the flux of sense and matter in time and space, Plato strives
to see a realm of fixed, immaterial Forms—qualities, values, types,
laws. Instead of Socrates' definitions and general concepts in
the minds of men, Plato thinks he sees eternal truths as Forms
or Ideas, or patterns in the spiritual world, existing independ-
ently of the mind. Plato held that these Ideas are invisible,
eternal, universal, self-existent, absolute, perfect, without beginning or end. They seem to point to a supreme Idea, a Form
of which all other forms partake—the Good.

Then Plato defines the Good as the goal of the individual and
society, until he contemplates the world as a teleological system.
He sees the Idea of Good as the end and principle of the whole;
a goodness which can communicate itself is the cause of being
and the well-being of all creatures. This is the cause of existence
of all things and of knowledge of all human minds, the reason
of the universe—*almost* a personal God. But is God to be conceived to be immanent in the universe, or transcendent, separate, alone, disinterested? Plato never gives the final answer.

Plato like Socrates was a man of deep piety and all the daring
of his rationalistic heretical thinking could not displace his
ineradicable belief in God. In his last unfinished Dialogue,
which was to have been a bequest to his people, he states his
theistic creed. He says: "My son . . . I can tell you that not a
single person of those who in their younger years shared the
opinion that there are no gods held to this conviction to his
old age." What seems to us defective in this world is doubtless
the best possible, at least the best in the making. There will be
a moral order and just reward and retribution in the life hereafter. It may be taken as a proved fact that there are gods, that
they are interested in human beings and that they never deny
justice.

If we examine his writings for the evidence of his discovery
of God and of the spiritual life, we are equally amazed at his

lofty flights to see how near he came to the summit of spiritual truth, but also to discover how far he fell short of it. In the *Laws* Plato created natural theology for a practical purpose. He refuted three false current beliefs which were fatal to moral character: atheism, the denial of the moral government of the world, and the belief that divine judgment in the moral order can be bought off by offerings. Plato passionately rejected the contemporary materialism and mechanism of Greek philosophy, he excluded pantheism as incompatible with the reality of evil, and was ever reaching out toward a sure theism. His three principal arguments for the existence of God are from design, from intuition or the universality of belief, and from the nature of the soul. He also adduced three strong arguments for the immortality of the mind. Plato believed he knew his own soul as self-conscious and self-determining, and looked from his own heart to what we would call the cosmic soul of the universe, although the idea of personality is not found in classical pagan literature.

Throughout Plato's writings, from the beginning God *is*. Like the sun in the heavens God is the central truth of philosophy. From the analogy of the soul Plato held that God is immutable, without blemish, self-conscious, self-determined. He maintained God's omniscience, his omnipotence, except as qualified by "necessity," and his ubiquity. God is perfect in thought and deed, he is beneficent, he desires to harm none but seeks the welfare of all. He does no evil and is not responsible for evil in man. He is wise, he sees and hears all, and well-nigh all things are possible with him. He is not identified with abstract ideas or values, nor is he denied personality. In some passages of the *Timaeus* the Creator is good as the Maker and Father of the world. The visible world, mutable and temporal, is only a copy or dim shadow of a model which is eternal, in the Forms or Ideas which God had before him, but even the copy is the work of God in his unceasingly active and generous goodness. The world had a beginning as God formed the world soul, and then subordinate gods and human beings. The immortal and rational element of the soul came straight from God himself, with a subordinate element in "necessity" in events. This necessity limits God but is under his beneficent purpose.

Monotheism and polytheism were to Plato but two sides of a single shield of reality, but he would impose the high God of philosophy upon a lower polytheism and mythology, though indignantly rejecting the man-made immoralities of the Greek pantheon. Plato could have said with Socrates in the *Phaedrus*: "Beloved Pan and ye other gods that are here, give me beauty in the inward soul and may my external possessions not conflict with my inner self. May I consider the wise to be rich. May my burden of gold be such as only the wise can lift and bear."[1] Men were "always to have intercourse with the gods by prayer," and the ear of Socrates is always attuned to the divine inhibition of his guiding spirit or "demon" within.

For both Socrates and Plato God is the measure of all things, not man, as held by the Sophists; and virtue is identified with knowledge. God, who is the beginning, the end, and middle of all, moves straight on to his goal. In the *Timaeus* we are in God's world and the universe is the radiation of the pattern of the good which is the goal of thought, of art, of love, and the sustaining constitution of all being. The mystic Plato reveals the light that never was on sea or land, though he confesses ignorance of God's inner nature: "It is hard to discover the maker and father of the universe, and impossible to express him to all men." Yet Plato is certain of a supernatural power ruling the world. Like the Platonic Kant he stands in awe before the witness of God in the starry heavens above and in the moral law within, in the still small voice of conscience. He sometimes feels the inadequacy of pure reason and agrees with Socrates that it was better to suffer even death by injustice than to gain the world by wrongdoing. Both in the *Laws* and the *Republic* Plato expressed a firm belief in God's providence and inexorable justice. He defends God's goodness, wisdom, truth, and immutability.

Plato says in the *Timaeus*:

Let me tell you why nature and this universe of things was framed by him who framed it. God is good; and in a perfectly good being no envy or jealousy could ever arise. Therefore, He desired that all things should resemble Himself as far as possible. This is the prime cause of

---

[1] *Phaedrus*, p. 257. This may be regarded as Plato's model prayer directed to the gods of the locality, and may be contrasted with the Lord's Prayer.

the existence of the world of change. God desired that everything should be good and nothing evil, so far as this could be. Now it is impossible that the best of beings should produce any but the most beautiful of works. The Creator therefore took thought and discerned that out of the things that are by nature visible no work destitute of reason could be made so fair as that which possessed reason. He also saw that reason could not dwell in anything devoid of Soul. This being his thought he put Spirit in Soul and Soul in Body, that he might be the maker of the fairest and best of works. Hence we shall probably be safe in affirming that the universe is a living creature endowed with Soul and Spirit by the providence of God.

He says in the *Laws*:

Neither let us suppose that God, the most wise, heeds the great things, but neglects the little things. All things have been ordered by God who has the world in his care to the salvation and virtue of the whole. That which happens to thee is best for the whole and for thee, so far as the common creation permits.

And in the *Republic*:

God and no other must be held the cause of what good we enjoy, whereas for the evils other cause must be sought, and not God.

Further in the *Theaetetus*:

It is not possible that evils should cease to be. Therefore our aim should be to escape hence to that other world with all speed. And the way of escape is by becoming like God insofar as we may, by becoming just and holy. God is most perfectly just.

By the virtues of wisdom, courage, and temperance, we shall attain the great end of justice. Justice is the inner law of measure, balance, health, and happiness, the well-being of the governing element of the soul, the *summum bonum*, the perfect good where every part of the soul performs its own function, where each man does the thing he can do best in the service of the state which should be the human realization of divine perfection. Finally the poet and lover of wisdom turns his eyes to the ineffable vision of the Absolute itself. Never was a more lofty view held of philosophy, of education, and of politics in the light of the divine, and that in the midst of all the corruption of a Greece that was already doomed.

Four centuries before Christ, Plato notes the intimate union between the vision of God, the love of God, the imitation of God, and the spiritual well-being of his fellow men. We abbreviate Plato speaking through Socrates in the *Phaedrus*:

Of the heaven which is above the heavens what earthly poet ever did or ever will sing worthily? Every soul which is capable of receiving the food proper to it rejoices in beholding reality. She beholds justice, and temperance and knowledge absolute in existence absolute. There was a time when with the rest of the happy band (of philosophers) we saw beauty shining in brightness—we philosophers following in the train of Zeus; others in company with other gods; and then we beheld the beatific vision and were initiated into a mystery which may be truly called most blessed, celebrated by us in our state of innocence, before we had any experience of evils to come; pure ourselves, and not yet enshrined in that living tomb which we carry about, now that we are imprisoned in the body, like an oyster in its shell.

How high Plato soars in his lofty flights, how near he comes to a firm ethical monotheism, to one God and Father and one Mediator between God and man "who loved us and gave himself for us," and yet how immeasurably he falls short of it is shown in his great *Symposium*:[2]

About the speeches in praise of love, which were delivered by Socrates, Alcibiades, and others, at Agathon's supper; no one has ever dared worthily to hymn Love's praises! So entirely has this great deity been neglected. Phaedrus began by affirming that Love is a mighty god, the eldest of the gods, the chiefest author and giver of virtue in life, and of happiness after death. Socrates then proceeded as follows: I will rehearse a tale of love which I heard from Diotima, a woman wise in this and in many other kinds of knowledge. What then is love? Is he mortal? No. He is neither mortal nor immortal, but in a mean between the two. He is a great spirit intermediate between the divine and the mortal. And what is his power? He interprets between gods and men, conveying and taking across to the gods the prayers and sacrifices of men, and to men the commands and replies of the gods; he is the mediator who spans the chasm which divides them, and therefore in him all is bound together. For God mingles not with man; but through Love all the intercourse and converse of God with man is carried on.

[2] A much abbreviated statement of Jowett's translation. Plato's word for love, *eros*, is a refining and ennobling principle but it is directed to self-realization and lacks the selflessness of *agape*.

The wisdom which understands this is spiritual. All men always desire their own good, for there is nothing which men love but the good. Love may be described generally as the love of the everlasting possession of the good. Love is not the love of the beautiful only. All men will necessarily desire immortality together with good. I am persuaded that all men do all things in hope of immortal virtue; for they desire the immortal. To ascend under the influence of true love, begin from the beauties of earth and mount upwards for the sake of that other beauty, arriving at the notion of absolute beauty, and at last knowing what the essence of beauty is. Beholding beauty with the eye of the mind brings forth, not images of beauty, but realities nourishing true virtue, to become the friend of God and be immortal.

For a thousand years the classic philosophy of Greece and Rome sought the Ultimate Reality, the First Cause, either as water, air, fire, form, the unknowable, Heraclitus' dialectic materialism, mind, idea, or gods many or one, personal or impersonal. Even Plato, greatest of them all, searching in his mighty synthesis for an ultimate One, a keystone to the mounting arch of his lofty thought, often ends in a rarefied impersonal mist of the transcendental, inaccessible, and unknowable. This breaks down in the final bankruptcy of classical reason, into a fatal dualism between abstract ideas above and the gross matter of a world of sense below. Six centuries later the great Augustine makes the needed synthesis between Plato and the Christian gospel, as he finds the keystone of the completed arch of thought and life: "*Thou* art the abiding light"—of nature, man, history, and human life, revealed in Christ.

Plato's views of God are often vague, pale and contradictory when compared with the Jewish prophets. A vein of agnosticism constantly reappears in his groping thought. Man's communion is not with the great God directly but with lesser gods, demons, the soul of this world, or some intermediary. Plato offers but cold consolation in his philosophy. There is no God and Father of the Lord Jesus Christ, no incarnation of God who so loved the world, no Comforter. There is no "Come unto me and I will give you rest," no "Blessed are the poor in spirit: for theirs is the Kingdom of God," no pure religion in service to the widow, the orphan, the poor, the slave, the harlot, the sinner; no passion of love for God and man, for one's neighbor and one's enemies.

Plato made the one great synthesis of spiritual thought before Augustine, but theistically it was a failure. It could not build a home for the spirit, nor overcome the deficiencies of the classical approach to experience. Paganism had decayed for lack of a spiritual dynamic after a thousand years of trial in Greece and Rome. Plato makes the natural but fatal blunder of his career when he identifies reality with the pattern or "Idea," and illusion and error with the concrete world of sense. Idealism failed to do justice to the problem of matter, and materialism to mind. All his life Plato sought a principle of unification and verification, an idea of ideas, the Form of the Good, but he ends as almost a prisoner in his own cave. This world and life are but a shadow and "time a moving picture of eternity." God was transcendent but not fully immanent. There was no salvation on earth but only the hope of heaven, often through a flight from the world or body. The followers of Plato devised a strange trinity of a Monad or One; a second creator, or demiurge, the First-born of the One; and a third creator, or Universal Soul, to establish contact between the heavenly Ideas and the world of sense. Their high idealism finally became a crypto-materialism. In his "truth apprehended in the cold light of reason" there is a break between the sensible and spiritual worlds. St. Augustine discovered a higher truth that makes men free in the Way, the Truth, and the Life, as he says in the *City of God* "with a faith that is different, a hope that is different, and a love that is different." That is the radical difference between the Christian and the non-Christian discovery of God. Yet no discoverer of God can ever ignore Plato or his great follower, Philo, whom we shall now study.

PHILO OF ALEXANDRIA, c. 20 b.c.—c. 50 a.d.

Philo, the Hellenistic Jewish philosopher of Alexandria, contemporary of Jesus and of Paul, tried to harmonize Hebrew religion and Greek philosophy by means of the Stoic art of allegory. He is the first great representative of Hellenistic Judaism. He went to Rome to represent the Alexandrian Jews in their refusal to worship the Emperor Caligula about 40 a.d. For Philo, God is a perfect Being, the primeval light, bare of all quality, eternal, unchangeable, free, self-sufficient, better than the good and the beautiful. In Philo's abstract *philosophic* conception, God is too perfect to have any active relation to the world or to men. He is not the God of the Old Testament, active in the world, loving and aiding his people, moved by repentance. Mediating between Philo's transcendent God and the mundane sphere, there are an infinite multiplicity of Greek divine Ideas, or forces, or angels. The supreme Idea is the Logos or the operative Reason of God, identified with the creative Word of God in Genesis, the Mediator between God and the world, the First-born Son of God, the archangel who is the vehicle of all revelation to men, the expiator of sins, the high priest who stands before God on behalf of the world. Here Philo follows Plato's conception of Ideas and the Soul of the World, and the Stoic doctrine of the Logos or Reason operative in the world. Inspired by Greek rationalism, Philo rejects the anthropomorphisms and unworthy superstitions of the Old Testament. For him as for Plato, man is a twofold being with a higher and lower origin, with a pure soul imprisoned in the body as a corrupt coffin or grave.

But Philo remained a Jew, holding that the Mosaic Pentateuch was of divine authority and embraced all truth. This he allegorically interpreted as containing all that is best in Plato and Greek philosophy. As a devout Jew his soul was athirst for God. He craved communion with a personal living God. Among monotheistic theologians he was the first mystic; among Platonic mystics he was a nationalistic monotheist, though he could never reconcile his Hellenism with his Hebraism.

Philo's doctrines were not accepted by orthodox Jews in Alexandria, but later they prepared some Jews for the acceptance of Christianity. Philo reads into his Judaism all he had learned from Greek philosophy, as today Gandhi in India sees in the Gita and the Hindu scriptures all that he finds in the Sermon on the Mount, and as we ourselves read our own ideas into almost everything we study. But whatever his sources, both in Hebrew religion and in Hellenic thought, *Philo had made the discovery of God.* He laid claim to all spiritual things whether they were taken from the teachings of Moses, or the prophets, or Plato. He thus describes his own experience when engaged in Greek philosophic study:

Sometimes when I have come to my work empty, I have suddenly become full, ideas being in an invisible manner showered upon me, and implanted in me from on high; so that through the influence of divine inspiration I have become filled with enthusiasm, and have known neither the place in which I was, nor those who were present, nor myself, nor what I was saying, nor what I was writing, for then I have been conscious of a richness of interpretation, an enjoyment of light, a most keen-sighted vision, a most distinct view of the objects treated, such as would be given through the eyes from the clearest exhibition.[3]

In his "Hymn of Faith," Philo says:

Faith is the only true and certain good—yea, faith in God; the consolation of life, the fulfilment of the highest hopes, the death blow to evils, the purveyor of benefits, the end of unhappiness, the knowledge of piety, the assurance of bliss, the progress of a soul which in all things rests assured upon God, the Author of all, who can do everything, but wills only what is best. It is faith alone which makes our path secure.

Concerning Moses and Aaron going up to the Lord at Sinai, he says:

Go up, O Soul, to the vision of Him who is—go up quietly, reasonably, willingly, fearlessly, lovingly. For these are the powers of the mind that is worthy to reign. It is dangerous for the soul to go up to the vision of Him who is, by itself alone, not knowing the path, and in ignorance and temerity; for ignorance and presumption breed great transgressions.[4] (He says elsewhere:) Ye initiates, whose ears have been purified, receive these things as the truly sacred Mysteries into your souls and babble them not to the uninitiated, but guard them as a treasure. For I myself have been initiated by the God-beloved Moses into the Greater Mysteries. Yet when I saw the prophet Jeremiah and recognized that he was not only an initiate but a capable hierophant I did not shrink from his company. Moses is the lawgiving Logos the purer and more perfect mind initiated into the Great Mysteries.

Philo and the Alexandrian Jews had been captivated by the Greek religion and culture about them. Endeavoring to remain

[3] *Migrat, Abrah,* p. 7.

[4] *Migrat, Abrah,* pp. 31, 45 (262), and *Cher.,* 48f. The central theme of Philo's *Allegory* is the development of the Greek Mystery. See also *de Migratione Abrahami,* the *Juis Heres* and *De Cherubim,* also E. R. Goodenough, *By Light, Light: The Mystic Gospel of Hellenistic Judaism.*

loyal Jews, they sought to appropriate all that was best in Hellenism. By representing Moses as Orpheus and Jewish Wisdom as identical with the female principle in nature, as Isis, by imaginative allegory Judaism was transformed and conceived to be the supreme and only true Mystery, or way of salvation. Here we see the power of Plato and of Moses, of Hellenism and Hebraism where these Jews sought to make a synthesis of both. God was now conceived as the Absolute connected with the lower material world by the emanation of his Light-Stream, by the Logos, or Wisdom. God was like the sun, self-sufficient, yet communicating himself by light and heat to the world of men, in life and creation. Philo sought to achieve the Greek mystic goal of salvation within Judaism. Wisdom was conceived as a mediating principle, God's agent in creation entering the souls of men, tending toward personality as a subordinate divinity. The Logos of Stoic pantheism was impersonal, but Philo equates Wisdom and the Logos, and Justin Martyr following him applies them both to Christ. Because of the confusion and danger in both terms, the Council of Nicea wisely dropped both words, wisdom and logos, in favor of "Son."

The Mosaic written law was conceived as an inferior material copy of the Platonic original spiritual law in the heavens. These Alexandrian Jews may even have had a mystic initiation, baptism, and a "sacred table." Philo allegorizes concerning the significance of the Ark, the Mercy Seat, the Cherubim and the Law. The two cherubim symbolize to him the creative and ruling powers of God. God's creative power guards the world from destruction, his royal power gives the Law, by which cosmic peace is preserved. The Cherubim have wings because all the powers of God "desire and struggle for the road up to the Father." Philo continues:[5]

God, who is One, is both Creator and King. Both incline toward the Mercy Seat. For if God had not been merciful to the things which now exist, nothing would have been created nor be given power. When God says: "I will speak to thee from above the Mercy Seat," the mind understands the Logos of God, which is a Mean, which leaves no void in nature, but fills all things and acts as a mediator, thus creating love

[5] An abbreviated quotation from Professor E. R. Goodenough's *By Light, Light: The Mystic Gospel of Hellenistic Judaism*, pp. 25-27.

and unanimity. For the Logos is always the cause and creator of fellow-ship. (Regarding the symbolism of the Ark:) First is the Being more primal than the One, the Monad, the Beginning. Second is the Logos germinative of things that exist. From the Logos come the two powers creative and ruling. From the creative powers stems mercy and from the ruling power the legal punisher (or power of judgment). The afore-said total seven in number comprise the conceptual world of forms. God is both ruler and good. (Philo concludes) Oh Mind, receive the uncounterfeited impression in order that you may win the blessed heritage, that you may possess the virtues that arise from these powers, love and piety toward God, through the kindliness of the great and bountiful God.

Though our scientific historical criticism cannot accept his allegorizing, we rejoice to find in Philo, as in Plato, a brother man who has discovered God. Philo and his followers, like many modern Jews, make a synthesis of much that is best in Moses and in Plato, in Hebraism and Hellenism. In the same way many a modern Jew, more even than he realizes, derives much from the Old Testament and from the New, from Judaism and from Christianity, just as he may be at once a Zionist and a loyal American.

Platonism gradually developed into Neoplatonism. As the Christian Platonist Clement of Alexandria found, truth is like a river receiving tributaries from every side, while Neoplatonism was like the flooded delta of the Nile. A trace of Greek thought is found in Paul and more especially in the Fourth Gospel. Platonism and Neoplatonism furnished Christianity with its scientific theology, its metaphysics, its mysticism. Neoplatonism was a syncretistic philosophy of Plato and Plotinus enriched by Aristotle and the Stoics. Though there was much in common between them, Christianity won and Neoplatonism lost in the inevitable battle between the two systems. Neoplatonism as a confused, semireligious philosophy was too abstract to become a popular religion. It interpreted emancipation from the sensible world materialistically and left man with an insoluble dualism, and a fatal chasm between the two worlds. Neoplatonism was entangled with the moribund Greco-Roman civilization, while Christianity sought to build a new world.

Most serious of all, Neoplatonism lacked passion and love. It was like the cold light of the frozen moon, not the blazing sun. It could not say "we know that we have passed from death unto life because we love the brethren." There was no God who so loved the world that he gave his Son, no incarnation, no Cross, no message in and for suffering, no sympathy and self-sacrificing love. "The intellectual love of God" was enough for Plotinus, Spinoza and Goethe; but not for Paul, Augustine, or Francis of Assisi. Neoplatonism, though it contributed its best to Christianity and its ethical culture, finally failed after long trial both as a philosophy and a religion. Under Porphyry, in seeking to protect the dying Greek and oriental religions from the formidable assault of Christianity, Neoplatonism became completely subservient to polytheism. But at its source, it was a pure life-giving stream, as when it enabled Augustine to rid himself of skepticism and the last dregs of Manichaeism, as he tells us in his *Confessions*. It reappears again and again in the great mystics, in the Cambridge Platonists, and in countless teachers like Coleridge, Ruskin, Carlyle, Tennyson, Browning, Matthew Arnold, Dr. A. N. Whitehead and a host of others. After this brief survey let us turn back to the finest embodiment of Platonism in Plotinus.

PLOTINUS, c. 205-270 A.D.

The most important philosopher of the Neoplatonic school was born of Roman parents in Egypt but, "being ashamed almost to live in a body," he strove to remain unknown. He was awakened to the study of philosophy in his twenty-eighth year; he continued for more than a decade in Alexandria, studied the philosophy of India and Persia and finally settled in Rome. Here he taught Platonic ideas in new garb to eager throngs of students who followed his ascetic piety in the contemplative life; some of them giving their fortunes to the poor and setting free their slaves. Plotinus held the doctrine of emanation, or the constant transmission of powers from the Absolute to the creation, through grades of pure intelligence, then to the soul of the world, to the souls of men and finally to matter. The whole universe is a living chain of being, the hierarchy of an unbroken series of ascending and descending values and existences, where the spiritual world is as vast and varied as is the visible material universe. Man

made in the divine image is homesick until he returns to the
Source of his life, the only home of the spirit. The material
world is like Plato's cave, or prison, as a tomb of the soul. Men
are amphibians living both in the sensuous and spiritual worlds.

Through the cardinal virtues, then purification of character
and the abandonment of all earthly things, the soul may rise
in the sphere of the intellect through the true, the good, and
the beautiful to final union with God. Plotinus attempted a
synthesis of the principal systems of Greek philosophy and his
influence upon the theology of Augustine and modern philosophy
from Spinoza to Schelling is remarkable. His whole impersonal
philosophy was an expansion of the truth that "God is light"
and that "The pure in heart shall see God." Plotinus' scheme
of ethics ascends, like the medieval and modern mystics who
follow him, through the threefold stages of purification, enlightenment, and final unification with the divine. His pupil,
Porphyry, edited his *Enneads* with a strong bias against both
the Gnostics and the Christians.

Plotinus is the great philosopher of mysticism; and mystics are
strangely alike in all ages. Mysticism is a spiritual philosophy
which demands the concurrent activity of the whole man in
thought, will, and feeling; through which man becomes a partaker of the divine nature. Much of Neoplatonism was absorbed
by Christian philosophy and theology, as Christianity gradually
became a syncretistic European religion. Plotinus' philosophy
contains two fundamental triads: the tripartite division of man
into spirit, soul, and body, which is a reflection of the Trinity
of divine principles—the Absolute, Spirit, and Soul. The third
person of Plotinus' Trinity is "the Soul of the All" which creates
and embraces the world and is its providence. Even Aristotle
believed only in three dimensions because "all things are three
and three is everywhere," as the number of perfection. Plotinus
refutes and abhors materialism. This world is framed in the
image of the spiritual world. It is as a whole good and God can
produce ultimate harmony out of its discordant elements, for
he has revealed the way to get back to him from whom men are
now lost or estranged.

The goal of the intellect is the One; the goal of the will is
the good; the goal of the affections is the beautiful; thus good-

ness, truth, and beauty are the attributes of spirit and the spiritual world. They are at once three lines of proof and three pathways to the divine. "The One" is not adequate to express the nature of the Absolute which is conceived as "beyond existence." The inner nature of the Godhead is unknown to us; but in the mystical state we may have an experience of intuition which is formless and indescribable. God is the Being and Reality of all things known. We may only know what he is not, for even Moses only "entered into the thick darkness" where God dwells. God is not unconscious but superconscious. Above all necessity and absolutely free, God is "the giver of freedom," so that men ultimately may be free indeed. God is fundamentally infinite, having his center everywhere and his circumference nowhere. He "would have been hidden" without a world, which dimly and imperfectly reveals him as his shadow. The path of beauty leads to the Absolute as the One and the Good, or Perfect. Man, himself a mystery, can spiritually know the unknowable because he is himself the unknowable. According to Plato, God is not far from every one of us, present with all, though they know him not. Man in fleeing from God flees from himself. If he comes to himself and knows himself he will know whence he is.

Though the vision of God and ecstasy are not the center of Plotinus' system, the Christian doctrine of mysticism on its metaphysical side is often derived from this great practical transcendentalist, Plotinus. Emerson had much in common with him. He is said to have attained the highest state of ecstatic vision three times in his life and has left us in the Sixth *Ennead* a description based upon his own experience, saying, "he who has seen it knows what I mean":[6]

In this choral dance (of life) the Soul sees the fountain of life and the fountain of Spirit, the source of Being, the cause of Good, the root of Soul. For we are not cut off from our source nor separated from it, but we are more truly alive when we turn towards it, and in this lies our well-being. In it our soul rests, out of reach of evil; it has ascended to a region which is pure from all evil; there it has spiritual vision, and

[6] The following much abbreviated portion of the *Enneads* is taken from Dean W. R. Inge's translation in his *Philosophy of Plotinus*, Vol. II, pp. 139-142.

is exempt from passion and suffering; there it truly lives. For our present life, without God, is a mere shadow and mimicry of the true life.

Life yonder is an activity of the Spirit, through its contact with the One, and with beauty, and righteousness, and virtue. For these are the offspring of a soul that is filled with God, and this is its beginning and end. For our life in this world is but a falling away, an exile, and a loss of the soul's wings. The soul is different from God and yet springs from Him, she loves Him of necessity. When she is yonder, she has the heavenly love, when she is here below, the vulgar. It is natural for the soul to love God and to desire union with Him. Let him who has not had this experience consider how blessed a thing it is in earthly love to obtain that which one most desires. *But yonder is the true object of our love, which it is possible to grasp and to live with and truly to possess, since no envelope of flesh separates us from it. He who has seen it knows what I mean,* that the soul then has another life, when it comes to God, and having come possesses Him, and knows, when in that state, that it is in the presence of the dispenser of the true life, and that it needs nothing further. On the contrary, it must put off all else and stand in God alone. We must then hasten to depart hence, to detach ourselves as much as we can from the body to which we are unhappily bound, to endeavor to embrace God with all our being, and to leave no part of ourselves which is not in contact with Him. Then we can see Him and ourselves, as far as is permitted. In this state the seer becomes another, he ceases to be himself and to belong to himself. He belongs to Him and is one with Him, like two concentric circles. Therefore, this vision is hard to describe. That which is divine is ineffable, and cannot be shown to those who have not had the happiness to see it. Caught up in an ecstasy, tranquil and God-possessed, one enjoys an imperturbable calm, and is in a state of perfect stability. *Such is the life of the godlike and blessed man; a liberation from all earthly things, a flight of the alone to the Alone.*

Despite the inevitable limitations of his abstract pantheism, and lacking the solid foundations of Philo's ethical monotheism, Plotinus was a kindred spirit of Plato rather than the prophets. Nevertheless, the mystic and the spiritual man find in Plotinus a brother whose language and experience remind us of the Psalmists and of the great Apostle of the Gentiles. He adds his witness to the other Platonists that man discovers God.

The high philosophy and the pale religion of Plato are both evident not only in Philo of Alexandria, in Plotinus and many Neoplatonists but in the life of a recent Platonist, the Princeton humanist, Paul Elmer More. Socrates and Buddha in their last moments had bade their disciples depend upon themselves alone, and the contemporary nontheistic humanist, Professor A. Eustice Haydon, constantly says, "You see, we have only ourselves." But Paul Elmer More had been saved from skepticism by the Ideas of Plato. In time, however, this great humanist felt the utter loneliness of an ideal world, as he said: "My longing for some audible voice out of the infinite silence rose to a pitch of torture. To be satisfied I must see face to face, I must as it were, handle and feel." He felt that all Plato's theistic reasoning never brought him to a vital personal relation with God at all, but was merely a name for the abstract sum of things considered as a unit.

Finally in his *Pages From an Oxford Diary* Dr. More discovers that "any true philosophy of God demands the incarnation." He tells us that he found at last sufficient evidence to believe in a personal God, and he was saved "from cosmic loneliness by the Incarnation of God in Christ and delivered by a Savior Friend." He says:

I can find no key to the Incarnation unless it reveals God as a personality somehow involved in the failure of his own handiwork and somehow redeeming the evil of the world by participating in the penalties of imperfection. . . . God voluntarily assumed, so far as that was possible, not only his own but man's share of responsibility for the wreckage of life. So was the Incarnation for us a work of vicarious atonement. . . . Only so could we be raised to God's point of view as he willingly lowered himself to ours. . . . Only of this I am assured, that some time and in some way, spirit to spirit, face to face, I shall meet the great Lord of life, and falling before him, tell my gratitude for all he has done, and implore pardon for all I have left undone.

We have found witnesses to the fact that man discovers God in Plato, in Philo of Alexandria, in Plotinus, in a long line of Christian Platonists and Neoplatonists, and finally in Paul Elmer More whose experience reminds us of that of St. Augustine whom we shall study later.

CHAPTER III

THE PROPHETS OF ISRAEL

GOD had revealed himself to Greece as well as to Israel, for knowledge was an essential phase in the quest of man for the divine. The difference between philosopher and prophet lies not in the character of God but in the character of the human agent. The Greeks were intellectualists, the Hebrews moralists. Hellenism found the *summum bonum* in truth, in metaphysics; Hebraism found it in righteousness and history. Aristotle's God is a calm thinker; the prophets' God is Will. Both are right in what they affirm; sometimes they are wrong in what they deny. Greek religion called itself natural religion but no true religion ends in nature, which always points beyond itself. We must realize God before we can fully grasp the meaning of nature. The Greeks and Hebrews had much in common. Both were looking for unity, constancy, dependability in the world. Upon these Plato based knowledge; the prophets, history. The first led to the problem of error, the second to the problem of evil which we shall find reappearing again and again to challenge all our adventurers.

The prophets come to grips with the deep moral and spiritual problems of human life and destiny, especially the central problem regarding the character of God. When in the dim prehistoric period, Israel entered Canaan, the Hebrews brought with them their tribal God Yahweh. He was their god but also their problem. In the opinion of many scholars, Yahweh had previously been a god of natural calamity, of storm, wind, hail, of sirocco, counted by the superstitious as an enemy of man. This awful storm god, this war god, this god of the mountain, brooding in the thunderclouds above Sinai, had finally by a sheer act of grace chosen Israel to be his people and made with them his solemn blood covenant. Thereafter he is on the one hand a God of mercy to those who keep his covenant and who remember and follow his precepts. But he remains the awful God to those outside the covenant and to those who disobey his precepts.

34

Much later, uncovenanted mercies appear in acts of further grace toward the undeserving. Yet to the end, there is in God an aspect of awful judgment and of terror. This is moralized by relating the wrath of God to the unrighteousness of man. It is exalted by transforming the terror into the majesty and holiness of God.

A certain dualism, however, runs through his character, the more so because he is but one God. Polytheism can avoid incompatibles in God by attributing one attribute to one god and another to another. That is why the devil is so useful in a monotheistic system. There are two elements in human experience, good and evil, light and darkness, the personal and impersonal, and man must conceive of something in the divine source of life to account for them. But the more nearly God is one, the more must he gather to himself all attributes, however much they apparently conflict. Greek and Roman polytheism had gods of peace and gods of war. Yahweh, being one, had to be now the god of battles and now the god of peace. The difficulty is not fully resolved even in the New Testament. There is apparent discrepancy between a God who marks the sparrow's fall, who numbers the hairs of our heads yet who prepares a place for sinners where "their worm dieth not."

The growth of the concept of the one God of Abraham, Isaac and Jacob belongs to the period when the Hebrews were a semi-nomadic people on the outskirts of Palestine. Actually there were still many other local gods attached to trees and springs, friendly gods who held converse with men but could not travel with them when hunger drove them into Egypt. Here the Hebrews fell into a period of servitude from which they cried for a deliverer.

The God of Moses was to lead them out. Though identified with the God of Abraham, Isaac and Jacob, his character was in part new and different. His had been the spirit of the storm cloud which brooded upon the summit of Sinai; or rolled up with thick darkness, thunder and lightning to terrify men. He was a god of natural calamity. Now to Moses came the amazing revelation that this god was also a god of mercy, who by a sheer act of grace had chosen Israel to be his people and to deliver them from the hand of Pharaoh. The people were summoned to the wilderness to make a covenant with Jehovah. This was one of the supreme acts in the history of religion because it meant that the favor of God was conditional; it was morally conditioned. Jehovah took Israel to be his people but they must keep his covenant. Thus was the door opened for the moralizing of religion and likewise for the explanation of defeat without a loss of faith.

Jehovah had several characteristics which set him above all the other gods. He was mobile. As the storm cloud he could go with his people from Egypt to the wilderness, from the wilderness to the Land of Promise, from the Land of Promise into exile. He was also sexless; no fertility rites could be associated with the god of the storm cloud. He gradually acquired other characteristics in the minds of his followers because he was their only God, who must supply all of man's religious needs, however inconsistent they might be. Hence in Israelitish religion we have almost from the outset a complex God of wrath and of mercy, of war and peace, of darkness and of light. Later we shall find St. Paul, Martin Luther, wrestling in his monk's cell, Karl Barth, Reinhold Niebuhr and Albert Schweitzer tormented by these tensions in their thought regarding the nature of God.

During the conquest, Jehovah became a God of war. Previously he had been simply a God of natural disaster. Now he fought for Israel. But when they became settled in the land, he was domesticated into a God of crops, of prosperity, and peace. He thus took to himself some of the characteristics of the Baalim, the gods of Canaan. But one of their characteristics he could never adopt, namely that of sex. Against the fertility cults, the prophets of Jehovah waged implacable war.

The next great stage of religious insights and illuminations begins with a turn in the external fortunes of the people, as marked by the rise of Assyria. Hitherto the Israelites had been able to take care of themselves in their conflicts with their neighbors. But except for the Maccabean interlude Israel lost her political autonomy forever on the day when tribute was paid to Tiglath-pileser. The great problem and the supreme achievement of Israel was to preserve her identity as a people after she had lost political freedom. Only through religion was Israel able to achieve this end, a religion built upon but vastly transcending the religion of Moses—the high moral monotheism that was developed by the prophets.

Defeat first of all required an explanation and the explanation lay at hand in the covenant relation. Israel had not kept the precepts, therefore God suffered her to be punished. The condition for deliverance is that she should obey the commands of the Lord and these are two, namely social righteousness and religious purity. The first is stressed by Amos and the second by Hosea. The latter at the same time introduces a new tone into the covenant relationship, for God is yearning for his people and is deeply grieved that they have been faithless to the compact.

The problem of defeat became ever more insistent as the Assyrians stood before the gates of Jerusalem. The Hebrews were taunted with the weakness of their God, who could not deliver them out of the hand of the Assyrians. To this jibe the prophet Isaiah replies with an assertion so amazing that one can call it only a divine illumination. His answer is that the little tribal god who has not saved his people from invasion is actually the God even of the invaders whom he is using as a scourge. Jehovah of the storm cloud now sits upon the circle of the earth.

The equation of rightness and security persisted in the covenant tradition. Men still felt that if only they could *do* enough to satisfy Jehovah, he would deliver them from the hand of their enemies. Hence the Deuteronomic reform. But the king who did so much to promulgate and execute this reform was brought back in a chariot dead from Megiddo. What was wrong? "Externalism," answered Jeremiah. "There must be a new covenant of the heart." Jeremiah learns in his own individual experience that Jehovah is the God of the individual, the God of personal relations, and that religion is a matter of the soul. Without Jerusalem or the Holy Land, without temple or synagogue, man, under a new covenant within the heart, can walk alone with God, with "a God who is near." But nothing helped to change the fortunes of Israel. Exile continued. Israel's cup was full to overflowing. She had received double for all her sins. Was there any fairness in this? Could it be explained in terms of the covenant? Here is the problem of evil and of unmerited suffering. Job wrestled with it and, if the last chapter be from another hand, then the real Job found no answer other than to prostrate himself upon his dunghill before the inscrutable ways of God. Then to the Second Isaiah came the unparalleled revelation that innocent suffering is a method employed by God for the healing of the nations, a method believed in and practiced by Gandhi today in India. To the "great unknown" Prophet of the Exile, whose writings were later affixed to the Book of Isaiah, Jehovah is revealed as the *God of the vicarious Suffering Servant*.

Finally God emerges, personal, spiritual, sole and supreme, of an unapproachable lofty ethical character. It is to be noted that it is first the conception of the righteousness of God that emerges in Amos, Micah and Isaiah, and only later his character of love and mercy. Religion first appears as a social function of the tribe or the nation of Israel, and only after several centuries as an individual personal experience. God is conceived as first tribal and only finally universal; at first in materialistic symbols as anthropomorphic; at last God is spirit, God is light, God is love. All this is evolved or developed for over a thousand years through the twofold co-ordination of the divine revelation, and the response of man's discovery of God.

AMOS, 765-750 B.C.

In passing from our study of Plato, the philosopher, to Amos, the rural shepherd, we cross a wide gulf. Plato sees a dim pattern in the heavens of abstract ideas, beautiful as sunset clouds. To Amos, God is as the sun blazing in the heavens. Man is not separated from God by an immeasurable distance upon a lower plane of existence as in Plato, but morally by his sins. Plato's dreams and speculations are as a mist. Amos is a flaming sword, piercing the conscience. Plato gropes in doubt; Amos flames and strikes in wrath with spiritual certainty from an immeasurably higher moral plane. Amos' brief prophecy, "minor" in length, short as a tract, but major in its moral might, its titanic strength and rugged grandeur, is one of the great achievements of the human spirit. It shows the incandescent illumination of a human soul, lit up by an authentic revelation of God, more sure and searching in its lofty ethical monotheism than the whole voluminous library produced by Plato and Aristotle combined, or than all the disquisitions of the philosophers and the moralists together.

This desert shepherd had discovered God in the solitude under the stars, but when he went to Bethel, Samaria, or Syria to sell his wool, attending the great fairs and festivals, his simple countryman's conscience was revolted by the fearful corruption of the people, and the oppression of the poor. At first, we seem to be listening to the words of Amos, one of the shepherds of Tekoa —six miles south of Bethlehem, the village of David, twelve miles south of Jerusalem, bordering on the wilderness of Judah, with its later association with John the Baptist and Christ's temptations in the wilderness—"Yahweh took me from behind the flock" (Amos 7:15). He left all to follow his God in one of the boldest missions ever undertaken by man. He scorns the thought that he was a disreputable professional prophet. There are autobiographical flashes in Amos as when he says, "I am a shepherd and a dresser of sycamores." As clear as thunder or lightning "the Lord said to me, 'Go prophesy to my people Israel,' " for "He will do nothing except he reveal his purpose to his servants the prophets." Amos begins, "The Lord roars from Zion." God's Word seems as clear to him as the voice of a desert lion. With consummate skill, after arraigning the seven surrounding nations for their sins—Damascus, Gaza, Tyre, Edom, the Ammonites, Moab, and Judah, the southern kingdom—he closes in upon Israel, the northern kingdom, complacent and blind to its impending doom because of its sins which cry to heaven: They have sold the innocent for silver and the needy for a pair of sandals, trampling upon the heads of the poor, robbing them with violence, oppressing the weak, crushing the needy, taking bribes, and denying justice in their courts. So recently nomadic and agricultural, in the first civilization that Israel had known they had already acquired ivory palaces, winter and summer resorts, and habits of luxurious debauchery and continual feasting.

Tiglath-pileser had just ascended the throne of Assyria in 745 B.C., his impending invasion providing the moving cause of the prophesying of Amos. Israel is blind, self-confident and "at ease in Zion" (Amos 6:1), but Yahweh drops a plumb-line over the crooked, crumbling wall of morally decaying Israel. Though God brought Israel up from Egypt, destroyed the Amorites and Canaanites before them, though he gave them repeated warnings, chastisement and judgment by famine, drought, blight, mildew and pestilence, sending them prophets to interpret his judgments, Israel has hardened its heart, and refused Amos' plea to repent that God may forgive them. Now there is left the swift sword of the Assyrian: "Prepare to meet thy God, O Israel" in certain invasion, destruction and captivity. This actually took place in 722 B.C., or in little more than two decades. Their very worship had become corrupt and sensuous and Amos sarcastically bids them come to Bethel and sin in their sacrifices. So the Day of the Lord will be darkness and not light to the wicked; judgment and not salvation. Amos shatters their comfortable eschatological hope of a Second Coming ushering in a new age. It is not Assyria nor any second causes but "I, Jehovah, will carry you into exile beyond Damascus." I, the God of nature and of history, not only brought you from Egypt, but have led the Philistines and Syrians also. You are not as spoiled privileged children but are to me like the Ethiopians or Africans. (Amos 9:7.) Amos is incredibly bold, for the complacent, smug and superior kingdom of Israel was more prosperous and powerful under Jeroboam II than it had been at any previous period. Amos' warning of doom comes like a bolt out of the blue. An economic "boom" had followed the victorious wars which had enriched the merchants and speculators of Israel. Just when they were saying peace and safety they were shaken by this prophetic volcanic eruption.

We have in Amos the very earliest of the prophets whose writings are extant and of undisputed date. Yet he is a master of language in this rhetorical masterpiece which gives a vivid picture of history and society in his day. Many scholars find his literary style astonishing; his clear rhythmical lines are grouped in strophes, characteristic of Hebrew prophecy and poetry. They seem to live and throb as a spoken word, struck off at white heat. Amos seems more than a rude peasant. He is absorbed in God and possessed by him, yet little did he dream in his denunciation at Bethel that he was to write the first prophetic book of a new ethical monotheism in the Bible of the whole human race —one hundred and thirty years before Deuteronomy was written, a century and a half before Jeremiah, two and a half centuries before Plato. A new epoch in literature and in religion began with Amos and the great literary prophets who followed him as this simple shepherd chanted before a vast assembly the funeral song of Northern Israel. In spite of their national prosperity under Jeroboam's splendid reign, blinded Israel was doomed by the holy Yahweh himself: "You only have I known of all the families of the earth, *therefore I* will visit upon you all your iniquities." Throughout Amos and all the prophets, God is conceived as immediately acting in history and in nature, in prosperity or adversity, in famine or pestilence, in war or judgment, using the conquerors and all the nations as his tools. But the basic note of Amos is the justice or righteousness of God. Amos struck this note so forcefully that it left an indelible impression. Men might not be able to rise at once to Hosea's good news of God's mercy, but after Amos for twenty-six centuries, nay to the end of time, men could never again doubt God's demand for justice.

HOSEA, 745-735 B.C.

Hosea was the prophet of the love of God as was Amos of his righteousness. A message of love proclaimed as an oracle in mere words would be well-nigh meaningless. It was deep in their own experience that the prophets had to learn the lesson which on the human side we may call "discovery," responding to the divine initiative of revelation. From the experience of human love they learned of its divine source. The Jewish prophets often embodied their message in symbolic acts which proved more effective than mere words. The supreme example of this is the marriage of Hosea. He marries a woman who afterward proves unfaithful to him. At the birth of the first son, whose father is another than Hosea, who is as yet ignorant of his wife's infidelity, the prophet gives him a name of symbolic character, as in the case of Isaiah's children. "Jezreel" refers to the great battleground where the wicked Jehu massacred the family of Ahab as a consequence of which God must "avenge the blood of Jezreel upon the house of Jehu and cause the Kingdom of Israel to cease"; a prophecy which was fulfilled some twenty years later. When the second child, a daughter, is born in sin, Hosea, now cognizant of his wife's unfaithfulness, names the child *No-love.* Another son is born. This one is called *Not-my-kin.* Apparently the woman now leaves home and falls into the hands of some man whose slave concubine she becomes. But Hosea who has loved her from the beginning, despite her shame, purchases her at the price of a slave.

While the character of Amos was stark and simple in his flaming righteousness, which knows little love, that of Hosea was complex. He had to learn the strength of endurance under incalculable agony and of patient persistence against the combined forces of the leaders of the time. But deepest of all it was the tragedy of his home that changed him and made him the first prophet of love. Through his own agony, he had to learn the merciful and long-suffering love of God for his unfaithful people. Though Israel must go into exile, this will not be due to Yahweh's punitive justice but to his redemptive love. Amos was the prophet of law and judgment; Hosea the prophet of the moral love of God, who is still a God of law with inexorable moral demands, but who is able in his vicarious love to triumph over law. Hosea writes brokenly in deep emotion in an "artless rhythm of sighs and sobs." Like Amos in passionate anger, the prophet first flames against Israel's wanton idolatry, their worship of the sensuous Baalim and the fat bull of Bethel, their degradation of Yahweh worship, their sacred phallic pillars and statues, their "sacrifice with temple prostitutes," or consecrated harlots who were connected with the ceremonial religious worship, as they still are today in many lands.

Hosea exposes Israel's "cursing, lying, murder, theft, and adultery," as "gangs prowl about." He flames against their insolent wooden images and idolatry, their flirting with Assyria and Egypt, their stubborn ignorance of their God and refusal to repent. Hosea is almost as scathing as Amos in his indictment of Northern Israel which has sunk even lower in sin a decade after Amos.[1] Having "dedicated themselves to Baal they became an abhorrence *like the thing which they loved.*" Beholding, they become like the object of their worship, whether sensuous or spiritual. And all because they had not known Yahweh: "My

---

[1] Hosea is the first known prophet to attack image worship, the crass misrepresentation of Yahweh as an idol in human or animal form. All Israel's sin is traced back to their failure to understand aright the character of Yahweh as righteous love.

people perish for lack of knowledge." "Therefore will I hew them by the prophets," like Jeremiah's "battle ax" or maul. For as it was I, Jehovah, not Moses, that brought Israel out of the bondage of Egypt; so I will erect a wall against her and destroy her cities and they shall go captive to Assyria, for "I am your destruction, O Israel." To Hosea he is the God of history, the God of judgment, the God of redemption, the God of love and providence. But he demands piety, not ceremonial sacrifice. Thus in Amos and Hosea we find not only that both make a genuine discovery of God in their own experience, but we see God's authentic and abiding revelation for all men and all time.

MICAH, 725-700 B.C.

Though Micah is a younger contemporary of Isaiah, though he was a humble peasant and Isaiah an influential aristocrat, Micah is nevertheless one of the great prophets. Like Amos he is a prophet of justice and is the protagonist of the peasants and the poor. In the last decade before the fall of Northern Israel, in 730-722, Micah announced the certain fall of Samaria and he was the first prophet to announce the fall of Jerusalem as well. More than a hundred years after this still unfulfilled prophecy, so deep was the impression that it made, that on the basis of it the elders plead for the life of Jeremiah.[2] The key to the whole prophecy is in Mic. 3:11-12: Jerusalem's "chiefs pronounce judgment for a bribe, they declare oracles for hire, and his prophets divine for cash. Yet they lean upon the Lord saying, 'Is not the Lord in the midst of us? No misfortune can befall us.' Therefore because of you, Zion shall be plowed as a field, and Jerusalem shall become a ruin, and the temple hill a high place in a forest."

As nominal religious people in after ages, whether Pharisees or orthodox Christians, would look upon themselves as the favorites of special privilege, saved as orthodox worshipers, whatever their moral lives or social injustice, these complacent, smug and wealthy religionists were to fall under the judgments of God both individually and nationally, whether in war or in peace. Micah joined with Amos, Hosea, and Isaiah, *seeking to*

[2] Jer. 26:16-19.

purify religion by a deeper discovery of the nature of God.
Jehovah seeks justice and mercy, not oxen and sheep; character
rather than right ritual, a changed moral life rather than right
opinion and orthodoxy. Here is the summary of the prophets
and of all true religion as to what the Lord requires of man:
*"Only to do justice, and to love kindness, and to walk humbly
with your God."* As in Amos, Hosea and Isaiah, God's first requirement is justice; yet it is to be feared that Anglo-Saxon
Christians are as blind at this point as in the days of these
prophets twenty-six centuries ago. There is probably more
blasphemous injustice today in so-called "Christian" nations than
in the days of Amos and Micah, or when the parable of Dives
and Lazarus was uttered. Many complacent Christians of our
own time are probably the chief obstacles to any new order of
justice for all and under an unjust system the poor are robbed
more effectively than in the days of Amos or Micah. Micah was
pre-eminently the prophet of the poor as their fearless champion,
combining Amos' passion for justice and Hosea's heart of love.

The text of Micah is corrupt and there are many additions
of later date, but taking the prophecy as it is today, we find the
first proclamation of a Messianic king:[3]

And you, O Bethlehem, too little to be among the clans of Judah,
from you one shall come forth for me, who shall be ruler over Israel,
whose origins are from of old. He shall feed his flock in the strength of
the Lord. And he shall be great unto the ends of the earth. (In that
Messianic Golden Age) It shall come to pass that the mountain of the
Lord's house will be established. Peoples will stream unto it, and many
nations will come, and say, Come let us go up to the mount of the Lord
that he may instruct us in his ways, and that we may walk in his paths.
For from Zion goes forth instruction and the word of the Lord from
Jerusalem. And he shall arbitrate for great nations and they shall beat
their swords into plowshares and their spears into pruning hooks.
Nation shall not lift up sword against nation, nor shall they learn war
any more. But we will walk in the name of the Lord, our God, forever
and ever.

JEREMIAH, c. 650-585 B.C.

Standing at the summit of Old Testament prophecy, Jeremiah
carries individual, personal religion to its highest and farthest

[3] Mic. 5:1-4; 4:1-5.

possible development in the Old Testament. He is the first intro-spective autobiographical prophet and his knowledge of psy-chology and of the human heart anticipates the Apostle Paul and Augustine. Living at the end of an epoch and on the threshold of a new order, Jeremiah illuminates one of the great crises in history as did Plato, Jesus Christ, and St. Augustine. He may even throw some light on our present world agony. There is a sense in which he is modern, and almost as our con-temporary he speaks to our own age. We shall find that in an extraordinary degree, he is not only an unconscious forerunner but in some ways prefigures the life of Jesus and of Paul.

In character he was nervous, shy, and sensitive, tender and loving, with poetic imagination, keen moral insight, and pro-found religious devotion, yet called to one of the boldest tasks ever assigned to man. In his complex character, Jeremiah is at once prophet and statesman, poet and mystic, patriot, rebel, an optimist-pessimist, a man of sorrows, and acquainted with grief, who yet foretells a glorious future. His very name is significant: "Jehovah my portion." From his deep-rooted love of nature and of man, his temperament demanded a life of quiet domestic obscurity. Yet his devotion to God and his calling flung him into the maelstrom of public life, always on the unpopular side. His impassioned love for God and for man led to his daily crucifixion. He sought to woo his people and unite them to Jehovah, yet saw them deliberately reject God, his covenant, and his prophet, and go stubbornly to their doom in captivity and ruin. He shares vicariously in responsibility for the evils of his age which he was powerless to divert. Yet through his suffering, he spiritual-ized religion for all time. He separates personal religion from all outward institutions, even the temple, the Law and the nation itself. He makes it available as a universal human possession, that all men might discover God, "for all of them shall know me, from the least of them to the greatest of them."

Jeremiah was the son of a devout priestly family in the village of Anathoth, some four miles north of Jerusalem. He had obvi-ously studied the writings of Amos, Isaiah, and Micah, and had been deeply influenced by Hosea. He was imperatively called to prophecy in 626 B.C. when the Scythian invaders appeared "from the North." Though he shrank back and pleaded his youth, he felt called to his divine mission almost as violently as Saul of Tarsus. This gave him a consciousness of prophetic mission unparalleled among the prophets, so that like Paul he felt that he had been predestined and prepared even before his birth. He saw all about him in Judah the flagrant apostasy and unrepented sin that had led to the ruin and captivity of Northern Israel, and boldly warned Jerusalem of its doom. He lived through the invasion of the Scythians and saw the adoption of the Deuteronomic law which was the finest system of national religion which the world had seen, but only and exclusively national. "He lived to see the Law fail, the nation dispersed, and the National Altar shattered; but he gathered their fire into his bosom and carried it with a purer flame toward its everlasting future."

With Jeremiah the human unit in religion, which hitherto had been mainly the nation, began to become the individual. The single soul is now revealed, charged and convicted as never before. Jeremiah's own mental and physical agonies oppress him with the problem of the unmerited sufferings of the righteous, and he incarnates what the great Prophet of the Exile later interpreted. While he does not understand it as yet, he himself becomes the Suffering Servant of the Lord. In his passionate identification of himself with the sorrows of his sinful people, in the unrealized possible atoning and redemptive value of his sufferings, he becomes "the likest to Christ of all the prophets."

Though six centuries separate Jeremiah and Jesus, both lived at the end of an age that was to witness the destruction of the Temple, as well as the captivity and dispersion of their people. Each foretold the destruction of Jerusalem and the national doom. Both loved nature and the history of their people; both were poets and spoke in vivid parables. Each delivered his oral message which was recorded by others, accompanied by rich biographical details. Each lived a lonely life without home or family, wedded to his nation. Each was accused of disparaging the Law and of being a destroyer; each said that to obey was better than sacrifice. Each arraigned the professional religionists of his day, whether priests or Pharisees. Each was accused of being "mad" by his kinsfolk. Each was a lamb led to the slaughter (Jer. 11:19). Jesus quoted Jeremiah and in his sufferings saw his own inevitable doom (Matt. 21:12). Each called the Temple "a den of robbers"; each was tried for treason and paid for the denunciation with his life (Jer. 7:11,14; Luke 19:41-47).

The likeness between the two was so great that the common people said Jesus must be "Jeremiah or one of the prophets" (Matt. 16:14). Each wept over Jerusalem. Jeremiah stands at the peak of the Old Covenant and Jesus at the climax of the New. Each was a man of sorrows and a Suffering Servant; Jeremiah cursed the day of his birth but Jesus recognized his suffering as "the cup which my father hath given me" and prayed "Father forgive them." Jeremiah foretold a New Covenant but only Jesus could say: "This cup is the New Covenant in my blood." Such a series of coincidences must be more than accidental. It seems to indicate that both Jeremiah and Jesus are in the midstream of the progressive and cumulative discovery of God in history and that each was an instrument of divine revelation.

In Jeremiah's discovery of God, though he confirms the early prophets, he dwells little upon the transcendent and infinite aspects of the divine nature. At his call he does not, like Isaiah, see the Lord upon a throne, high and lifted up, nor behold the awful vision of Ezekiel. Rather God talks with Jeremiah as his friend, while he speaks to us as a gentle lyric poet. Like wrestling Jacob, like Job, like Luther centuries later, he struggles with the divine will and is left amazed and perplexed. He finds Jehovah a God of deeds, who has done and is always doing things, working in nature and providence. The Living God had delivered his people from Egypt, led them through the desert, brought them to a land of blessing, made them a chosen nation, and ever watched over his Word to perform it. His Word destroys the evil as it pulls up and tears down; but it creates the good as it builds and plants. Even in late Deuteronomy, there lingered a belief in the existence of other gods, but for Jeremiah there is the grandeur of a pure ethical monotheism where all idols are an abomination.

God is holy, demanding justice, but Jeremiah dwells rather on the everlasting mercy of a God of love, yearning for the love of his children in return. When Israel is faithless, Jeremiah is "full of the rage of the Lord"; and God corrects his people by the scourge of their own sins, as men reap what they sow. Among the new titles for God that Jeremiah uses are: The Fountain of Living Waters, the Hope of Israel and the Saviour thereof in time of trouble, and Loyal-in-Love.[4] Though God is transcendent, and omniscient, he says: "I am a God who is near, not a God who is far. Can any man hide him in secret, and I not see him? Do I not fill heaven and earth?" In the early oracles of Jeremiah, God deals with Israel as a whole and with the nations as units, but he comes later to grips with individuals in personal religion. He turns from Israel to "ye men of Israel." He reads the heart of man as no previous prophet had done, and sees original sin in every man almost as clearly as Paul. Finally, beyond the destruction of everything of value—the Temple, the Holy City, the Holy Land, the failure of the Law and the apostasy of the people, he sees a New Covenant "written on their hearts" (Jer. 31:31-34):

Behold, days are coming when I will make a new covenant with the house of Israel, not like the covenant which I made with their fathers on the day that I took them by the hand to lead them out of the land of Egypt. I will put my law within them, and will write it on their hearts; and I will be their God, and they shall be my people. And they shall teach no more every one his neighbor, and every one his brother, saying, Know the Lord; for all of them shall know me, from the least of them to the greatest of them, for I will pardon their guilt, and their sin will I remember no more.

THE PROPHET OF THE EXILE, 546-539

In passing from the first thirty-nine to the last twenty-seven chapters of the prophecy of Isaiah, we enter upon a new period of history, a new scene with a completely new style of writing, a new vocabulary, and authorship. Hitherto Isaiah's message has been one of judgment for the impending doom of captivity for sinful Judah; now there is a message of comfort for the discouraged exiles in Babylon, more than a century and a half later. Cyrus the Great of Persia (546-529 B.C.) is pictured as already advanced in his conquests, showing that the former prophecies of Isaiah are at last being fulfilled. There is nothing in these chapters to indicate that they were written by Isaiah, but much to show that they were not. If prophecy is moral and not magical,

[4] Jer. 2:13; 14:8; 17:13; 3:12.

this message of comfort, imperatively needed by the despairing captives in Babylon, would not only have been premature but disastrous, blunting and taking the edge off the warnings of doom by the earlier Isaiah.

A young patriot Jew, whose name is unknown to us, who is now generally called the Second or Deutero-Isaiah, had watched with a prophet's insight the rising victories of Cyrus who might conquer Babylon and set Israel free to return to their Promised Land. The hopeless pessimists among the exiles who had turned to the gods of Babylon could not believe that anything could deliver them, while the rigidly orthodox could look for nothing less than the miraculous intervention of Jehovah, scorning all second causes such as God's working through this pagan idolater Cyrus. But if Jeremiah could refer to Nebuchadnezzar as his "servant" and "battle ax," might not God use this imperfect human instrument even better than a bigoted orthodox Jew, thus making not only the righteousness but also the wrath of man to praise him? As God's human instrument had taken Israel captive to Babylon, so his servant from Persia should now restore them. Cyrus was stamped with the signature of "God, character and success." Conquering Media in 550 B.C., he was well-nigh as tolerant as Rome was to be, benevolent toward Israel, which might serve him as a buffer against Egypt and the West.

In connection with Isaiah's view of history in counting Cyrus as God's instrument we may note that Hegel closes his *Philosophy of History* with the words: "This is the true theodicy, the justification of God in history. The human spirit is capable of being reconciled with the course of past and present history only when it sees that that which has happened and which is daily happening has been and is, not only not without God, but is essentially the work of God himself." If God could use Nebuchadnezzar and Cyrus, however evil, does this suggest the possibility that he might use Stalin, Hitler and the leaders of Japan? They are surely not "the wave of the future" but may unconsciously accomplish God's ultimate purposes for good when his destructive judgments are abroad in the earth. As in the charge to Jeremiah, does the God of righteousness still work through human instruments "to root up and to pull down to wreck and to ruin," as well as to build and to plant? Is God any more complacent with regard to the monstrous injustice of man's economic order and of his conquering imperialism today among "Christian" nations than he was in the days of Amos, Jeremiah or Isaiah? All the prophets seem to be our contemporaries and the same human problems are perennial.

With a conviction that Yahweh is the Supreme Director of all movements in history and in the lofty language of a poet, the great Prophet of the Exile's vivid imagination sees heavenly beings in the desert preparing a miraculous highway for weak and weary Israel. With a prophet's certainty, he counts it already done; he sees Babylon fallen and Jerusalem rebuilt. All is possible in the light of his discovery of God. The prophet declares there is no other God beside Yahweh, he alone is God in the light of this blazing monotheism. It had taken several centuries to wean the Jews from their ubiquitous idolatry and from lower sensuous views of Yahweh and his nature. After the Babylonian exile, however, the Jews, the later Mohammedans who were influenced by them, and Protestant and Puritan Christians for all time have had a horror of idolatry. One must read again the first thousand years of Israel's history or live in lands of idolatrous polytheism to appreciate the significance of this fact.

This prophet's ethical monotheism proclaims the unity of the God of all mankind. Indeed, this writer has almost the humanity and catholicity of the parable of the Good Samaritan. Such prophets were the crowning glory of Israel. They began their course amid the mists and the low-lying valleys in their protest against the sensuous worship of both the Baalim and Yahweh. They ended upon the sunlit mountaintops with their blazing faith in the righteous and loving character of the God of the whole earth. They began by making Israel the favorite of God. They ended by making Israel the "Servant of God" upon whom great sufferings were imposed by God himself.

The Second Isaiah is a thinker, a theologian and a poet as well as a prophet. He employs a "singing style." His poet's imagination and intense enthusiasm break into rhapsody and live in the future rather than in the depressing present of Babylon. He is in the process of transforming the national religion of Israel's ethical monotheism into a universal religion for all. He looks forward to a day when all men will worship Jehovah as their only God and be saved by him. This prophet could have said, "There is no God but God and Israel is his prophet." His prophecy furnishes the transition to and preparation for the New Testament. "His spiritual epic not only inflamed the faith of Israel, but surpassed all other writings of the Old Testament in its influence on mankind. Reaching the highest level of Old Testament religion, he passed on the torch to Christianity and the world."

This is the great evangelical pre-Christian prophet. Without offering any proofs, he regards his contagious monotheism as axiomatic and tries to rekindle a burning faith in God in his people. This writer combines the faith of the prophets of Israel with the philosophy of Job, identifying the national God of Abraham and the prophetic international God of justice and love, with Job's almighty creator of all the starry host of heaven and all that exists in one universe. He points his people to the stars on that barren Babylonian plain and to God as their only hope of escape. Thus a universal God and a universal religion are the consummation of history, the spiritual goal of the world. No prophet had ever expressed so clearly the universal implications of Israel's religion.

For nearly half a century during the captivity (from 586 to 538 B.C.) the Jews had been deprived of all the ordinances and sacraments of their religion. They could not sing the songs of Zion among their enemies and they were homesick for their own promised Holy Land. The Prophet of the Exile is unique in his majestic description of the character of God as holy and loving, universal yet passionately tender, and in his portrayal of the Suffering Servant of Jehovah as probably an unconscious prophecy of Christ. He seems to be writing better than he knew, and was probably beyond his depth in experience and understanding in these great passages. He is often vague and contradictory and shifts from the actual to the ideal, from the nation to the holy remnant and then to an individual, historic or symbolic. He takes the thought of social solidarity and makes it applicable to Israel and to the world at large.

The Servant is often undoubtedly a collective term for suffering and persecuted Israel, the chosen people of God, who as a nation are to be a light to the Gentiles, his witnesses to the end of the earth, for "salvation is of the Jews."[5] Yet many are called but few are chosen. When Israel fails as a nation, God turns to the purified remnant, from Israel after the flesh to Israel after the spirit, to "the seed of Jacob" as his instrument. In Isa. 49:3-6, the Servant, as the holy remnant of spiritual Israel, is to raise up the tribes of Jacob and to restore Israel as a whole, as well as to be a light to the nations and salvation to the end of the earth. Though the nation crucified their Messiah, Paul, the twelve apostles, and the early Jewish church as a holy remnant and God's Servant are used to proclaim the universal gospel for all mankind.

But in Isa. 52:13 to 53:12, the Servant has suddenly become a personification or an individual person, and as George Adam Smith says, the passage "was fulfilled in One Person, Jesus of Nazareth, and achieved in all its details by Him alone. But Christ's personal fulfilment of it does not necessarily imply that our prophet wrote it of a Person."[6] In the New Testament, the phrase the Servant of the Lord is used both for his people and his Person. At Nazareth, Jesus read his own commission from Isa. 41:1: The Spirit of the Lord is upon me. His acts and words repeatedly show his consciousness of fulfilling more than a human martyrdom and of the significance of his death as in some way an expiation for his people's sins, and the basis of the New Covenant in his blood. As the writer describes this suffering and crucified Servant, the style is no longer eloquent and flowing but "broken, sobbing, and recurrent:"

> See! my Servant, whom I uphold;
> My chosen one, in whom I delight.
> I have put my Spirit upon him,
> He shall bring forth justice to the nations.
> He was despised, and avoided by men,
> A man of sorrows, and acquainted with pain.
> Yet it was our pains that he bore,
> Our sorrows that he carried.
> He was wounded for our transgressions.

[5] Isa. 41:8 "Thou Israel art my servant, Jacob whom I have chosen," and in 44:1, 21, "Now hear O Jacob my servant; and Israel whom I have chosen."
[6] G. A. Smith, *Isaiah*, Vol. II, p. 283.

> He was crushed for our iniquities;
> The chastisement of our welfare was upon him,
> And through his stripes we were healed.
> All we like sheep had gone astray,
> We had turned everyone to his own way;
> And the Lord made to light upon him
> The guilt of us all.

As we recall the witnesses summoned to support the thesis that man discovers God, there is no more clearly marked period of the correlative operation of divine revelation and human discovery throughout the last three millenniums of history than the three hundred years from Amos to Malachi, or the seven centuries from Hosea to Jesus Christ. These prophets, not only of Israel but of our common humanity, seem to be in the very midstream of the self-revelation of God to man. They take a commanding place in the permanent Bible of the human race. We find that men like Amos, Hosea or Jeremiah are faulty and fallible like the rest of humanity but there is morally a piercing quality, a self-evidencing power in their message that is inescapable. Many may be skeptical as to the moral and spiritual contribution of Hellenism, but no one who has discovered the reality and importance of ethical monotheism can fail to see that it lies at the very foundation of all that is best in our civilization. It is the salt of the earth without which the rest would have perished long ago, as did Babylon and Rome.

We saw how Amos once for all strikes the clear note of the righteousness or holiness of God. Logically and chronologically this is the first, the foremost, the absolutely imperative element in ethical monotheism and in man's relation to God and his fellows. A holy God *must* demand social justice of man in his dealing with his fellow men. No ceremonial trivialities, no philanthropic charity even though one give his body to be burned —nothing can ever be a substitute for justice which Jesus counted so weighty a matter of the law. A man must leave his unacceptable gift at the altar of God and first go and be reconciled to his brother man if he is wrong in this crucial all-important matter which is inseparable in divine and human relations. Many see in this truth the crux of what is wrong in our disintegrating social order today. If righteousness is ever to exalt a nation these prophets are living forces in our individual and national life at this hour.

We saw how Hosea realized out of the depth of suffering in his own heart and home the equally sure conviction of the love and mercy of God. From this fountainhead, the truth is later derived that God not only forgives a repentant Israel but like a father he seeks and will receive a prodigal individual or prodigal humanity when they return to him. This mighty truth of the love of God who seeks his children and freely forgives them when they repent, is forever central and from it is derived the later generalization that God is love. Thus we have in the very first two literary prophets the two correlative aspects of God's nature which must abide for all time. Here also is the source of the two eternal commands of all high religion to love God with all our hearts and our neighbor as ourselves.

Micah and succeeding prophets sum up the whole duty of man forever. Even the most sophisticated modern writer like George Bernard Shaw can find no better summary of human duty for universal man than to do justice, to love mercy and to walk humbly with his God. Once this universal truth is discovered, it becomes part of what we have called throughout this volume the central core of experience and of man's moral certainty which can never be denied nor destroyed. And these prophets proclaim not only man's duty and God's arduous requirement but the provision of God's grace in the Messianic fulfillment for all nations in the universal Kingdom of God. The ultimate realization of the possibility of peace on earth and good will among men—only realizable through this spiritual kingdom— was never more desperately needed than in our own day and presumably it can never be realized until man returns to God.

In Jeremiah we found the first clear prophetic note of personal religion where a man can walk alone with God even though the earth be moved or the heavens seem to fall about him. Here we found the first promise of a new covenant written in the heart for all men and all time, regardless of all externals, institutional or ecclesiastical. Finally, in the great unknown Prophet of the Exile, we found in the type of the Suffering Servant the promise on the divine side of the solution of the problem of evil. Thus, however veiled in vague prophecy or hidden type, we have progressed in the prophets from the thundering judgment of Amos to the foreshadowing of the cross of Christ in the Prophet of the Exile; from the inexorable demand for human justice, to the divine work of redemption, from "wrath" to mercy, from judgment to vicarious atonement, from human despair to the prophetic truth that man discovers God.

CHAPTER IV

THE DISCOVERY OF GOD IN THE NEW TESTAMENT

IN OUR study of man's discovery of the divine, we now turn to the New Testament as the chief source of our knowledge of God. These twenty-seven human documents in themselves constitute a "library." Here is a collection of books which differ widely, not only in the style and viewpoint of these authors, but in their teaching, which is at times contradictory. No extended saying of Jesus is given in the same words in the Four Gospels, or in any three, or even two of them. There is no possibility for bibliolatry in the critical study of these widely varying documents. Yet, quite as remarkable as their differences, there is an underlying unity in the common experience which they record and in their testimony as to man's discovery of God.

In this library of documents three groups are dominant. These are the three Synoptic Gospels which have a prevailingly Jewish background, the Fourth Gospel and Johannine writings in the Greek tradition, and the epistles of Paul who is the first Christian theologian. The Four Gospels give four portraits of Jesus. Fortunately human portraits always differ—as do even mechanical camera snapshots, but they help to form an authentic composite picture of the most human figure found in the Bible or in any literature.

THE SYNOPTIC GOSPELS

The first three gospels present a fairly consistent picture of Jesus as a man. Four and a half centuries after Malachi, there suddenly appeared a young prophet in Galilee proclaiming an amazing message: "The time has come and the reign of God is near; repent and believe this good news." Beginning as Amos the shepherd-prophet had done, and as Jeremiah and John the Baptist who had called the people to repentance, Jesus announced this thrilling good news of the near approach of the reign of God on earth. This supernatural catastrophic event would transform and transfigure the present world. It was a religious hope of personal and social redemption. In spite of his sublime teaching and blameless life in complete obedience to the will of God, Jesus encountered the fierce opposition of the Jewish and Roman authorities and was crucified. Yet in some unaccountable and seemingly superhuman way, this unlettered artisan in less than three years had suddenly launched the greatest spiritual movement in history.

In Nazareth they had asked how this man could read when he had never gone to school. He had left the silence of his village shop to call all men to be his brothers and the children of one heavenly Father. Without writing a word himself, this peasant carpenter stimulated the production of the greatest volume of literature known to the world, greater than that created by Socrates, Plato, Aristotle and their followers all combined. The book which contains the record of his life has had a circulation of over a billion copies in more than a thousand languages. It is the world's one universal book. And this same Galilean carpenter has given the world its highest moral standards. At the cost of his life Jesus cut away a labyrinthine forest of nonessential traditions, including the six hundred and thirteen fine points in which the Pharisees had meticulously elaborated the enslaving Law. In place of this he gathered, centered and simplified, not only Judaism, but religion for all time, under the single universal principle of righteous love; focusing all life in the love of God and man.

In a unique way, Jesus experienced and revealed God as Father. The word "god" was as old as man, and the conception of a divinity as a "father" is found in various contexts in Hebrew and Hellenic literature. But on Jesus' lips the words had a new significance, for Jesus himself was new. Out of his own deep fellowship with the divine, he introduced his followers to a new experience of God which resulted in a new way of life. Henceforth there is a new title for Deity; a new summit, a new Mount Everest of spiritual meaning is opened to view in "the God and Father of our Lord Jesus Christ." It is only in the light of Jesus that most of us can believe that we have a Father in heaven who makes his sun to rise upon the evil and the good, who sends his rain upon the just and the unjust, and who marks even the sparrow's fall. He bids us love our enemies and attempt what seems to us the morally impossible—to be perfect and all-encompassing in our love, as is our heavenly Father. It is only in the light of the truth of the God and Father of Jesus that we realize the incalculable value, the priceless worth, rights and responsibilities of each individual soul. Even the humblest is now a brother for whom Christ died. And it is only in the light of the universalism of the love of Jesus that we can grasp the full dynamic of the potential spiritual brotherhood of all men.

Even Jesus' calamitous and catastrophic death had strange consequences, in a way, for instance, that the moving death of Socrates completely lacked. Later, men thought they saw in his Cross the fulfillment of the cosmic law of sacrifice. They thought they found there the convergence of two streams of history in man's long search for God and God's long search for man. The Jew had looked to the last judgment for the final vindication of God. But in reflection, as men stood before the cross of Christ, they began to see a better way, not of sin punished but borne, not of evil destroyed but overcome and converted to good. Men like the great Prophet of the Exile had looked at the stars and dared to believe God could do anything he would. Now they looked at the cross and dared to believe God would do anything he could. In nature they saw God's power, in Jesus' life and death they believed they saw his love.

However we may explain it, not only were Jesus' power and influence not destroyed by his death, but in an unprecedented and almost unbelievable way they were intensified, multiplied and universalized by it. His followers had felt in him an absolutely unique and unbroken relationship with God. After his death, in some strange way this suddenly became available for all men. Culminating at Pentecost in a new spiritual fellowship, the disciples made the great discovery of God for themselves, for they found in principle the same experience of God that he had had. Whatever the reason, the days that followed upon his death witnessed the most wonderful outburst of moral and spiritual energy the world had ever known. The men who had lived with him in Galilee never had any doubts that this carpenter was truly a man. Yet they also felt that God was in his life in a unique way. Jesus henceforth seemed to tower above them in sheer moral grandeur, the one central figure of human history, the commanding spiritual character of all time.

We started with the synoptic picture of this young Galilean peasant. But as always and inevitably happens in the case of this Man, we start with his humanity but soon find ourselves face to face with God in his life. We early discover that he himself is asking us, "Who say ye that I am?" And we know that the answer he seeks, as in the case of Peter, is not a speculative theory, but the searching, personal and transforming reply, "Thou art the Christ of God."

Throughout the Synoptic Gospels, God is Father. This is the most characteristic and profound of all the analogies used to describe his character. He is the creator of human personalities, and men become spiritual sons by accepting his spiritual fatherhood. He is a God of stern justice but his justice is always tempered with mercy. The divine-human Suffering Servant on the cross cries: Father forgive them for they know not what they do. Evil is in part ignorance and all evil is relative. It is only God who is absolute and who can in the end overcome it. And God is love. Because he is so, and because he first loved us, his children are to love God, their neighbor, and triumphantly, even their enemies. Throughout the New Testament, as in the Old, he is a personal God, known in personal relations such as prayer, trust and obedience. The only alternatives to a personal God are that the fundamental reality of the universe is not spirit, or that it is impersonal spirit. Materialism and pantheism are philosophic conceptions which cut the nerve of worship and make personal religion practically impossible. Personality in God is the very opposite of anthropomorphism. God is not a limited person, beside and outside of other personalities. To discover God as personal is to know him in terms of the highest attribute of our own being, and in a way which alone enables us to escape from petty self-centered limitation. It is not an attempt to conceive God in our own likeness. Rather it is the discovery of infinite personality in God which can remake us by that in man which is likest to God whose image we bear.

It would take a volume to analyze the teaching of Jesus. We may say briefly, however, that instead of the Greeks' absolute abstract values of the true, the good, and the beautiful, for Jesus there are three ultimate concrete realities in the fatherhood of God, the brotherhood of man, and the priceless worth, rights and responsibilities of each individual soul. In place of the four self-centered, self-attained cardinal virtues of the Greeks: wisdom, courage, temperance and justice, there are for Jesus four vital attitudes or *individual* relationships of the spiritual, God-centered life: *humility, faith, purity and love.* There are also four *social* implications of Jesus' teaching. These are *justice, liberty, brotherhood and peace.* If Jesus was right in his life and teaching regarding the character of God and the duty of man, we shall never put the world right, whether in war or peace, until we return to these eternal principles, individual and social, which embody Jesus' way of life. And we shall hold the character and teaching of Jesus as a frame of reference by which to judge our various adventurers who discover God.

THE FOURTH GOSPEL

When we pass from the first three gospels to the fourth, we have moved into a new world of thought. We have turned from the Hebraic to the Hellenic, from historic fact to philosophic interpretation. We must view this gospel from two standpoints, historic and religious. Historically it contradicts the first three gospels at literally a hundred points, and could not have been written by a member of the original group that produced the first three. But religiously it supplements and completes them. The author is not trying to write history; any more than was Plato. Both held a high view of philosophy and a low view of history. Like Plato, this writer cared little for concrete fact, everything for abstract and absolute spiritual truth. Consider, for instance, one of his typical anachronisms: "As I said to the Jews" (John 13:33). To what other people had Jesus as a Jew ever spoken save to the lost sheep of the house of Israel? But this Hellenist—as much a Greek in his thought as Philo, almost as much as Plato—is now speaking to Greek Gentiles in Ephesus a century later. Here he counts the Jews as the crucifiers of their Messiah, and now the enemies of Christianity.

This writer cares as little for particulars, for concrete facts and events as Plato, and thinks rather of eternal spiritual Ideas, *sub specie aeternitatis*. He sees the eternal Logos who was with God before the foundation of the world as the agent of creation entering history in the incarnation: "So the Word became flesh and blood and lived for awhile among us . . . the divine Only Son, that has made God known." Where the groping synoptics were baffled by unsolved mystery in the person of Jesus and wrote a truer history because of their undogmatic uncertainty, this great mystic Hellenist writes his gospel in the sure certainty of the incarnation. In the first three gospels Jesus is expected to come again suddenly on the clouds of heaven. But a century had passed and he had not come. The Fourth Gospel tries to show that Christ has come already in spiritual experience, for "he that believeth *hath* eternal life." This writer had discovered God in his own soul; he had the same experience of the living Christ as the Apostle Paul, and seems to feel that the living Christ is speaking through him. Mark had sought to tell of the acts of Jesus, Matthew to record his teaching, Luke to write a history of the Son of Man, but this "John," just possibly John the Elder of Ephesus of whom Papias speaks,[1] strives to give him eternal meaning.

This great anonymous writer resembles the unknown Prophet of the Exile. Writing in the first person, which Deissmann shows was then common in Ephesus, he retells the whole story. He puts into the mouth of Jesus the whole body of his teaching as he understands it, in terms of the life in Ephesus and of the Graeco-Roman world of that day. This made it more understandable and helpful for the whole Gentile world and for succeeding centuries. As perhaps the world's greatest mystic, probably far greater than the actual fisherman son of Zebedee, of

---

[1] Papias, Bishop of Hierapolis, writing about 140 A.D. says: "On any occasion when a person came in my way who had been a follower of the Elders—what was said by Andrew, or by Peter . . . by John or Matthew . . . and what Aristion and the *Elder John*, the disciples of the Lord, say . . ." The Elder John ranked after the apostles themselves. Papias contrasts what Peter and John *had said* and what "John the Presbyter" *was saying*. The second and third epistles of John are ascribed to the "Elder" or "Presbyter." Dionysius says the tombs of the two Johns were to be seen in Ephesus and the Syriac calendar celebrates the apparently early martyrdom of the two sons of Zebedee on the same day long before the Fourth Gospel was written.

whom we know little, this author writes not a prosaic record of fact, but a philosophic interpretation of truth. No wonder Clement counted it "a spiritual gospel" and Luther "the precious and only gospel, far to be preferred above the others." This great Hellenistic Jew thus summarizes the whole Galilean gospel: "For God so loved the world, that he gave his only begotten Son, that whosoever believeth in him should not perish, but have everlasting life."

In this gospel, however, the Logos who became flesh never ceases to be God. From the point of view of the synoptics and Paul this distorts the meaning of the incarnation. The writer does not sufficiently safeguard the real humanity of Jesus, as do the first three gospels, but the human is often in danger of being absorbed in the divine. Nowhere is Jesus tempted in all points like as we are. There is no bloody sweat, no cry "My God, My God, why hast thou forsaken me."

Unlike the picture in the Synoptic Gospels, Jesus knows everything and needs not to learn from any man. Christ is the absolute, the pre-existent Logos before Abraham was, the eternal I Am: the Way, the Truth, the Life, the Light of the World, the Door, the Good Shepherd, the Bread of Life, the Fountain of Living Water within, the True Vine, the crucified, glorified Lamb of God, the Resurrection and the Life—God incarnate in man. In a word, the union of Hebraism and Hellenism has begun and Christianity is now acclimatized to the Gentile world. It is providential for us, however, that the three Synoptic Gospels come first with their historic human record, and that the fourth comes last with its deeper spiritual interpretation. Perhaps each states a half-truth needed to comprehend the whole; each emphasizes one side of reality needed for the full discovery of God.

PAUL'S DISCOVERY OF GOD

It was the conversion experience of Saul of Tarsus on the road to Damascus that revolutionized his whole life. The chief persecutor of the followers of the Nazarene is suddenly transformed as by a volcanic psychological upheaval. He finally becomes Christ's foremost apostle and his greatest follower of all time. In agony of mind from such experiences as the stoning of the radiant Stephen, he had been trying to determine who this crucified Galilean really was. Suddenly he was met by such an inward revelation of "his Son in me" and by an outward blinding light that robbed him of sight for days and seemed of such reality that he was faced with the inescapable fact of the risen living Christ as the chief spiritual force at work in the world. But if God was in Christ, and Jesus was a crucified Messiah, then it involved a transvaluation of all values, and a revolution in Paul's conception of God, of man and of destiny. God was no longer then a Pharisaic Lawgiver, but the Father whose nature is revealed in the Cross. Jesus, instead of a crucified criminal, was the Saviour of humanity. Salvation was not man's slavish legal attainment by merit, but God's free gift to simple faith. Thus the face of all the world was changed, of all history, of God himself, by the vision of the reality of Christ. Jesus' experience of the discovery of God is now repeated in Paul, as it had been in the disciples at Pentecost, and Christ becomes the first-born of a great brotherhood which Paul was to gather over the Roman world.

Jesus had proclaimed "the gospel of *God*," the good news of his swiftly coming Kingdom and a life of moral obedience by which men might enter it. Paul's gospel is that of *Christ*— Crucified Saviour, Risen Lord, Incarnate Son of God, human and divine.[2] The emphasis is now shifted from the life and message of Jesus as recorded in the Synoptic Gospels to the person and work of Christ; from the Messianic Jewish carpenter-rabbi, to the Saviour of the world. Jesus had lived the life, Paul interpreted it. Rooted in his own imperative experience Paul becomes the first Christian theologian. Augustine, Thomas Aquinas, Luther, Calvin, Wesley and all the great Christian teachers of the centuries build their systems upon him. It was inevitable that this new way of life which was turning the world upside down should become a way of thought also. Paul with his fine Pharisaic Jewish training under the liberal Gamaliel, his Roman citizenship, his Greek language and culture had, as a citizen of the world, the unique background that enabled him to interpret Christianity as a world religion.

We believe that Harnack's humanistic view of Jesus is quite

[2] I. Cor. 15:1-9.

out of date. Harnack and his school of modernists held that Jesus was a benevolent Teacher proclaiming the fatherhood of God and the brotherhood of man, almost in the accents of the nineteenth century, and that when Paul and the Greek Christians interpreted the religion "about Jesus" in terms of the incarnation and the atonement they were misrepresenting the simple almost naturalistic religion of this young Galilean prophet. Instead, as a Jew that believed in a personal God, as Jesus himself did, Paul, in his interpretation of Christ, came to grips with man's central and inescapable problem of the relation of the divine to the human. Paul was not disputing about mere words and artificial dogmas; he was concerned with eternal values. The best minds wrestled for centuries with the problems Paul raised and modern philosophy and theology have not outgrown them. Can God reveal himself to man? Can man be the organ of revelation and the manifestation of God? If God was revealed to and in Christ, was Christ real man?

In Jesus, God and man meet. Dualism was always latent in both Hebrew and Greek thought. But this is forever transcended and the breach is bridged if God was in Christ. Paul saw that if God was revealed in man, in creation and in the incarnation, if God could enter history and be manifest in flesh, he could draw all mankind to himself. God could then manifest himself to man wherever man surrendered himself to God. If in the face of the fiercest evil Jesus could make us sure of the divine goodness in nature and providence, if in Jesus' perfect obedience, in his achieved human goodness, God had found a Son who could completely reveal him, then here was the long-sought Logos, groped after by Jew and Greek alike. Here was the Mediator and connecting link between God and man. For a true Mediator must be both divine and human if he is to unite both. For Paul, the seat of evil was in the consciousness and will of man and must be eradicated in sinful men by conversion, redemption, regeneration and reconciliation. If actually Jesus can achieve these things for all who fully follow him, then he becomes the key to all the antagonisms of thought developed in Greek philosophy—the antagonism between matter and spirit, the finite and infinite, the temporal and eternal, the human and divine. All in principle are related to One in whom all is embodied. Here is the missing keystone of the broken arch that had sought to span the gulf which had hitherto separated God and man in all religions and in all life. Here in this first full personality, in this most human Son of Man, One comes to terminate forever the impassible separation between the human and divine.

In our interpretation of Christ, if we take the Synoptic Gospels together with Paul, we have a fine balance between the divine and the human, the Hebraic and Hellenic, the rigorist and humanist elements in life. There are no crystallized dogmas, no hard and fast categories of thought in him. He attempts no impossible "Athanasian" creed with its omniscient but unintelligible account of the inner nature of Deity. Whenever Neoplatonism left the solid rock of Hebraic history and soared away to exalt Christ above the clouds, it introduced a whole hierarchy of beings in the mediation of the Virgin, saints, angels, and other-worldly ideas. This for a time conquered Greece and captured Rome and the Roman Church. There was an inevitable revolt in modern life and philosophy in the Renaissance, the Reformation, and modern science, to reassert the positive side of ethics and religion that had been realized in Jesus and in Paul. The central idea of Christianity is the unity of the divine and human in Christ. All things are reconciled in this great unity.

There is discernible a certain dialectic advance in the view of Christ which the New Testament presents. The Synoptic Gospels suggest a view of Jesus that is truly human, but perhaps too simply human; the Fourth Gospel presents a Jesus truly divine, but perhaps too simply divine; Paul holds a more balanced view of Jesus who is both human and divine. But throughout the New Testament, Christ, though a mystery, is both Son of Man and Son of God.

Even in the earliest and basic Gospel of Mark, the introduction states his theme as "The beginning of the gospel of Jesus Christ," a Jesus who is already an object of faith of a cult. The first part of this gospel committed to writing, and deemed worthy of the dignity and precision of a written account was that of the Passion, which occupies about half of the extent of the rest of the gospel. The first half of the gospel was written in the light of the second, to show how Jesus' death came about and that it was God's will. The resurrection was undoubtedly central in the lost fragment at the end, and the whole gospel, like the other three, is written in the light of this triumphant certainty, with a high and full Christology that was probably Pauline.

Let us remember again that the Apostle Paul had discovered God and was related to God through the instrument of the Law, before which he was found "blameless." Suddenly he finds himself in the midst of a new experience of an infinitely closer relation to God. In some unaccountable way Jesus was stronger than Moses, the sponsor and mediator of the Law. He had become Paul's way to the Father, despite his almost hysterical opposition to him. This had made Paul dissatisfied with Moses and placed Jesus above the great giver of the Law who had hitherto been Paul's supreme mediator. There is a finality in his conviction about Jesus when he is declared to be the Son of God with power by the resurrection, where, last of all, in the series of resurrection appearances, "he was seen by myself." In the light of this overwhelming experience, Paul is forced to reinterpret Jesus, his view of the Messiah, and of the character of God himself. He rediscovers his own life in Christ. Though he had been accepted under the Law he is forced to give this new experience of assurance a new name—justification. And the new relation of believers had to be characterized by a new name—sons of God. For the Apostle to the Gentiles the whole world is new in its new focus in Christ.

As Plato proposed the chief problems for philosophy for all time, so Paul raises the major problems of theology and throws light on their solution. As Jesus reveals God fully for the first time in a human life, so Paul first interprets that revelation. He bends language to new uses as he lays hold on a hundred new terms, sacred or secular, Hebrew or Greek, Christian or pagan, to express in manifold metaphors the one great central reality of the transformation that had taken place in human experience through Jesus Christ. Jesus' revelation of God and Paul's experience of him were so much richer than our own, that we shrink from the full blinding light of the Sun of Righteousness, like Plato's denizens of the dark cave in a world of shadows. Especially in a naturalistic and materialistic age, the unbelief and inexperience of many stumble before such overwhelming conceptions as revelation, the incarnation, the atonement and a Triune God.

Paul starts with the simple fact that in some unique way God was in Christ. But how fully was he in him? Was the goodness, the character, the purpose that his followers saw in Jesus really fundamental in the very being of God? Then was not God Christlike in character? Or, must we say that this Galilean carpenter was better than God and more loving? There are no intellectual convincing "proofs" of God, and we cannot discover him unless life brings us the possibility of an inward experience of him such as Paul and all the characters in this book had, independent of any knowledge that comes from without. If we have that all-satisfying experience we ask no proofs any more than we do of our own existence. But if Jesus as man was a Son, we also through him may be sons. No other ever entered or can enter so deeply into the experience of the world's sin. Jeremiah can tell us of a new covenant but only Jesus can create it and hand us the cup in which in symbol we dimly share his agony. The great Prophet of the Exile can envisage the vague figure of a Suffering Servant, but in Jesus we see the reality of God suffering in man.

Paul shows that fully and finally God was in Christ. Plato pictured a divine Idea, Socrates believed in God's wisdom, Aristotle in an Unmoved Mover, Confucius in an impersonal heaven as a moral lawgiver, Lao-tse spoke of a mystic Way and of human forgiveness, Buddha of almost impossible self-control by the elimination of desire. But in one who was himself the Way, the Truth, the Life, God as Father, in his Son, offers to enter the hearts of all men as his sons. Paul shows that God, not as an individual person, but an all-pervasive Spirit, entered into Jesus and his disciples; and from that time on, God was less transcendent and more immanent, less potential and more actual in his world than he had ever been. For God had entered history in the incarnation. Of no other human being could it be said, "he that hath seen me hath seen the Father." Jesus has "the full value of God," for no other had lived so nearly the life of God on earth. He seemed the very focus of the divine immanence, all of God that could be revealed in a human life.

Paul also struggles to express in human language the mystery of the atonement. In some unique and dynamic way "God was in Christ reconciling the world unto himself." In a score of metaphors the apostle finds in Jesus' death in some way a vicarious suffering for sin, a bearing of it, or the payment of a "ransom." Jesus offers to God in his complete obedience a perfect penitence which his moral obedience made possible. He affords the supreme manifestation of God's love, as a powerful moral influence, moving man to repentance. No one or all of these figures of speech fully explain the meaning of Christ's cross, nor the fact that men were changed by it. Paul seemed to see in the cross both Jesus' participation in the sorrow of God and the experience of God himself in his relation to man.

Paul also found in Jesus a new revelation of the nature and being of God. He and the other devout and bigoted Jews of later date who were followers of the Galilean would gladly have gone to their death rather than cast a few grains of incense upon the pagan fire in the worship of the emperor, for their assertion "Christ is Lord." They were steeped in fierce monotheism, for it had taken the Jews well-nigh two thousand years to learn to have no other gods beside the awful Jehovah of Sinai, and they were the only people who had attained to a consistent ethical monotheism. Yet these men, including the twelve who had all forsaken him and fled, place this man beside God on the very throne of the universe. As they sum up their threefold experience, they close their letters and their meetings with the amazing words, "The grace of the Lord Jesus the Messiah, and the love of God, and the fellowship of the Holy Spirit be with you all."

We have found no hard crystallized dogma in the New Testament regarding the nature of God or Christ, the incarnation, the atonement, the Trinity or anything else. We repeat that the various books in this sometimes self-contradictory library are utterly unlike the harsh finality of the Koran. In a few passages there are the roots of the adoptionist belief that Jesus was a man who by virtue of his constant obedience was at some point elevated to divine rank. In others, Christ is credited with full pre-existence.[3] In the same way passages vary as between a Binitarian and Trinitarian view of God. In most passages the Spirit is regarded as an influence, a gift, or power sent by the Father and the Son and not yet a clearly defined person.[4] St. Paul is clear on God the Father and his Son Jesus Christ, but sometimes identifies the risen Christ with the Spirit, as, "The Lord is the Spirit" (Cor. 3:17). We find in him both a Binitarian and Trinitarian strain of thought. In the first great council at Nicaea in A.D. 325, the religious formula of the Christian belief in the Godhead, as Father, Son and Holy Spirit, was officially stated. The controversy was formally ended only at the Council of Constantinople in 381. The doctrine of the Trinity is not finally settled in the New Testament, nor in early philosophy or theology, but the fully developed *Christian experience* of God has been prevailingly threefold.

The recognition of the limitation of human speculation has wisely agreed with John Calvin when he says: "How can the infinite essence of God be defined by the narrow capacity of the human mind . . . How can the human mind, by its own efforts, penetrate into an examination of the essence of God, when it is totally ignorant of its own? Wherefore let us freely leave to God the knowledge of himself. For he alone is a competent witness for himself, being only known by himself."[5] Christian experience, however, from the Apostle Paul, throughout the early, medieval and modern church, has prevailingly agreed that it has discovered God and known God in his three-

[3] As in Col. 1:13-20; Phil. 2:5-11; Heb. 1:3. In Acts 2:22, 33, 38; 3:13; 10:38. Before the resurrection Jesus was a Servant, a man approved by signs and miracles, who went about doing good, thereafter exalted to the right hand of God, made Lord and Christ and glorified.

[4] Of thirteen of the seventeen epistles which open with the invocation "grace and peace," gifts come from "God our Father and the Lord Jesus Christ." In I Peter 1:2, God the Father, Jesus Christ and the Spirit are mentioned. In II Cor. 13:14, we have "the blessing of the Lord Jesus Christ, the love of God, and the communion of the Holy Spirit." In New Testament formulae, twenty-two are Binitarian and one Trinitarian. The baptismal formula in Matt. 28:19, "baptizing them into the name of the Father, the Son and the Holy Spirit" is probably of very late date. The original Christian baptism was apparently simply in the name of Christ.

[5] Calvin's *Institutes*, Book I, chap. 13.

fold self-manifestation as Father, Son and Spirit; God creating, redeeming, and indwelling; God as transcendent, Incarnate Redeemer and immanent quickening Spirit as helper, and sanctifier—one God, known to us not absolutely but relatively in our threefold experience.

We are not concerned throughout this volume with creedal orthodoxy, for many of our adventurers were accounted revolutionary or heretical in their day, including the prophets, Jesus and Paul. Our sole interest is the adequate discovery of God. It is not the mere fact of God's existence but of his plenary nature gradually revealed, progressively discovered, and known first in personal and then in social experience that concerns us. It can hardly be denied, however, that from the time of the New Testament, most of our witnesses testify to an essential, threefold experience of God. Whatever his inscrutable inner nature may be, we find the God of the Old Testament experienced as creating, redeeming and ruling. He is revealed in Christ as Son, and he is experienced in the Spirit, as God present in the heart. The deeply spiritual Juliana of Norwich (c. 1400) holds a hazelnut in the palm of her hand and quaintly asks: "What might this be? It is (a type of) all that is made. In this little thing I saw three properties. God made it. God loveth it. God keepeth it. All-thing hath being by the love of God." Here is no theological or philosophical Trinity but a threefold spiritual experience continuously known for nineteen centuries.

There is only one way of regarding Jesus as both truly divine and human, and that is by seeing in him the culmination and creative focus of an incarnation that began with God's out-going and self-giving in creation and persisted until it found victorious achievement in Jesus. If we start with the belief in a God whose eternal self-giving is known in Jesus, then we see in Jesus the truth of what God was, is, and ever shall be to men. Jesus is thus the full emergence of the divine immanence in the universe.

By A.D. 150, the brief confessional formula used at the baptism of believers included: "I believe in God the Father Almighty and in Jesus Christ his Son . . . I believe in the Holy Spirit." We are neither entitled to inquire nor are we interested in intruding the question as to whether any man can repeat this as a creedal formula, for it would be quite futile—the very devils believe and tremble. We shall be contrained to ask, however, at the end of the volume, how many have found the threefold experience to which our adventurers testified. To this the Apostle Paul testifies:

Present suffering, I hold, is a mere nothing compared to the glory that we are to have revealed. . . . With all my labours, with all my lashes, with all my time in prison I have been often at the point of death; five times have I got forty lashes (all but one) from the Jews, three times I have been beaten by the Romans, once pelted with stones . . . through labour and hardship, through many a sleepless night, through hunger and thirst, starving many a time . . . but I am strong just when I am weak . . . As sorrowful yet always rejoicing! We know that all things work together for good to them that love God . . . Now what follows from all this? If God is for us, who can be against us? The God who did not spare his own Son but gave him up for us all, surely he will give us everything besides! What can ever part us from Christ's love? Can anguish or calamity or persecution or famine or nakedness or danger or the sword? No, in all this we are more than conquerors through him who loved us. For I am certain neither death nor life, neither angels nor principalities, neither the present nor the future, no powers of the Height or of the Depth, nor anything else in all creation will be able to part us from God's love in Christ Jesus our Lord . . . For the sons of God are those who are guided by the Spirit of God. And when we cry, "Abba! Father!" it is this Spirit testifying along with our own spirit that we are children of God; and if children, heirs as well, heirs of God—for we share his sufferings in order to share his glory.

CHAPTER V

THE SYNTHESIS OF HEBRAIC AND HELLENIC THOUGHT

ST. AUGUSTINE, 354-430

WHEN on August 28, 1930, the fifteenth centenary of St. Augustine's death was celebrated, it was widely recognized that he had left a profounder impress upon the human soul in the Western world than any other since the Christian Era, save the Apostle Paul. He had contributed more to the essence, the definition and the theological substance of Christianity than anyone else since New Testament times. He was the creative figure of the Catholic Church and the chief architect of the Middle Ages. As a brilliant philosopher and teacher of rhetoric, he was counted by many "the greatest man that ever wrote Latin." In his doctrine of grace, he was the spiritual ancestor of Protestantism. William James calls him the first modern man. There is a revived interest in our own day in Augustine and also in Francis of Assisi.

St. Augustine lived in the midst of one of the major crises of history resembling that in the days of Jeremiah or the time of Christ. As Rome perished, a world was falling about him. When Augustine was a boy, the prosperity and peace of the ordered civilization of the Empire still "seemed as stable as the solar system; when he died all was chaos." With the Goths and Vandals thundering at the gates, the church, which had lost its visible center, was rent by schisms and heresies. In A.D. 410, after the third siege, Rome was sacked and given over to savage cruelty and rapine. For a century Christianity had supplanted paganism as the state religion and the superstitious ascribed the fall of Rome to the anger of the gods at the desecration of their temples. Throughout the crisis, Augustine remained serene, and to answer this charge he devoted the first ten of the twenty-two books of his *City of God*.

Aurelius Augustinus, later known as St. Augustine, was born

in Thagaste, a little town near Carthage, in the Roman province of North Africa. Although forbidden by his father to become a Christian, his saintly mother, Monica, gave him most earnest spiritual training during a period when the Christian religion was the one stimulating element in the intellectual and social life of the dying Empire. At the University of Carthage he made a brilliant record, outstripping all competitors, and became an adept in rhetoric. But here he lived a life of dissipation, having an illegitimate son by a young woman who was his mistress for fourteen years. Here also he joined the heretical dualistic sect of the Manichaeans, professing to have received from their founder Manes, who claimed to be the Paraclete, a higher form of truth than Christianity.

After his brilliant university career, Augustine took up the teaching of rhetoric, or oratory, as a profession, training young lawyers in the art of pleading, first in his native town and then in Carthage and Rome. He was in Italy during the five crucial years of his life. At about the age of twenty-seven, he had serious doubts of Manichaeism and entered upon a period of earnest religious inquiry, with deepening conviction of sin. When he received a state appointment as professor of rhetoric in the University of Milan, he came under the spell of the commanding intellect and eloquent preaching of the saintly Bishop Ambrose. Augustine's deep study of Plato and then of skepticism was followed by an agonizing search for personal salvation. His insatiable passion was the search for truth, goodness and beauty. He tried in turn but finally abandoned in despair every other human hope: the dualistic and ascetic Manichaeans, the teaching of Plato, Cicero, Plotinus—and every pagan leader he had sought in Carthage, Rome, or Milan—until at last he was shipwrecked upon Christ. Repeatedly he thus writes of his slavery to sin: "My ancient mistresses still held me," and in answer to the quesion, "Why not now?" he had prayed, "Give me chastity, but not yet." For a time the Platonic doctrine of the divine Word as unchangeable, coexistent with the Father and pouring his fullness into all things, provided him with a weapon against Manichaean dualism. But it was not the saving Word made flesh, humbled and obedient unto death. Though he entered Christianity through the gate of Platonism he tells us that it was always powerless to overcome his lusts and make him a new man: "I sought a way of acquiring strength sufficient to enjoy Thee but I found it not till I embraced that mediator between God and Man, the man Christ Jesus, who is over all, God blessed forever."

After the famous scene of his conversion in the garden which Augustine describes for us so vividly in his *Confessions*, he was baptized by Ambrose on Easter Day A.D. 387. Dr. Kenneth Kirk, Bishop of Oxford, shows that Augustine had experienced a *moral* conversion, over the temptations of the flesh and his besetting sins of lust and pride; a *mystical* conversion, with his account of his ecstasy at Ostia when with his mother; and an *intellectual* conversion when his whole attitude toward life, toward God and toward the person of Christ was profoundly changed. His conversion was followed by his retreat at Cassiciacum which corresponded to Paul's retirement to Arabia. He now resigned his worldly professorship in rhetoric and returned to Africa where, after giving all his money to the poor, he formed a religious settlement, like an Indian ashram with a group of intimate friends to spend his time in prayer and study. The rest of his life was spent in his North African province as monk, priest and bishop.

Several years after his conversion, on a visit to the neighboring town of Hippo, he reluctantly yielded to the coercion of the aged bishop and became a priest. In A.D. 395, he became Bishop of Hippo and remained for the next thirty-five years until his death in this small and obscure little town, dying there during its siege by the Vandals in A.D. 430. In Hippo he lived a penitent's life of extreme simplicity and self-denial. Here he trained a large number of disciples who became leaders in the church, while he became a saintly character and one of the most distinguished ecclesiastical figures in the Empire. Much of his literary activity was devoted to controversy with the heretics of his time, including the Manichaeans, the Donatists, and finally the Pelagians. It was in writing against these last opponents that he developed his doctrines of original sin, predestination, irresistible grace and final perseverance through which he left his mark upon later creeds and theologians. His doctrine of predestination must not be confused with determinism in the sense that man's free will and moral responsibility before God are denied. He simply meant that salvation is God's act, giving man the gift of faith in Christ and enabling him to find reconciliation with his Creator.

Augustine lived at a time of social disintegration when the classical civilization of pagan antiquity, after a thousand years of trial in Greece and Rome, was dying and the new Christendom had not yet arisen. Ours is a similar period, for Christendom has been disintegrating since the Renaissance, and our industrial civilization with its class strife and World War is cracking and crumbling as surely as was ancient Rome. Skepticism and frustration always prevail in such a period. Greek philosophy, despite its early vigor, had ended in skepticism. In opposition to its intellectual autonomy and secularization, Augustine laid the basis of civilization in revealed religion, relating all existence, thought and life to an ultimate unity with the abolition of all dualism. This he had found in the revelation of God in Christ. Thus for Augustine the mind was saved from skepticism, the heart from world-weariness, the will from impotence, and society could be saved from decay. The Christendom of the Middle Ages was a working out of the Augustinian synthesis between religion and life, between Hebraism and Hellenism.

Augustine knew Plato adequately but not Aristotle, and that robbed him and his age of scientific interest. For Augustine, creation is continuous and things are known only from within by knowing God. But this gave an other-worldly character to the Middle Ages. The decadent civilization amid which Augustine lived was sinking in sin, and he saw no hope for the world save in the Christian Church saved by grace.

Augustine was occupied through thirteen stirring years in writing his great *Civitas Dei*. The Latin word *civitas* has no local meaning and corresponds more to our organized community, commonwealth or nation, rather than to the city. Augustine held a philosophy of history that believed in a divine all-ruling providence as a principle of unity and purpose in the world. All his life seemed a series of accidents or fortuitous events which, however, when looked back upon appeared a chain of providences. And as God guides individuals so he overrules nations. Amos had maintained that God had led both the Israelites and the Philistines; the Prophet of the Exile declared that Cyrus was God's shepherd, Daniel had a scheme of world events; and Paul at Athens proclaims a God of the nations and of history. Augustine as the first thinker seriously to undertake a philosophy of history sees two communities in conflict, Christianity and secularism, representing the two principles of good and evil: one motivated by the love of God, the other by the love of self and earthly goods. All history records the struggle between the principles of faith and unbelief. Throughout history, as Abel was opposed to Cain and Israel to Assyria, and as Abraham was a prophecy of the Divine Community that was to be realized in Christianity, so Christ and his church are opposed to Rome, head of the earthly community, "by which God was pleased to conquer the world, bringing it into one fellowship of government and laws." But both the church and the world are within the plan of God: "Behold then the goodness and the severity of God," who makes even the wrath of man to praise him. Augustine utterly repudiates the theory of cycles or repetitive patterns in history held by the early Greek philosophers and the modern Spengler. Under a sovereign God with man relatively free, history is marked by a sure if unsteady advance to an ultimate goal. On the human side the clue to history is found in the inborn impulse of human beings to attain happiness. On the divine side, God, through Christ, by his Spirit is working out his sovereign plan of the Kingdom of God, which is to be realized in part in history but fully and finally only beyond it. In history the love of God is the power of God, of the fully integrated will for the final triumph of the good over all evil in the world.

Augustine held that the Christian should obey the state *except* when its action is contrary to the will of God. War is opposed to every Christian ideal but it is still a necessary evil when it is a just war for the defense of a higher way of life. Augustine held that Christianity had never condemned all wars nor told soldiers to cast away their arms. Rather they were to be content with their wages. Augustine is not enslaved by prosaic literalism like Tolstoy on the passage "Resist not evil." Rather, he believed that the Sermon on the Mount was to prevent our taking satisfaction in private revenge, not to make us neglect our duty of restraining evil men or nations. The Christian citizen is responsible for maintaining justice in the state and peace by its defense, however secular or imperfect the state may be. Like Paul before him and Luther who was to follow him, Augustine was never an absolutist, a perfectionist, nor a pacifist, though he would turn the other cheek and not forcibly defend his own life or property.

Augustine attempted the great synthesis of experience in thought and life where Plato failed. The Greek philosophers for centuries had striven to determine the frontiers of nature, the principle or cause underlying nature, as ultimate being or reality. Differing philosophers had conceived the ultimate principle as water, or air, or fire; as "substantial cause," as "pure being" or "creator." But Greek philosophers had found in the end three independent first principles. They had turned to naturalism, materialism, idealism, the positivism of science, subjectivism, sophistry or cynicism; but they had found no final explanation or solution. Plato tried to diagnose the desperate sickness of philosophy in his day and to find a remedy. He came within a hair's breadth of stumbling on the truth, but he disastrously failed when he identified reality with the inaccessible transcendent pattern or Idea, and identified illusion and error with sense perception.

Plato had sought the keystone of his broken arch in an abstract idea of ideas; the Form of the Good, the One. But this inaccessible One required a Logos, or "second creator," and then a "third creator," or Universal Soul. Plato's missing links were an unprovable hypothesis, in the shadows of which lurked a host of demons and all the superstitions of polytheism.[1] Thus Plato failed to emancipate himself or his followers. In his treatment of transcendence he never finds the Absolute which lies in an unknowable realm "beyond all existence." And in Plato's problem of immanence he never finds "a God who is near." His noble speculation of a lifetime comes to an ignominious end in a yawning and impassible gulf. This was the best that the reason of man could do; including the finest minds of

[1] I am indebted throughout this section to Charles N. Cochrane's excellent treatment of this subject in *Christianity and Classical Culture*, pp. 380-420.

Greek civilization, which excelled the rest of the ancient world.

As Paul had plumbed the depths and the limits of Judaism in his experience recorded in the seventh of Romans, so Augustine had agonized his way through Plato and Plotinus, through skepticism and moral defeat, till he finally found Christ and the whole Pauline Christian experience. In place of the missing links of Plato's three abstract principles, he finds a Triune God—transcendent, immanent and redemptive in history; a God creating, redeeming and indwelling; God the Father, revealed in his unique Son, and acting by his spirit in all the world. He finds this reality not as dogma, anthropomorphism, or myth, but in the rejection of these. Plotinus' monad or One was "beyond knowledge and being" and this rare philosopher and saint had had contact with him—or it—only three times in his life by ecstasy. The dumb masses of common men could never hope for this philosophy or ecstasy.

Augustine, after testing Plato and Plotinus, had seized upon an historic fact; rather he had been seized by it. This fact was personal, the God of ethical monotheism, known for a thousand years by prophets and humble believers; a God entering history and working out man's redemption in it. And this way of life, theoretically and practically, actually worked in experience. The historic Jesus Christ had changed fickle Simon into the rocklike Peter, Saul into Paul, Augustinus, the libertine, into Augustine, the saint. These three were only individual instances of a great multitude of humble folk, ideally and potentially called "saints" in morally rotten Corinth or decaying Rome. God was able and ready to achieve this extension of the incarnation from the First-born Son of Man, as a new type or pattern, into "a great brotherhood" of common men. Augustine sought and found no impersonal Platonic Logos, no "Unmoved Mover," to explain being and motion. His Logos was made flesh and died upon a cross. He was not a dead Jesus but a living Christ! Knocking at the door of every heart, piercing the conscience with conviction as in the case of Augustine, and if he be lifted up, drawing all men with the cords of love.

Augustine found the providence and universal sovereignty of God, but for him as a Roman it is a constitutional not an arbitrary sovereignty. Socrates and Plato both thought that knowledge necessarily implied virtue and ignorance vice. Aristotle held that "virtue and vice are both alike in our power." Augustine knew the human heart better, after thirty years of agony in his own soul. He knew there was no perfectability through knowledge. In his own experience he had cried, "O wretched man that I am!" and had personally known the meaning of "original sin." In short Augustine like all men required a revelation, for man was impotent to discover God by himself. But also in his own experience he had discovered a new technique of salvation in his Pauline doctrine of sin and grace. Augustine knew that he was himself utterly undone, lost and sunk in sin, and all his philosophy could not save him. But he knew also that he was saved and had become a new man in Christ. The libertine was now a saint. All the philosophy and religion of Greece and Rome had never accomplished this. Beyond the fall of classical civilization here was hope for the world.

Augustine had discovered at last a new philosophy of history in terms of a living Triune God. He had found what classicism failed to find; an adequate philosophic basis for humanism, that could at last cry "All things are yours." At last the promise both of Hellenism and Hebraism could be realized. Augustine had now turned forever from the bankruptcy and breakdown of Greek and Roman classicism after a thousand years of trial. Decayed Greece and fallen Rome were the answer of history to the philosophy and religion of paganism. But a new Augustine and a myriad "saints" in an ever-imperfect church were the promise of the eternal *City of God* that lay beyond history and man's last failure. Augustine had received a kingdom which could not be shaken. He had found life, abundant and eternal, for himself and all who would enter the kingdom with the spirit of a little child. In place of the classical search for truth, goodness, and beauty, Augustine had seen the glory of God in the face of Jesus Christ. He had found Truth, Goodness, and Beauty, incarnate in man, as the Way, the Truth, and the Life.

Augustine may be seen best in contrast with his great philosophical predecessor: in Marcus Aurelius is disclosed the best that Hellenism could accomplish. The *Meditations* of Aurelius the emperor (A.D. 121-180) and the *Confessions* of Augustine are characteristic of these two great Romans. Marcus Aurelius is the Stoic successor of the cold Aristotle. By nature he was "sweet, pure, self-denying and unaffected." As a practical moralist, following reason and conscience, believing that "man is a social animal," he consistently practiced the four self-centered Greek virtues of wisdom, justice, temperance and fortitude. Yet with equal consistency he conscientiously persecuted Christianity in his day. Augustine, a greater Roman was, philosophically, the son of the more impassioned Plato, and spiritually a son of God in Christ. He was a more profound philosopher and historian than Marcus. In place of the Stoic virtues he sought to embody in his life the Christian relationships of humility, faith, purity and love. Humble as a child, he was an uncrowned moral and spiritual emperor in the church which was to outlive the Empire. By nature he was more complex, brilliant and passionate than the great Marcus. Repudiating himself, he shone with the incandescent sustained light of God in Christ to the whole Roman spiritual world of his day, and to succeeding centuries. While Marcus Aurelius, greatest of the Roman Emperors, characteristically addresses his *Meditations* to himself, Augustine addresses his individual *Confessions* to God, or to the universe. This fact, together with their frequent rhapsody and panegyric, makes them hard reading for the unspiritual modern man.

St. Augustine shows both in his *Confessions* and the *City of God* that he believes that every man's life and all history is a plan of God, however marred by man's sin. As the greatest of the Latin fathers, he had come to Christ by a Greek road. Plato had already taught him that the Word was made flesh. In his experience, his philosophy and his theology, he had to make the great synthesis for which the world was waiting between the Hebraic and the Hellenic, humanism and rigorism, the aesthetic and the ascetic sides of life. The light came to him first through his certainty of God. The sense of the love of God and of his unchangeable goodness broke upon him like the rising sun. He was consciously pursued by God's love, as the Hound of Heaven. In God's light, he sees the darkness of sin: "I enquired what iniquity was and found it to be no substance, but the perversion of the will turned aside from Thee,

O God." Augustine was a man of fierce passion, tempted in all points, physically and mentally, as we moderns are, not like the gentle and relatively passionless Pelagius. All Europe needed just what Augustine found.

In Augustine's *Confessions*, as a document rare in all literature, we have the full record of the winning of a human soul by God. In Saul of Tarsus, we see a man pass from Judaism to Christianity. In Augustine we see not only the passage from paganism to Christianity, but the birth of a soul, and of a new order in the world, with the falling of the old order. We see the promise of Catholic Christendom at its best. In him we see the deepening sense of the reality and overwhelming sovereignty of God in a great heart and a great mind. Here also he is a pathfinder for the Western world, who is to furnish a doctrinal form which was dominant for a millennium and a half.

Our space will now permit only a few brief excerpts in a much abbreviated statement from St. Augustine's *Confessions*. Augustine as a master psychologist and with a deep knowledge of the human heart, and especially of his own, in simple integrity and utter humility thus addresses these *Confessions* to God:

Great art Thou, O Lord, and greatly to be praised; for Thou madest us for Thyself, and our heart is restless, until it repose in Thee. . . . Passing from infancy I came to boyhood and began to pray to Thee, my aid and refuge. I had already heard of an eternal life, and even from the womb of my mother, who greatly hoped in Thee, I was sealed with the mark of His cross. . . . But how many and great waves of temptation seemed to hang over me after my boyhood. I loved Thee not. I committed fornication against Thee. I was thus carried away to vanities, and went from Thy presence, O my God. This was the world at whose gate unhappy I lay in my boyhood; with innumerable lies deceiving my tutor, my masters, my parents; thefts also I committed. I will now call to mind my past foulness, reviewing my most wicked ways out of the muddy concupiscence of the flesh. I strayed further from Thee, and I was tossed about, and wasted, and dissipated, and I boiled over in my fornications in that sixteenth year of the age of my flesh, when the madness of lust took the rule over me, and I resigned myself wholly to it. My friends meanwhile took no care by marriage to save my fall; their only care was that I should learn to speak excellently, and be a persuasive orator.

To Carthage I came, from my seventeenth to my nineteenth year in the university there, where sang all around me a cauldron of unholy

loves. Stage-plays also carried me away, I became infected with disease.
. . . And now I was chief in the rhetoric school, whereat I joyed
proudly, and I swelled with arrogancy. In that my nineteenth year, my
father being dead two years before, I fell upon a certain book of Cicero,
an exhortation to philosophy called *Hortensius*. This book altered my
affections, and turned my prayers to Thyself, O Lord. I resolved then
to bend my mind to the holy Scriptures, but they seemed to me unworthy to be compared to the stateliness of Tully: for my swelling pride
shrunk from their lowliness.

For this space of nine years then, from my nineteenth to my eight-
and-twentieth, we lived in divers lusts. In those years I taught rhetoric,
and, overcome by cupidity, made sale of a loquacity. . . .

Augustine as a teacher of rhetoric was now guided to Rome
and then Milan where he hears the saintly Bishop Ambrose,
finally leaves the dualistic Manichaeans, and becomes again
a catachumen in the Church Catholic, in answer to the prayers
of his saintly mother, Monica:

. . . To Milan I came, to Ambrose the Bishop, known to the whole
world as among the best of men. Thenceforth I began to love him,
trying his eloquence. I hung on his words attentively; but of the matter
I was as a careless and scornful looker-on. I heard him indeed every
Lord's day, and I was more and more convinced; (yet) I panted after
honours, gains, marriage; and in these desires I underwent most bitter
crosses.

From that my nineteenth year, wherein I had begun to kindle with
the desire of wisdom, now in my thirtieth year, sticking in the same
mire, I said to myself, "To-morrow I shall find it," but I delayed to turn
to the Lord, loving a happy life and sought it by fleeing from it. (Still
the slave of his own lusts, Augustine now turned from one concubine
to another, and from teacher to teacher, breaking away unsatisfied from
the Manichaeans, the astrologers, the Stoics, and the Platonists, until he
finally turns in desperation again to the Scriptures, "chiefly the Apostle
Paul." He now describes the memorable scene of his conversion in a
garden, near Milan in his thirty-second year, in company with his
friend, Alypius, and his illegitimate son, Adeodatus.)

For many of my years, some twelve, I wretched, most wretched, had
said, "Give me chastity and continency, only not yet." And now was the
day come wherein I was to be laid bare to myself? I retired then into the
garden, and Alypius on my steps. In the very fever of my irresoluteness,
I tore my hair, beat my forehead. I said within myself, "Be it done now,
be it done now." I all but did it, yet my ancient mistresses still held me.

Choked with weeping, I cast myself down under a certain fig-tree, when, lo! I heard from a neighboring house a voice, as of boy or girl, I know not, chanting, and oft repeating, "Take up and read; Take up and read." Interpreting it to be no other than a command from God to open the book, I seized, opened, and in silence read that section on which my eyes first fell: *Not in rioting and drunkenness, not in chambering and wantonness, not in strife and envying; but put ye on the Lord Jesus Christ, and make not provision for the flesh.* No further would I read; nor needed I: for instantly at the end of this sentence, by a light as it were of serenity infused into my heart, all the darkness of doubt vanished away.

I made it known to Alypius. Without any turbulent delay he joined me. Thence we go into my mother; we tell her; she rejoiceth: she leaps for joy, and triumpheth, and blessed Thee, for thou converted me unto Thyself, so that I sought neither wife, nor any hope of this world, standing in that rule of faith, where Thou hadst showed me unto her in a vision so many years before.

How sweet did it at once become to me, and what I feared to be parted from, was now a joy to part with. For Thou didst cast them forth from me. Now was my soul free. Now I was indeed to be freed of my Rhetoric Professorship. Thou didst rescue my tongue, whence Thou hadst before rescued my heart. We were baptised (with Alypius and his brilliant son, Adeodatus, nearly fifteen, who died soon after) and anxiety for our past life vanished from us. How did I weep, in Thy Hymns and Canticles, touched to the quick by the voices of Thy sweet-attuned Church!

(There follows a beautiful description of the death of Augustine's saintly mother, Monica, at Ostia on their way from Italy to Africa. He then makes a masterly psychological analysis of human nature, before he rises to the contemplation of the divine nature, beginning with the noble passage: "And I came to the fields and spacious palaces of my memory, where are the treasures of innumerable images." He then analyzes his own temptations under "the lust of the flesh, the lust of the eyes, and pride," and thus closes his *Confessions*:)

Thus then have I considered the sicknesses of my sins in that threefold concupiscence, and have called Thy right hand to my help. Whom could I find to reconcile me to Thee? A mediator between God and man must have something like to God, something like to men; lest being in both like to man, he should be far from God; or if in both like God, too unlike man. But the true Mediator, the Man Christ Jesus, appeared betwixt mortal sinners and the immortal Just One. For as Man, He was a Mediator; but as the Word, equal to God. How hast Thou loved us, good Father, who sparedst not Thine only Son, for us to Thee both

Victor and Victim, Priest and Sacrifice, making us to Thee, of servants, sons, by being born of Thee. He, Thine only Son, hath redeemed me because I meditate on my Ransom, and eat and drink, and communicate it; and poor, desired to be satisfied from Him, amongst those that eat and are satisfied, and they shall praise the Lord who seek Him.

As the Apostle Paul with his Jewish ethical monotheism, his Greek culture and Roman citizenship, was prepared to make the great Christian synthesis in the first century, his spiritual son, Augustine, was qualified to make the needed synthesis between Hebraism and Hellenism. For decades, he had tried Platonism, Manichaeism and every available substitute, alternative or escape from the arduous way of the gospel. His fine mind had explored all the spiritual possibilities of human reason in the pale light of natural religion. At last out of the gloom of his own moral despair, the Sun of Righteousness had risen upon him. He had discovered God: not Plato's Form of the Good, nor Aristotle's Unmoved Mover, but the God and Father of Jesus Christ. He had found and reaffirmed the core of moral certainty at the heart of universal religion, that all that the Lord required of him or of any man since the Prophet Micah was to do justice, to love mercy and to walk humbly with his God. Augustine reaffirms the universal spiritual experience: "Thou hast made us for Thyself and the heart is restless until it finds rest in Thee."

CHAPTER VI

THE MYSTICS' DISCOVERY OF GOD

Every man has in him something of the mystic and of the rationalist and every normal man has the capacity to respond to reality in science, art, and religion. By mysticism we mean simply the *immediate experience of God*. Mystical states of consciousness are states of feeling which often defy expression. They are also states of knowledge, as illumination or insight, into depths of truth unplumbed by the intellect. They are usually passive and receptive in an experience which may modify or transform the inner life or character. St. Paul and the author of the Fourth Gospel were among the greatest of the mystics. Philo, the deeply mystical Jew of Alexandria, united Greek mysticism and Hebrew realism. Clement of Alexandria first adapted the language of the pagan mystery-cults to the Christian way of life and was followed by his great pupil Origen. Plotinus, the Neoplatonic philosopher of Alexandria, one of the greatest practical mystics after St. Paul derived his system from the philosophy of Plato, the Mysteries of Greece and oriental cults. He deeply influenced Christian mysticism from St. Augustine to the Cambridge Platonists of the seventeenth century. St. Augustine purified the mysticism of Neoplatonism and transmitted it in the Christian tradition. Bernard of Clairvaux was followed by St. Francis of Assisi, who came into the open sunshine of glad communion with God and Christlike service for men. In the thirteenth century in Italy the great lay Franciscan Dante, in Germany, the Dominican scholar, Meister Eckhart, and in Flanders, the friar-preacher, Johannes Tauler, the Friends of God, and the great mystic, Jan van Ruysbroeck, shared in the immediate experience of God.

Ever since Clement of Alexandria, spiritual writers have frequently divided the progress of the Christian disciple toward his end into three stages or ways which they have often called the Purgative, Illuminative, and Unitive. Following Purgation, for the imperative purification of character—for only the pure in heart can see the holy God—comes the stage of Liberation or enlightenment; and finally Union with God by love. These mark the stages of the Novice, the Proficient, and the Perfect or full-grown. They may be thought of as Servants, Friends, and Sons. The Servants *do*, Friends *know*, Sons *are*. To break the chains which the ego weaves around the growing soul, with deep psychological insight the three vows of the monastic orders of poverty, chastity, and obedience were worked out in experience, patterned after the simple, surrendered life of Jesus of Nazareth.

There is a strong similarity of experience among mystics, whether Christian or non-Christian, from the Greek Mysteries before the time of Plato, from the pagan Plotinus, or the Mohammedan Sufi, al Ghazali, to the medieval Christian mystics and the modern Gandhi. All true mystics would agree with al Ghazali, the Persian philosopher and theologian of the eleventh century, when he says in his autobiography that the first condition for the true mystic is to purge his heart entirely of all that is not God. The mysticism of Ignatius Loyola "made him assuredly one of the most powerful human engines that ever lived." St. John of the Cross warns us that "the soul during its purgation endures grievous afflictions of spirit," but writing of the intuitions and "touches" by which God later reaches the soul, he says: "A single one of them may be sufficient to abolish at a stroke certain imperfections of which the soul during its whole life had vainly tried to rid itself, and to leave it adorned with virtues and loaded with supernatural gifts." Jacob Boehme, the saintly shoemaker, thus describes the mystic's full realization of the love of God:

The soul here saith, *I have nothing*, for I am utterly stripped and naked; *I can do nothing*, for I have no manner of power but am as water poured out; *I am nothing*, for all that I am is no more than an image of Being, and only God is to me I AM; and so sitting down in my own nothingness, I give glory to the eternal Being, and *will nothing* of myself, that so God may will all in me, being unto me my God and all things.

Many volumes could profitably be written on what the mystics discovered of God. Lack of space compels us to confine ourselves to two or three of the greatest of them who are comprehensible to the majority of us who are still on the lower rungs of the ladder of earthly experience. We shall look briefly at the life of Francis of Assisi, then at the *Imitation of Christ* generally ascribed to the German ecclesiastic Thomas à Kempis, at Brother Lawrence and at Pascal who was both mystic and rationalist, and then at George Fox, the greatest of the Quakers, with their sacrament of silence. As we study these mystics and their teachings, let us remind ourselves that, though the way is still straight and narrow, and though they be few that find it, there are men and women all over the world today, in monasteries or in God's open sunshine out of doors, who are having the same experience—priests and laymen, Christians and non-Christians, in the Church Militant or Triumphant—who fulfill the conditions or pay the price of the open vision or the full discovery of God.

FRANCIS OF ASSISI, 1182-1226

Francis, the son of a rich cloth merchant, was educated in the medieval priests' school of Assisi, acquiring a slight knowledge of Latin and as a young merchant, some French. A poor scholar himself, he retained a lifelong aversion to the pride of learning as he did to the greed of wealth. All his life he wrote little and awkwardly, usually dictating his letters, like the Apostle Paul, and ending them with the sign of the cross. Paul Sabatier thinks the gaps in his education were of marvelous service to him. He knew without learning. Endowed with a romantic and emotional temperament, spoiled by his ambitious parents and association with gay, dissolute companions, he wasted his youth in worldly pleasures and sin.

The early thirteenth century in Italy was characterized by gross materialism and incessant feudal wars. The sins of the world had invaded the church and even of the Roman *curia* it was said: "They are stones for understanding, wood for justice, fire for wrath, iron for forgiveness; deceitful as foxes, proud as bulls, greedy and insatiate as the minotaur." The romantic Francis during this age of chivalry lived in the midst of seven long crusades, which were the church's resort to violence, while the rich Benedictine abbeys as fortresses crowned the hilltops.

From the age of twenty-two Francis began to hear mysterious voices, like St. Augustine or Joan of Arc, summoning him to the sacrificial service of the Lord. He gave away every cent he possessed, stripped off his rich clothing and severed every worldly tie. At the age of twenty-seven, he believed he heard a personal call when Matthew 10:7-16 was read in the church: "As you go, preach 'the Kingdom of Heaven is at hand!' Cure the sick, heal lepers, give without payment. Do not accept gold or silver or copper money; do not take a bag, nor two shirts, nor shoes. I am sending you like sheep among wolves." Francis arose straightway to follow his Master. He was soon joined by the wealthy merchant, Bernardo, who gave all that he had to the poor; Pietro, the canon of the cathedral; a laborer, Egidio; and Brother Leo, the Apostle of Love; until twelve young men made up the Penitents of Assisi.

In poverty, in joy and song, as joyful troubadours of God, they went out to call all Italy to repentance. When the noble lady, Clare, left all to follow Christ, Francis founded the Franciscan Second Order for Women, and later the Third Order of those who could not leave their ordinary vocations. His orders included the great friar, Roger Bacon, the father of modern scientific investigation, the poet Dante, the philosophers, Duns Scotus and William of Occam, and four of the most godly popes. The devoted lay Franciscan Friars Minor numbered a hundred thousand at the time of the Reformation, and there are still today some thirty-five thousand of these simple Franciscans and Capucins in the ends of the earth. With stubborn spiritual persistence these little brothers of the poor have consistently maintained the spiritual stigmata of their crucified Lord in poverty, chastity, and obedience. For full seven centuries the impetus of this life upon myriads has been reproduced because Francis of Assisi was only one of a long line of mystic saints who were the handiwork of God. Francis led the way to the glad springtime of the Renaissance and was the unconscious herald of a desperately needed religious reformation.

Francis early felt he heard the call: "Go repair my house that is all in ruins." At first he applied this literally to three ruined chapels in the neighborhood, and then to the degenerate spiritual church of his day. When he had drawn up his simple Rule for the restoration of primitive apostolic Christianity and had obtained its confirmation at Rome, he led his ragged enthusiasts across Italy as a flaming preacher of the love of God. When nobles and peasants and sometimes whole populations were moved to declare themselves his disciples, he drew up the Rule for his Third Order of Continents or Penitents.[1] The poor *minores* had found in Francis sympathy and a mouthpiece as the masses in India have found in Gandhi in our day. The delirious enthusiasm of the people of Italy was a living testimonial to the unique service of the saint. Indeed the life of Francis reads strangely like the record of the early springtime in Galilee. A few years later it passes swiftly to its Calvary, in "the dark night of the soul," and then on to the resurrection morning and eternal day.

Between 1212 and 1215, Francis sought martyrdom in two attempts to reach the infidels in Egypt, Palestine and Morocco, and in 1219, the foreign mission of the Franciscans was organized. Sixty friars went to Germany, others to France, Tunis, Spain, Hungary, Morocco, where many suffered martyrdom. Later the friars penetrated to other parts of Europe, Asia and Africa.

During the absence of Francis in the East arose the first crisis in the affairs of the Franciscans under the rule of the powerful, worldly Friar Elias. The new Order with a vast organization covering the whole civilized world had now grown beyond the statesmanship of its guileless founder. This crisis and division marked the agony of St. Francis. He had returned from the East broken in health and suffering from a disease which was shortly to end his life. An infection of his eyes, contracted in Egypt, inflamed by incessant weeping, rendered him almost blind and, as his biographer Father Cuthbert says, his mental suffering "brought black night into his soul." The glad troubadour had

[1] This first extant Rule of 1228 was a precious find of Paul Sabatier whose *Life of St. Francis of Assisi*, published in 1894, is the best we have. In this Rule of the Third Order, the Penitent vowed to make restitution of all ill-gotten gain, to become reconciled with his enemies, to live in peace and concord with all men, to pass his life in prayer and works of charity, to keep certain fasts and vigils, to pay tithes regularly to the church, to take no oath save under exceptional conditions, never to wear arms, to use no foul language, and to practice piety to the dead.

now become a heartbroken penitent. In 1224, he retired to the wild hermitage of La Verna to prepare himself for death. At the end of the forty days, Michaelmas fast, longing "to suffer or to die," he experienced his Calvary. After the long night watches, as the day broke, he is said to have borne upon his body the marks of the Crucified. Paul Sabatier, after years of study, was finally convinced of the historic reality of the stigmata, or likeness to the nails upon his hands and feet: "Thus I have come to conclude the reality of the stigmata. They may have been a unique fact without being more miraculous than other phenomena." When Francis repaired to St. Damien, now quite blind and helpless, Sister Clare built him a cell of reeds, and with sympathy and courageous good cheer nursed him back to normal life. One day at the monastery table while in conversation with her he seemed caught up in ecstasy, and upon coming to himself sang his famous Canticle of the Sun.

During the last year of his life Francis, though broken in body, sent his friars up and down the country preaching the good news, singing his glad canticle. As his strength failed, he cried with joy, "Welcome Sister Death." He went to meet death singing as he feebly dictated his last spiritual will, to recall the Order to the simple life once more, in spite of the influence of the powerful Pope Ugolini, Gregory IX. On October 1, 1226, as his last act, he requested that he be stripped of his clothing and laid naked upon the ground, to die in the arms of his Lady Poverty. Asking that bread be brought, he broke it, and gave to his disciples, celebrating the Lord's Supper without an altar and without a priest or wine, for with all his brother friars upon conviction he had remained a layman.

"The Brothers were still gazing on his face, hoping yet to catch some sign of life, when innumerable larks alighted, singing, on the thatch of his cell, as if to salute the soul which had just taken flight and give the Little Poor Man the canonization of which he was most worthy." Within two years, Gregory IX set the official seal on the canonization which the universal voice of Europe had already conferred. Paul Sabatier says: "By an ineffable mystery he felt himself the Man of his age, him in whose body are borne all the efforts, the desires, the aspirations of men; with him, in him, by him, humanity yearns to be renewed, and to use the language of the gospel, born again. In this lies his beauty. By this, far more than by an exterior imitation, he is a Christ."

Brother Leo, Francis' dearest friend, and for the last six years of his life his sick nurse, secretary, and confessor, wrote within a year of his death the *Mirror of Perfection*, which is the best record of his teaching, completed about 1318. *The Little Flowers of St. Francis* is an Italian translation of a Latin original which preserves the quaint memorials and traditions of the early Franciscan Order, compiled about 1322.[2] The little brothers write of Francis' miracles as simply as children speak of fairies. Sabatier considers it one of the most exquisite religious works of the Middle Ages. Though legendary, it shows the atmosphere and local coloring of the environment of the early Order. Francis' chief characteristics were humility, love and joy; and in him Beauty lived content. Many believed that in this simple medieval saint, the Jesus of the gospels had found his purest incarnation. He was probably the world's best loved saint. He sought nothing less than a brotherhood whose cloister was the world.

In prosaic English we have a hopelessly inadequate translation of the liquid Italian of Francis' glowing Canticle of the Sun, as follows:

Most High, Omnipotent, God Lord.
Thine be the praise, the glory, the honour, and all benediction.
Be Thou praised, my Lord, with all Thy creatures,
    above all Brother Sun,
    who gives the day and lightens us therewith.
And he is beautiful and radiant with great splendour,
    of Thee, Most High, he bears similitude.
Be Thou praised, my Lord, of Sister Moon and the stars,
    in the heaven hast Thou formed them, clear and precious and comely.
Be Thou praised, my Lord, of Brother Wind,
    and of the air, and the cloud, and of fair and of all weather,
    by the which Thou givest to Thy creatures sustenance.
Be Thou praised, my Lord, of Sister Water,
    which is much useful and humble and precious and pure.
Be Thou praised, my Lord, of Brother Fire,

---

[2] The quotations which follow are from the Everyman's Library edition of *The Little Flowers of St. Francis* and *The Life of St. Francis* by St. Bonaventura. See pp. 1-4, 29, 98, 115, 126, 244-246.

by which Thou hast lightened the night,
and he is beautiful and joyful and robust and strong.
Be Thou praised, my Lord, of our Sister Mother Earth,
which sustains and hath us in rule,
and produces divers fruits with coloured flowers and herbs.
Be Thou praised, my Lord, of those who pardon one another for Thy
love and endure sickness and tribulations.
Be Thou praised, my Lord, of our Sister Bodily Death,
from whom no man living may escape,
woe to those who die in mortal sin:
Blessed are they who are found in Thy most holy will,
for the second death shall not work them ill.
Praise ye and bless my Lord, and give Him thanks,
and serve Him with great humility.

Space will permit only a few brief quotations from *The Little
Flowers of St. Francis*:

In this book are contained certain little flowers, miracles, and devout
ensamples of Christ's poor little one, St. Francis, and of some of his
holy companions; to the praise of Jesus Christ. It is first to be considered
that the glorious St. Francis in all the acts of his life was conformable to
Christ the Blessed. And that even as Christ, at the beginning of his
mission, chose twelve Apostles who were to despise all worldly things and
follow Him in poverty and in the other virtues, so St. Francis in the
beginning chose for the foundation of his Order twelve companions who
were possessed of naught save direst poverty.

The first companion of St. Francis was Friar Bernard of Assisi, who
was one of the noblest and richest and wisest of that city. He invited
St. Francis to sup and lodge with him. And St. Francis, to conceal his
holiness, flung himself on his bed immediately he entered his chamber
and feigned to sleep. Believing that Bernard slept, Francis arose, in the
stillness of the night; lifting his eyes and hands to heaven he cried with
great devotion and fervour until morning, ever repeating, "My God,
my God!" and naught else. Now Bernard, when he beheld these most
devout acts of St. Francis was moved to change his manner of life, and
spake thus, "Friar Francis, I have fully determined in my heart to
forsake the world and obey thee in all things thou commandest me."
Then (after delay and prayer) said St. Francis to Bernard, "Behold the
counsel that Christ giveth us. Go, therefore, do faithfully what thou
hast heard, and blessed be the name of our Lord Jesus Christ, who hath
deigned to reveal to us the life evangelical." Hearing this, Bernard departed and sold all he had, for he was very rich, and with great joy

distributed all to widows and orphans, to prisoners and hospitals and pilgrims.

And then Francis bethought him of the third Order which he established for the universal salvation of all people. And journeying on, he lifted up his eyes and beheld some trees by the wayside whereon were an infinite multitude of birds; so that he marvelled and said to his companions, "Tarry here for me by the way and I will go and preach to my little sisters the birds." And all stood still the while St. Francis made an end of his sermon; and even then they departed not until he had given them his blessing.

Touching the sacred and holy stigmas of St. Francis and some considerations thereon, Christ appeared in a seraphic vision, and revealed to St. Francis certain secret and high things. "Knowest thou," said Christ, "what I have done to thee? I have given thee the stigmas that are the marks of my Passion, in order that thou be My standard-bearer." This wondrous vision having vanished, after a great space, this secret converse left in the heart of St. Francis a burning flame of divine love, exceeding great, and in his flesh, a marvellous image and imprint of the Passion of Christ. For the marks of the nails began anon to be seen on the hands and on the feet of St. Francis, in the same manner as he had then seen them in the body of Jesus Christ crucified: the heads whereof were in the palms of his hands and in the soles of his feet, outside the flesh; and the points came out through the backs of the hands and the feet. Of a surety he had the image and similitude of our Lord Jesus Christ crucified, expressly imprinted on his hands and feet, and likewise on his side, albeit he strove much to conceal and to hide those glorious, sacred, and hallowed stigmas.

Of his sufferings and death, he kept faith with the Lady Poverty even unto the end, and raising his hands unto heaven, he glorified his Christ for that, freed from all burdens, he was going unhindered unto Him. He was verily minded in all things to be made like unto Christ Crucified. He charged the Brethren that stood around him, on their loving obedience, that when they saw that he was dead, they should leave him lying naked on the ground for so long time as a man would take leisurely to compass the distance of a thousand paces. St. Francis, glorious confessor of Christ, passed from this life in the year of our Lord one thousand two hundred and twenty-six; and that year was the twentieth year of his conversion and it was the second year after the imprinting of the sacred and hallowed stigmas, and the forty-fifth year of his life. St. Francis was canonised by Pope Gregory IX, in the year one thousand two hundred and twenty-eight.

THOMAS A KEMPIS, c. 1380-1471

The Augustinian monk and writer, Thomas Hammerken, was born in Kempen, near Cologne, about 1380, and early joined the convent of poor monks at Mount St. Agnes. He became the biographer of the good Father Florentius and of Gerhard Groot who together had founded the Brothers of the Common Life. He accepted their motto "Abide in lowly simplicity and Christ will abide in thee," making it his lifelong aim, in seeking to be hid with Christ, to "strive to remain unknown." Thomas was trained in the mystical theology and practical benevolence of Ruysbroeck, the Flemish mystic. He was a devout copyist of manuscripts, working joyfully in the spirit of the saintly artist, Fra Angelico, a lover of books, of meditation and of quiet corners. The cloister record says: "In the year 1471 died our wel-beloved brother, Thomas à Kempis, in the ninety-second year of his age. He fell asleep blessed of the Lord." So little do we know of his life that, as he himself would have wished, we are not even sure that he was the author of the *Imitation*.

The famous medieval devotional work, *The Imitation of Christ,* was lived before it was written. It appeared in Latin early in the fifteenth century. No other Christian writing except the Scriptures has had so wide a vogue in the last four hundred years, for it has been translated into some fifty languages and appeared in more than six thousand editions. The *Imitation* was typical of some of the best of early Western mysticism and incorporates much of the earlier mystics, though it differs from the mysticism of Augustine, of Bernard, of Eckhart, Tauler, and Ruysbroeck. It is nonscholastic, non-Platonic, free from arid intellectualism, written with limpid clarity out of deep practical experience of the human heart, and it has appealed to the religious sense of readers in many lands over the centuries. The writer would not have boldly said, as did St. Paul: "Imitate me as I imitate Christ," but seems to say this to us in the *Imitation* as from the other world. His whole experience is a valuable corrective of the oversimplified Protestantism of those who almost reduce the Christian life to the moment of an instantaneous conversion and lazily leave the whole process of purgation and sanctification to the supposed miraculous and immediate work of God at death in another world. The author of the *Imitation* apparently lived the most placid and outwardly uneventful life of any writer mentioned in this book, but the following excerpts from *The Imitation of Christ* show how much he had discovered of God, of the human heart, and of the meaning of life in the solitude of his monk's cell and in his ministry among the poor:

"He that followeth me shall not walk in darkness," saith the Lord. These are the words of Christ; and they teach us how far we must imitate His life and character, if we seek true illumination, and deliverance from all blindness of heart. Let it be our most earnest study, therefore, to dwell upon the life of Jesus Christ. His teaching surpasseth all, and such as have His Spirit find therein the hidden manna. He, therefore, that will fully and with true wisdom understand the words of Christ, let him strive to conform his whole life to that mind of Christ.

What doth it profit thee to enter into deep discussion concerning the Holy Trinity, if thou lack humility? For verily it is not deep words that make a man holy; it is a good life which maketh a man dear to God. I had rather feel contrition than be skilful in the definition thereof. If thou knewest the whole Bible, and the sayings of all the philosophers, what should all this profit thee without love. All is vanity, save to love God, and cast the world behind us. It is vanity to seek after riches, to covet honours, to follow the desires of the flesh, to love that which quickly passeth away. What profiteth knowledge without the fear of God? Better is a lowly peasant who serveth God, than a proud philosopher who neglecteth the knowledge of himself. Be not high-minded; love to be thyself unknown and to be counted for nothing.

He to whom the Eternal Word speaketh is free from multiplied questionings. From this One Word are all things, and all things speak of Him. The man to whom all things are one, who seeth all things in one, he is able to rest in God. O God, who art the Truth, make me one with Thee in everlasting love. Let all creation keep silence before Thee: speak Thou alone to me.

The more a man hath unity and simplicity in himself, the more things and the deeper things he understandeth. The spirit which is pure is not distracted though it hath many works to do. Who hath a harder battle to fight than he who striveth for self-mastery? All perfection hath some imperfection joined to it in this life. A lowly knowledge of thyself is a surer way to God than the deep searchings of man's learning, but a good conscience and a holy life is better than all. At the Day of Judgment it will be demanded of us, not what we have read, but what we have done; not how well we have spoken, but how holily we have lived.

It is Truth which we look for in Holy Writ. All Scripture ought to be read in the spirit in which it was written. We must seek for what is profitable in Scripture. Ask not, who hath said this or that, but look to what he says. Without respect of persons God speaketh to us in divers manners. Read humbly, simply, honestly. Ask freely, and hear in silence . . . Do what lieth in thy power, and God will help thy good intent. Count not thyself better than others. Be not proud. If thou hast any good, believe that others have more. Peace is ever with the humble. Seldom do we entirely conquer even a single fault, nor are we zealous for daily growth in grace. And so we remain lukewarm and unspiritual. If each year should see one fault rooted out from us, we should go quickly on to perfection. Zeal and progress ought to increase day by day. It is a hard thing to break through a habit, and a yet harder thing to go contrary to our own will. Yet if thou overcome not slight and easy obstacles, how shalt thou overcome greater ones? Withstand thy will at the beginning, and unlearn an evil habit.

It is good for us that we sometimes have sorrows and adversities. It is good that we sometimes endure contradictions, and are hardly and unfairly judged. Therefore ought a man to rest wholly upon God. So long as we live in the world, we cannot be without trouble and trial. Temptations turn greatly unto our profit, for through them we are humbled, purified, instructed. All Saints have passed through much tribulation and temptation. Always we shall have somewhat to suffer. He who only resisteth outwardly and pulleth not up by the root, shall profit little. The beginning of all temptations to evil is instability of temper and want of trust in God. Temptation revealeth to us what we are. Check the beginnings. Look well unto thyself, and beware that thou judge not the doings of others. Often some secret thought lurking within us, or even some outward circumstance, turneth us aside . . . He doth well who ministereth to the public good rather than to his own. He who hath true and perfect charity, in no wise seeketh his own good. He envieth none, because he longeth for no selfish joy. He ascribeth good to none save to God only, the Fountain whence all good proceedeth.

Those things which a man cannot amend in himself or in others, he ought patiently to bear. If one who is once or twice admonished refuse to hearken, strive not with him, but commit all to God, for He knoweth well how to convert the evil unto good. Endeavour to be patient in bearing with other men's faults and infirmities, for thou thyself also hast many things which have need to be borne with by others. If thou canst not make thine own self what thou desireth, how shalt thou be able to fashion another to thine own liking. How seldom we weigh our neighbor in the same balance with ourselves. How hath God thus ordained, that we may learn to bear one another's burdens, because none is without defect, none sufficient of himself. How much strength each man hath is best proved by occasions of adversity. Learn to mortify thyself in many things.

There is a whole literature upon the authorship of the *Imitation* just as there is upon the Fourth Gospel. Perhaps as in the case of Homer, Shakespeare, and Dante, this author did but give final form to the spirit and tradition of his age in this treatise on the Christian life in the monasteries of medieval Europe. As Michelet well says: "*The Imitation of Christ,* after the gospel the most wonderful of Christian books, is come as the gospel came out of the womb of death. Out of the death of the ancient world came the gospel; out of the death of medievalism came the *Imitation.* These two dying worlds have borne such germs of life."

The *Imitation* inhabits eternity, not time. It is oblivious to the rise of Joan of Arc and the crowning of the king of France at Rheims, of Columbus and his vision of a round world, of the fall of Constantinople, the birth of the Renaissance and the rule of the de' Medicis in Florence. It flees the wicked world of temptation without, and dwells in the stillness of the inner world of the spirit. It knew nothing of the geographical areas that we now call France, Germany, or Italy. Rather heaven, hell, and purgatory were its only destinations; God and the soul its immediate realities. The monk and the warrior were the real men of the day, representing the battlefield of chivalry and the monastery. The *Imitation* considers only the spiritual world of the monastery. Here speaks the medieval mind as in Dante who was "the voice of twelve silent centuries." It emphasizes a side of life in which the modern feverish world of activity is weak or wholly wanting, and so it may have a message for many to whom Christ would say: "Go into thy closet and when thou hast shut the door pray to thy Father who is in secret."

Since monasticism was to the medieval mind the very imitation of Christ, Thomas à Kempis reveals the inner epic, or the soul of monasticism at its best. Though it represents but one neglected side of life, it speaks the nontemporal, eternal language of mysticism to all ages. Living on this side of the great divide of modern science, we in our day would never be content to imitate this one contemplative side of Christ, but rather the whole Christ in the imperative alternation between worship and work, contact with God and the world, rhythmic inflow and overflow, solitude and society. We can be, what was impossible for Thomas, both catholic and protestant; we can claim both the prophetic and the sacramental side of life, whatever our philosophy or theology. And here the *Imitation* may have a message for us at our weakest point as it continues:

O the coldness and negligence of our times! May progress in holiness not wholly fall asleep in thee. The life of a Christian ought to be adorned with all virtues. Verily it should be yet better within than without. We ought daily to renew our vows, and to kindle our hearts to zeal. According to our resolution so is the rate of our progress. Most of all, we must strive against those sins which most easily beset us. Both our outer and inner life should be straitly examined. If thou canst not be always examining thyself, thou canst at least twice in the day, at evening and at morning. In the morning make thy resolves, and in the evening inquire into thy life. Be thou never without something to do; be reading, or writing, or praying, or meditating, or doing something that is useful to the community. Take heed that thou be not careless in the common duties, and more devout in secret.

Seek a suitable time for thy meditation. Study such matters as bring thee sorrow for sin rather than amusement. He, therefore, that seeketh to reach that which is hidden and spiritual, must go with Jesus "apart from the multitude." . . . Enter into thy chamber and shut out the tumults of the world. In silence and quiet the devout soul goeth forward and learneth the hidden things. Lift up thine eyes to God on high! Remain with Him in thy chamber, for thou shalt not elsewhere find so great peace. . . . Arise, begin this very moment, and say, "Now is the time to do: now is the time to fight, now is the proper time for amendment." When thou art ill at ease and troubled, then is the time when thou art nearest unto blessing. Watch over thyself, stir thyself up, admonish thyself, neglect not thyself.

Accuse thyself and excuse thy brother. Behold how far thou art as yet from the true charity and humility which knows not how to be angry or indignant against any save self alone. By two wings is man lifted above earthly things, even by simplicity and purity . . . Thou art what thou art; and thou canst not be better than God pronounceth thee to be. If thou considerest well what thou art inwardly, thou wilt not care what men will say to thee. To walk inwardly with God is the state of a spiritual man. Blessed is he who understandeth what it is to love Jesus . . . When Jesus is present all is well and nothing seemeth hard, but when Jesus is not present everything is hard. How dry and hard art thou without Jesus! To be without Jesus is the nethermost hell, and to be with Jesus is sweet Paradise.

. . . Love is swift, sincere, gentle, strong, patient, never seeking her own. He who is not ready to suffer all things is not worthy to be called a lover of God. My Son, I must be thy supreme and final end, if thou desirest to be truly happy. Therefore refer everything to Me first of all, for it is I who gave thee all. So look upon each blessing as flowing from the Supreme Good, and thus all things are to be attributed to Me as their source. From Me, the humble and great draw water as from a living fountain. O Fountain of perpetual love, what shall I say concerning Thee? Behold all things which I have are Thine, and with them I serve Thee. And yet verily it is Thou who servest me, rather than I Thee.

My Son, thou must give all for all, and be nothing of thine own. Why art thou wearied with superfluous cares? Is anything too hard for Me? Where is thy faith? Wait for Me; I will come and heal thee. When thou thinkest thyself far removed from Me I am often the nearer. All is not lost when something goeth contrary to thy wishes. I know thy hidden thoughts: and that it is very needful for thy soul's health that sometimes thou be left without relish. . . . This is not the work of a day, nor children's play. My Son, trust not thy feeling. As long as thou livest thou art subject to change, so that thou art found now joyful, now sad. But the wise man standeth above these changeable things, attentive not to what he may feel in himself, being steadfastly fixed, through the manifold changes of the world, upon Me.

Behold, God is mine, and all things are mine! O delightsome and sweet world! My God, my all! When Thou art present all things are pleasant. Thou makest the heart to be at rest, givest it deep peace and festal joy. My Son, lose thyself and thou shalt find Me. My Son, if thou set thy peace on any person, thou shalt be unstable and entangled. He who attributeth anything good to himself, hindreth the grace of God from coming to him. Learn in all things to conquer thyself for thy Creator's sake.

. . . The Voice of Christ: "Take, eat: this is My Body, which is given for you; this do in remembrance of Me." Thou commandest that I draw near to Thee with firm confidence, if I would have part with Thee, and that I receive the food of immortality. Oh, sweet and lovely word in the ear of the sinner, that Thou, O Lord my God, dost invite the poor and needy to the Communion of Thy most holy body and blood. But who am I, O Lord, that I should presume to approach unto Thee? Trusting in Thy goodness and great mercy, O Lord, I draw near, the sick to the Healer, the hungering and thirsting to the Fountain of life, the poverty-striken to the King of heaven, the servant to the Lord, the creature to the Creator, the desolate to my own gentle Comforter. I need two things, even food and light. Thou hast therefore given to me who am so weak, Thy sacred Body and Blood, for the refreshing of my soul and body, and hast set Thy Word for a lantern to my feet. Without these two I could not properly live; for the Word of God is the light of my soul, and Thy Sacrament the bread of life. These may also be called the two tables, placed on this side and on that, in the treasury of Thy holy Church.

. . . Go forward therefore with simple and undoubting faith, and draw nigh unto the Sacrament with supplicating reverence. And whatsoever thou art not enabled to understand, that commit without anxiety to Almighty God. For faith and love do here especially take the highest place, and work in hidden ways. If the works of God were of such sort that they might easily be comprehended by human reason, they should no longer be called wonderful or unspeakable.

BROTHER LAWRENCE, 1611-1691

The simple Brother Lawrence stands in striking contrast to his brilliant French contemporary, the mathematical genius Pascal. Spiritually far greater than Pascal was this lowly and unlearned peasant, Nicholas Herman, of Lorraine, who came to be known as Brother Lawrence. He had first served as a soldier, and afterward as a footman in a great French family, where he clumsily broke everything of his master's. He told the anonymous reporter of his conversations, supposed to be M. Beaufort, who about 1660 was grand vicar of Cardinal de Noailles that "God had done him a singular favor in his conversion at the age of eighteen. That in the winter, seeing a tree stripped of its leaves, and considering that within a little time, the leaves would be renewed, and after that the flowers and fruit appear, he received a high view of the providence and power of God, which had never since been effaced from his soul. That this had set him perfectly loose from the world and kindled in him such a love for God that he could not tell whether it had increased in above forty years that he had lived since." Everywhere he saw the Uncreated Light manifesting itself in and through created things as had his Master in Galilee. From the time of his spiritual awakening he endeavored with single eye constantly to walk *"as in His presence."* When he was between fifty and sixty years of age, in Paris in 1666 he entered the barefooted Carmelite Order as a lay brother and was thenceforth known as Brother Lawrence. His letters, "spiritual maxims" and conversations of this period were published after his death in 1691. His is almost the simplest record of any of the saints of the nineteen centuries. As an utterly consecrated man, he lived his life as a steward, not an owner; a pilgrim, not a possessor; a servant of all and master of none, dying at the age of eighty. His words *seem* simple and childlike, but there is an at first unsuspected depth in his teaching like that of his Lord and Master. M. Beaufort continues:[3]

That he had desired to be received into a monastery, thinking that he would there be made to smart for his awkwardness and the faults he should commit, and so he should sacrifice to GOD his life, with its pleasures: but that God had disappointed him, he having met with nothing but satisfaction in that state. That we should establish ourselves in a sense of God's Presence, by continually conversing with Him. That we should feed and nourish our souls with high notions of God; which would yield us great joy. That we ought to *quicken*, i.e., to *enliven, our faith*. That it was lamentable we had so little.

That we ought to give ourselves up to God, with regard both to things temporal and spiritual, and seek our satisfaction only in fulfilling His will, whether He lead us by suffering or by consolation, for all would be equal to a soul truly resigned. That there needed fidelity in those drynesses, or insensibilities and irksomenesses in prayer, by which God tries our love to Him; that *then* was the time for us to make good and effectual acts of resignation. That to arrive at such resignation as God requires, we should watch attentively over all the passions which mingle as well in spiritual things as those of a grosser nature.

That he had always been governed by love, without selfish views; and that having resolved to make the love of God the *end* of all his actions, he had found reasons to be well satisfied with his method. That he was pleased when he could take up a straw from the ground for the love of God, seeking Him only, and nothing else, not even His gifts. That he had thus reasoned with himself: *I did not engage in a religious life but for the love of God, and I have endeavoured to act only for Him;*

[3] The quotations are not continuous, but are excerpts from *Brother Lawrence: The Practice of the Presence of God*, published by the Fleming H. Revell Company, New York.

*whatever becomes of me, whether I be lost or saved, I will always
continue to act purely for the love of God. I shall have this good at
least, that till death I shall have done all that is in me to love Him.*
That his trouble of mind had lasted four years; during which time he
had suffered much. That since that time he had passed his life in
perfect liberty and continual joy.

That in order to form a habit of conversing with God continually, and
referring all we do to Him; we must at first apply to Him with some
diligence: but that after a little care we should find His love inwardly
excite us to it without any difficulty. That when an occasion of practising
some virtue offered, he addressed himself to God, saying, *LORD, I cannot do this unless Thou enablest me;* and that then he received strength
more than sufficient. That when he had failed in his duty, he only
confessed his fault, saying to GOD, *I shall never do otherwise, if You
leave me to myself; 'tis You must hinder my falling, and mend what is
amiss.* That after this, he gave himself no further uneasiness about it.

That he said to GOD, *It was His business he was about,* and that he
afterwards found it very well performed. So, likewise, in his business in
the kitchen (to which he had naturally a great aversion), having accustomed himself to do everything there for the love of GOD, and with
prayer, upon all occasions, for His grace to do his work well, he had
found everything easy, during the fifteen years that he has been employed there. That he was very well pleased with the post he was now
in, doing little things for the love of GOD.

That he was very sensible of his faults, but not discouraged by them.
When he had committed his limitations to God he peaceably resumed
his usual practice of love and adoration. That in his trouble of mind,
he had consulted nobody, but knowing only by the light of faith that
GOD was present, he contented himself with directing all his actions
to Him. . . . That all bodily mortifications and other exercises are use-
less, save as they serve to arrive at union with GOD by love. He found
it the shortest way to go straight to Him by a continual exercise of love,
doing all things for His sake. That our only business was to love and
delight ourselves in GOD.

When he had business to do, he did not think of it beforehand; but
when it was time to do it, he found in GOD, as in a clear mirror, all
that was fit for him to do. That he was more united to GOD in his
outward employments than when he left them for devotion in retirement. That the worst that could happen to him was to lose that sense
of GOD which he had enjoyed so long; and therefore that he feared
nothing, and had no occasion to consult with anybody about his state.
That many do not advance in Christian progress, because they stick
in penances, and particular exercises, while they neglect the love of

GOD, which is the *end*. That there needed neither art nor science for going to GOD, but only a heart resolutely determined to apply itself to nothing but Him, or to things done for *His* sake, and to love Him only.

He told me, that all consists *in one hearty renunciation* of everything which we are sensible does not lead to GOD. . . . That, without being discouraged on account of our sins, we should pray for His grace with a perfect confidence. That GOD always gave us light in our doubts, when we had no other design but to please Him. That the most excellent method he had found of going to GOD, was that of doing our common business without any view of pleasing men, purely for the love of GOD. That his prayer was nothing else but a sense of the presence of GOD, his soul being at that time insensible to everything but Divine love. That we ought not to be weary of doing little things for the love of GOD, who regards not the greatness of the work, but the love with which it is performed.

That the whole substance of religion was faith, hope, and charity; by the practice of which we become united to the will of GOD. That all things are possible to him who *believes*, that they are less difficult to him who *hopes*, they are more easy to him who *loves*; that the end we ought to propose to ourselves is to become, in this life, the most perfect worshippers of GOD we can possibly be. That when we enter upon the spiritual life, we should consider, and examine to the bottom, what we are. And then we should find ourselves worthy of all contempt, and such as do not deserve the name of Christians, subject to all kinds of misery, and numberless accidents, which trouble us, and cause perpetual vicissitudes in our health, in our humours, in our internal and external dispositions: in fine, persons whom GOD would humble by many pains and labours, as well within as without. After this, we should not wonder that troubles, temptations, oppositions and contradictions, happen to us from men. We ought, on the contrary, to submit ourselves to them, and bear them as long as GOD pleases, as things highly advantageous to us.

It was observed, that in the greatest hurry of business in the kitchen, he still preserved his recollection and heavenly-mindedness. "The time of business," said he, "does not with me differ from the time of prayer; and in the noise and clutter of my kitchen, I possess GOD in as great tranquillity as if I were upon my knees at the Blessed Sacrament."

Excerpts from his Letters

I renounced, for the love of Him, everything that was not He; and I began to live as if there was none but He and I in the world; for at all times, every hour, every minute, even in the height of my business, I drove away from my mind everything that was capable of interrupting my thought of GOD, because we can do nothing without Him; and *I* still less than any. But when we are faithful to keep ourselves in His holy Presence, and set Him always before us, it also begets in us a holy freedom, and if I may so speak, a familiarity with GOD, wherewith we ask, and that successfully, the graces we stand in need of. In fine, by often repeating these acts, they become *habitual,* and the presence of GOD is rendered as it were *natural* to us.

For the first ten years I suffered much: the apprehension that I was not devoted to GOD. During this time I fell often, and rose again presently. When I thought of nothing but to end my days in these troubles, which served only to increase my faith, I found myself changed all at once; and my soul, which till all that time was in trouble, felt a profound inward peace, as if she were in her centre and place of rest. Ever since that time I walk before GOD simply, in faith, with humility and with love. I hope that when I have done what I can, He will do with me what He pleases. I have no pain or difficulty about my state, because I have no will but that of GOD; I make it my business only to persevere in His holy presence, wherein I keep myself by a simple attention, and a general fond regard to GOD, which I may call an *actual presence of* GOD. . . . I am assured beyond all doubt, that my soul has been with GOD above these thirty years. As for my set hours of prayer, they are only a continuation of the same exercise. Sometimes I consider myself there, as a stone before a carver, whereof he is to make a statue: presenting myself thus before GOD, I desire Him to make His perfect image in my soul, and render me entirely like Himself. . . . It is not necessary for being with GOD to be always at church; we may make an oratory of our heart, wherein to retire from time to time, to converse with Him in meekness, humility, and love. I am almost eighty. Let us live and die with GOD: sufferings will be sweet and pleasant to us, while we are with Him.

Be satisfied with the condition in which GOD places you. Pains and sufferings would be paradise to me, while I should suffer with my GOD. I must, in a little time, go to GOD. What comforts me in this life is, that I now see Him by *faith*; and I see Him in such a manner as might make me say sometimes, *I believe no more, but I see.*

From his Deathbed

GOD knoweth best what is needful for us, and all that He does is for our good. If we knew how much He loves us, we should be always ready to receive equally and with indifference from His hand the sweet and the bitter; all would please that came from Him. Let all our employment be to *know* GOD. And as *knowledge* is commonly the measure of *love,* the deeper and more extensive our *knowledge* shall be, the greater will be our *love*. Let us cast everything besides out of our hearts; He would possess them alone. I hope from His mercy the favour to see Him within a few days.[4]

BLAISE PASCAL, 1623-1662

Pascal, the brilliant mathematician and religious philosopher, was a contemporary of Descartes and of Brother Lawrence and in some ways he resembled both. His father supervised at home the entire education of this excessively precocious genius. We may abbreviate Chateaubriand's summary of his life:

Pascal at twelve had created mathematics, at sixteen composed the most learned treatise on conic sections, at twenty-three demonstrated the weight of the atmosphere. Having traversed the whole round of human knowledge, he turned all his thoughts toward religion, from that moment till his death, constantly beset by infirmity and disease. He fixed the tongue that Bossuet and Racine spoke, and finally in the short respite that his bodily pains allowed him, solved unaided one of the deepest problems of geometry, and set down in random order *Thoughts* that seem as much divine as human. This stupendous genius was known as Blaise Pascal.

Many consider that Pascal was one of the greatest physicists and mathematicians of all time. His worldly life in fashionable society gave him an intimate knowledge of men and of the sinfulness of the human heart, but he never descended to dissipation or debauchery. His eighteen *Letters to a Provincial* are beautiful prose that lie at the foundation of the French classical style. However unfair, they are as brilliant a polemic as that of Demosthenes, Cicero, or Swift.

Pascal's whole family finally came under the influence of the Catholic Jansenist school which sought to apply St. Augustine's teaching to contemporary France. The Jansenists turned from reason to spiritual experience, and from Stoic self-sufficiency to complete dependence upon God. They emphasized the need of a conversion like that of St. Augustine to realize the love of God by grace, and hoped to reform the Roman Catholic Church in France. As between free will and supernatural grace, both of which are required for salvation, Jansenius, Bishop of Ypres, emphasized the latter as did St. Augustine and John Calvin,

[4] He took to his bed two days afterward and died within the week.

while the Pelagians and Arminians emphasized human freedom. Jansenism was a severe morally Puritan movement in the
Roman Church which attacked a particular school of casuistry
among the Jesuits.

Pascal is often said to have experienced conversion in two
stages. He first felt he must seek purification and perfection and
yield all to God, yet realized that he had not made the final surrender of his life. He threw himself into the study of theology
until he injured his frail health, and being forced to abstain from
intellectual labor, he returned for a time to the gay world of
Paris society. He now "turned his attention to the world" until
he realized at last that all that is in the world left him in satiety
and disgust.

At the age of thirty, Pascal began to realize that the void in
his heart could only be met by God himself. Epictetus and Montaigne had failed to satisfy him. After the age of eighteen, no
day was without pain but he now "joyfully turned all his sufferings into his penitential sacrifice. In these we know Jesus Christ
the Crucified, who must be the Christian's sole knowledge and
the unique glory of his life." He writes: "Now Thou dost send
me illness to chasten me; render me unable to enjoy worldly
pleasures that I may enjoy but Thee alone. May I, being ill,
glorify Thee in my sufferings. Unite me with Thyself, that Thou
mayest live and suffer in me, that Thou mayest fill me wholly
with the glory they have brought to Thee."

In 1654 came his great experience of rapture which he recorded
in his Memorial. On this scrap of parchment around a rough
drawing of the Flaming Cross are written in abrupt and broken
words the record of his ecstatic experience which escaped human
language. This paper and strip of parchment, always worn upon
his person, were found sewn in the lining of his coat a few days
after his death. They read as follows:

This year of grace 1654,
Monday, November 23, day of St. Clement,
From about half-past ten at night, to about half an hour after midnight.
FIRE
God of Abraham, God of Isaac, God of Jacob,
    not of the philosophers and the wise.

Security, security. Affection, joy, peace
> God of Jesus Christ.

Thy God shall be my God.
He can be found only in the ways taught in the Gospel
> The greatness of the human soul.
>> Joy, joy, joy, tears of joy.
>> I have separated myself from Him.
>> My God why hast Thou forsaken me?
>> That I be not separated from Thee eternally.
>>> Jesus Christ
>>> Jesus Christ

I have forsaken Him; I fled from Him, renounced and crucified **Him.**
> May I never be separated from Him!
He maintains Himself in me only in ways taught in the Gospel
> Absolute sweet renunciation.

Pascal's two hours of ecstatic vision of light, life and love were indescribable and incommunicable. Henceforth in the light of that spiritual reality he knows God with his heart, by faith working through love. He had never found God by his unaided reason, but now God had found him through grace. Pascal henceforth lived a life of ascetic austerity, self-denial, lavish almsgiving, seeking absolute obedience to his spiritual director. He now engaged in controversial theological writing against Jesuit casuistry on behalf of the Jansenists of the Cistercian Abbey of Port Royal which he joined for a short time as a solitary. He died at the age of thirty-nine after spending his last years in an ecstasy of self-denial, of charity, and of aspiration after God.

Pascal's *Pensées* or *Thoughts* were planned about 1660 as an ambitious apology or defense of Christianity to convince the intellect of the doubting; first of all his own. Never a theologian or systematic philosopher, but rather a genius as a scientist, mathematician and literary artist, his work should have been a noble spiritual autobiography like St. Augustine's *Confessions*. But the form in which we have his thoughts are only a rough draft and fragmentary notes for his unfinished work. His great adversary is Montaigne (1533-1592) who seemed to him to express the worst side of the skepticism of every human being, and who infected French thought and literature for the three succeeding centuries, including men like Voltaire, Renan and

Anatole France. As T. S. Eliot says, "Montaigne is a fog, a gas, a fluid, insidious element"; while Pascal is one of the noblest of French moralists. His disillusioned analysis of human bondage is the intellectual analogue of the spiritual drought or "the dark night of the soul" experienced by the great mystics. He makes a discerning study of human motives with all their vanity, pride, and self-deception. He succeeded spiritually where Descartes failed. Pascal finds evil man and the evil world inexplicable by any nonreligious theory. They are only finally understandable in the light of the incarnation. He broods on the misery of man without God. With his piercing intellect, his passionate hungry heart and his whole personality he is ever groping after God, seeking the discovery of God. He relies on faith and revelation to justify each other.

Pascal's unfinished *Thoughts* are fragmentary, incomplete and frequently incoherent. They often combine, however, mental precision and fervid imagination. He writes as a devout ascetic Catholic always assuming that "if you die without worshipping the True Cause you are lost." The first part of his *Thoughts* are an amplification of the text: "All have sinned"—in selfishness, pride, lust and unbelief; but the very nature of sin is to blind us to it. All the world is vanity as the author of Ecclesiastes found. God is the great Reality. Since there is no order in his fragmentary sayings, we may follow them in the logical progress from doubt to God and the reasons for his existence, then to the sense of sin, the need of Christ and the completeness of the life abundant one finds in him. In brief excerpts, Pascal says concerning doubt:

There is, humanly speaking no human certainty, but we have reason. I look on all sides, and I see only darkness everywhere. Nature presents to me nothing which is not matter of doubt and concern. If I saw nothing there which revealed a Divinity, I would come to a negative conclusion; if I saw everywhere the signs of a Creator, I would remain peacefully in faith. But, seeing too much to deny and too little to be sure, I am in a state to be pitied; in my present state, ignorant of what I am or of what I ought to do, I know neither my condition nor my duty. I envy those whom I see living in the faith. It is incomprehensible that God should exist, and it is incomprehensible that He should not exist, that the soul should be joined to the body, and that we should have no soul; that original sin should be, and that it should not be. Draw this conclusion: that there remains an infinity for you to know. The finite is annihilated in the presence of the infinite. So our spirit before God, so our justice before divine justice. The justice of God must be vast like His compassion. We know that there is an infinite, and are ignorant of its nature. We may well know that there is a God without knowing what He is. By faith we know His existence; in glory we shall know His nature. Now, I have already shown that we may well know the existence of a thing, without knowing its nature. Who then will blame Christians for not being able to give a reason for their belief?

Reason can decide nothing here. You must wager. It is not optional. You are embarked. You have two things to lose, the true and the good; and two things to stake, your reason and your will, your knowledge and your happiness; and your nature has two things to shun, error and misery. Let us weigh the gain and the loss in wagering that God is. If you gain, you gain all; if you lose, you lose nothing. Wager then without hesitation that He is. There is an eternity of life and happiness. Now what harm will befall you in taking this side? You will be faithful, honest, humble, grateful, generous, a sincere friend, truthful. You will thereby gain in this life. . . . Religion is not certain. But how many things we do on an uncertainty, such as sea voyages and battles! I say then we must do nothing at all, for nothing is certain, and that there is more certainty in religion than there is as to whether we may see to-morrow. When we work for tomorrow, and so on an uncertainty, we act reasonably.

Those who have the living faith in their heart see at once that all existence is none other than the work of the God whom they adore. Scripture says that God is a hidden God. There are three sources of belief: reason, custom, inspiration. The Christian religion, which alone has reason, does not acknowledge as her true children those who believe without inspiration. The mind must be opened to proofs, must be confirmed by custom, and offer itself in humbleness to inspirations, which alone can produce a true and saving effect. Faith is different from proof; the one is human, the other is a gift of God. This faith that God Himself puts into the heart makes us not say I know, but I believe. . . . Faith indeed tells what the senses do not tell, but not the contrary of what they see. It is above them, and not contrary to them. The last proceeding of reason is to recognize that there is an infinity of things which are beyond it. But if natural things are beyond it, what will be said of supernatural? If we submit everything to reason, our religion will have no mysterious and supernatural element. If we offend the principles of reason, our religion will be absurd and ridiculous. The heart has its reasons, which reason does not know. I say that the heart naturally loves the Universal Being, and also itself naturally, and it hardens itself against one or the other at its will. It is the heart which experiences God, and not the reason. This, then, is faith: God felt by the heart, not by the reason. We know truth, not only by the reason, but also by the heart. It is in this last way that we know first principles; as space, time, motion, number. And reason must trust these intuitions of the heart.

Let man then contemplate the whole of nature in her full and grand majesty. It is an infinite sphere, the centre of which is everywhere, the circumference nowhere. Returning to himself, let man consider what he is. It is natural for the mind to believe, and for the will to love. Love or hate alters the aspect of justice. Our own interest is a marvellous instrument for nicely putting out our eyes. The most powerful cause of error is the war existing between the senses and reason. Man is a subject full of error. Reason and the senses deceive each other in turn. It is a deplorable thing to see all men deliberating on means alone, and not on the end. The will is one of the chief factors in belief. Human life is only a perpetual illusion. . . . Man is disguise, falsehood, and hypocrisy. . . . How hollow and full of ribaldry is the heart of man! Man is obviously made to think. His whole duty is to think as he ought. The order of thought is to begin with self, and with its Author and its end. Vanity is so anchored in the heart of man (that he) boasts, and wishes to have his admirers. Even philosophers wish for them. We even lose our life with joy, provided people talk of it. He who does not see the vanity of the world is himself very vain. We do not rest satisfied with the present. Let each one examine his thoughts, and he will find them all occupied with the past and the future. The present is never our end. The past and the present are our means; the future alone is our end. We know ourselves so little.

The conduct of God, who disposes all things kindly, is to put religion into the mind by reason, and into the heart by grace. Men despise religion; they hate it, and fear it is true. Religion is not contrary to reason; we must make it lovable, because it promises the true good. This religion says that men are in darkness and estranged from God, that He has hidden Himself from their knowledge. He will only be perceived by those who seek Him with all their heart. The immortality of the soul is a matter which is of so great consequence to us, and which touches us so profoundly, that we must have lost all feeling to be indifferent on this subject, whereon depends all our conduct. The Christian faith goes mainly to establish these two facts, the corruption of nature, and redemption by Jesus Christ. Eternity exists, and death must open into it. The sensibility of man to trifles, and his insensibility to great things, indicates a strange inversion. When I consider the short duration of my life, swallowed up in the eternity before and after, the eternal silence of these infinite spaces frightens me. We shall die alone. We should therefore act as if we were alone. We should seek the truth without hesitation. It concerns all our life to know whether the soul be mortal or immortal. If the Gospel be true, if Jesus Christ be God, what difficulty is there?

The greatness of man is great in that he knows himself to be miserable. It is great to know that one is miserable. What in animals is nature we call in man wretchedness; he has fallen from a better nature which once was his. Notwithstanding, we have an instinct which we cannot repress, and which lifts us up. There is internal war in man between reason and the passions. Having both, he cannot be without strife. Thus he is always divided against, and opposed to himself. Man must not think that he is on a level either with the brutes or with the angels, nor must he be ignorant of both sides of his nature. It is good to be tired and wearied by the vain search after the true good, that we may stretch out our arms to the Redeemer. God Himself is our true good, and since we have forsaken Him, it is a strange thing that there is nothing in nature which has not been serviceable in taking His place; the stars, the heavens, earth, pestilence, war, famine, vices. God says: "Man wanted to make himself his own centre, and independent of my help. He withdrew himself from my rule; by the desire of finding his happiness in himself, I abandoned him to himself."

. . . Your chief maladies are pride, which takes you away from God, and lust, which binds you to earth. What a chimera then is man! What a novelty! What a monster, what a chaos, what a contradiction, what a prodigy! Judge of all things, imbecile worm of the earth; depository of truth, a sink of uncertainty and error; the pride and refuse of the universe! Know then, proud man, what a paradox you are to yourself. Humble yourself, weak reason; be silent, foolish nature; learn that man infinitely transcends man, and learn from your Master your true condition, of which you are ignorant. Hear God. It clearly seems that man by grace is made like unto God, and a partaker in His divinity, and that without grace he is like unto the brute beasts. If man is not made for God, why is he only happy in God? If man is made for God, why is he so opposed to God? Original sin is foolishness to men, but it is wiser than all the wisdom of men. If we do not know ourselves to be full of pride, ambition, lust, weakness, misery, and injustice, we are indeed blind. And if, knowing this, we do not desire deliverance, what can we say of a man? The wisdom of God says, "I alone can make you understand who you are." God has willed to make Himself quite recognizable to those who seek Him with all their heart, and to be hidden from those who flee from Him with all their heart. There is enough light for those who only desire to see, and enough obscurity for those who have a contrary disposition. Lift your eyes to God, see Him whom you resemble, and who has created you to worship Him. Men before Jesus Christ did not know where they were.

True religion consists in annihilating self before that Universal Being. It consists in knowing that there is an unconquerable opposition between us and God, and that without a mediator there can be no communion with Him. Christianity is strange. It bids man recognize that he is vile, even abominable, and bids him desire to be like God. We know God by Jesus Christ. Jesus Christ had nowhere to rest on earth but in the Sepulchre. Jesus will be in agony even to the end of the world. We must not sleep during that time. "Thou wouldst not seek Me, if thou hadst not found Me."

If God discovered himself continually to men, there would be no merit in believing him. He remained concealed under the veil of the nature that covers him till the Incarnation; he concealed himself still the more in covering himself with humanity. All things cover some mystery; all things have veils that cover God. Christians ought to recognize him in everything. Temporal afflictions cover eternal goods to which they lead. Let us pray God to make us recognize and serve him in every thing.

Pascal's prayer in sickness: Lord, whose spirit is so good and so gentle in all things, like a true Christian I may recognize thee for my Father and my God, in whatever condition I may find myself. Thou gavest me health to serve thee, and I made a profane use of it. Thou sendest me sickness now to correct me; suffer not that I use it to irritate thee by my impatience. Grant that I may consider myself in this sickness, separated in thy presence. Grant, O my God! that I may adore in silence the order of thy adorable providence in the direction of my life. Nothing that is less than God can fulfil my expectation. It is God himself that I ask and seek; and it is to thee alone that I address myself to obtain thee. O God, who lovedst so much these suffering bodies that thou hast chosen for thyself a body more oppressed with suffering than any that has ever appeared on earth! Love my sufferings, Lord, and let my ills invite thee to visit me, to join thy consolations to my sufferings, that I may suffer like a Christian, to feel at the same time both the sorrows of nature and the consolations of thy Spirit through thy grace. I ask of thee neither health, nor sickness, nor life, nor death; but that thou wilt dispose of my health and my sickness, my life and my death, for thy glory. Enter into my heart and soul, to bear in them my sufferings, and to continue to endure in me what remains to thee to suffer of thy passion, that thou mayest complete in thy members even the perfect consummation of thy body, that it may be thou that livest and sufferest in me, O my Saviour! And that thou wilt fill me entirely with the glory in which thou wilt live with the Father and the Holy Spirit through ages upon ages.

GEORGE FOX, 1624-1690

In rural England out of the religious ferment of the Reformation George Fox led the extreme left wing movement, seeking to recover the simplicity of primitive apostolic Christianity. This unlettered shoemaker, with his leather breeches, was in the direct line of descent of the Old Testament prophets, of John the Baptist and the medieval mystics. His vivid *Journal* reads like the self-revelation of St. Augustine's *Confessions*, though it is more crude and violent. Fox's early life shows an unstable psychic constitution, resembling many other prophets and mystics. Only after long discipline in silence and in public service did he achieve an integrated personality with complete self-control, which he believed to be God-controlled.

The one central certainty of his life was that he had come into direct and immediate correspondence with God, who was the undeniable reality of all existence. With all his inward silence and waiting in stillness, this unseen God was to him far more real than the whole material universe. He says: "I came to know God experimentally and was as one who hath a key and doth open." Like the Apostle Paul, he lived not only in the material world but possessed some of the psychic gifts mentioned in the twelfth and fourteenth chapters of I Corinthians and in the twelfth chapter of II Corinthians, and like the Apostle he refers to "gifts and endowments" as well as of "visions and revelations." Though he speaks with reserve in these matters, throughout his *Journal* from first to last he has his visions, voices and trances, yet he finally became a practical prophet of doom like Amos. As he thunders his message through rural England of the Day of the Lord and of judgment, he is more like these rugged prophets than he is like the gentle St. Francis, though love and peace were ever his gospel.

The early Quakers were so nicknamed because they were bidden to "tremble at the word of God," and because they often quaked with emotional fervor in their meetings. They were much more violent and bold than the quiet, proper and prosperous Friends of today, and they were far more persecuted than any other sect in the Old World or the New at this period. They refused to doff their hats, insisted on the singular Thee and Thou instead of the plural honorific You, refused to take oath in court because they sought to obey the literal command to "swear not at all," and declined to conform to what seemed to them the frivolous and worldly conventions of a corrupt society and a dead and formal church. They challenged an artificially built religion with its creeds, rituals and "hireling priests." For two decades every prison in England was filled with them. Even more violently than the Apostle Paul, for twenty years Fox himself was stoned, mobbed, beaten and imprisoned, and his sufferings in filthy, verminous jails finally broke his iron constitution.

Fox was not only a prophet and mystic saint but a practical organizer who built, on the principle of group fellowship, not a new church or sect but a simple body, "the Society of Friends," with no essential officers, ritual, program or creed. His most famous and gifted disciple, William Penn, thus describes Fox's character:

From a child he was religious, inward, still, solid and observing beyond his years. He was of an innocent life, so meek, contented, modest, easy, steady, tender, it was a pleasure to be in his company. With love, compassion, and long-suffering, a most merciful man. He was an incessant labourer in England, Scotland, and Ireland, turning many to God. He visited the Churches of Christ in the plantations in America, and in Holland and Germany. God visibly clothed him with a divine authority and his very presence expressed a religious majesty. His authority was inward and not outward and my witness is true, having been with him for weeks and months together and that by night and by day, by sea and by land, in this and in foreign countries: and I can say I never saw him out of his place, or not a match for every service or occasion. Many sons have done virtuously in this day, but dear George, thou excellest them all.

The following brief excerpts, which are not continuous but are given in his own language, show the nature of Fox's remarkable *Journal*. They reveal his transparent character with all its strength and limitations, and tell us much of his discovery of God:

That all may know the dealings of the Lord with me I think fit briefly to mention how it was with me in my youth. When I came to eleven years of age, I knew pureness and righteousness; inwardly to God, and outwardly to man; and to keep to Yea and Nay in all things. My relations thought to make me a priest;[5] but I was put to a man, a shoemaker by trade. At the command of God, in 1643, I left my relations, and broke off all familiarity or fellowship with old or young. I continued in that condition some years, in great troubles. I went to many a priest to look for comfort, but found no comfort from them. I fasted much, and walked in solitary places many days, and often took my Bible, for I was a man of sorrows. I was never joined in profession of religion with any, but gave up myself to the Lord, for I saw there was none among them all that could speak to my condition. Then, oh! then I heard a voice which said, "There is one, even Christ Jesus, that can speak to thy condition." Then spiritual discerning came into me. Then came people from far and near to see me. The Lord's power brake forth; and I had great openings and prophecies; and spake unto them of the things of God.

When the Lord sent me forth into the world, He forbade me to put off my hat to any, high or low; and I was required to Thee and Thou all men without any respect to great or small and this made the sects and professions to rage. About this time I was sorely exercised in going to their Courts to cry for justice, in warning such as kept public-houses and in testifying against their wakes or feasts, may-games, sports, plays, and shows. In fairs also and in markets forewarning them of the great and terrible day of the Lord, which would come upon them all. I was moved also to cry against all sorts of music, and against the mounte-banks on their stages, for they burthened the pure life and stirred up people's minds to vanity. I was much exercised, too, with school-masters, fathers and mothers in private families. But the black earthly spirit of the priests wounded my life; and when I heard the bell toll to call people together to the steeple-house, it struck at my life.

Now as I went towards Nottingham, I espied the great steeple-house; and the Lord said unto me, "Thou must go cry against yonder great idol, and against the worshippers therein." The priest, like a great lump of earth, stood in his pulpit above. I could not hold, but was made to cry out and say, "Oh, no it is not the Scriptures," but the Holy Spirit whereby opinions, religions, and judgments were to be tried. Now as I spake thus amongst them, the officers came and took me away, and put me into a nasty, stinking prison. In Mansfield the people fell upon me in great rage, struck me down and I was cruelly beaten

[5] Here and elsewhere applied to all persons who were in receipt of money for preaching, irrespective of the particular sect to which they belonged.

and bruised by them with their hands, Bibles, and sticks. The rude people stoned me out of the town, and threatened me with pistols. I was scarce able to move or stand but the Lord's power went through me and healed me.

In the year 1651, after I had been a prisoner in Derby almost a year, being set at liberty again, as I was walking, I lifted up my head and espied three steeple-house spires, and they struck at my life. Immediately the word of the Lord came to me that thither I must go. I was commanded by the Lord, of a sudden, to untie my shoes and put them off. It was winter, and the word of the Lord was like a fire in me. The word of the Lord came to me again, to cry, "Woe unto the bloody city of Lichfield!" As I went thus crying through the streets, there seemed to me to be a channel of blood running down the streets. The fire of the Lord was so in my feet, and all over me, that I did not matter to put on my shoes any more. Afterward I came to understand that in the Emperor Diocletian's time a thousand Christians were martyred in Lichfield. So the sense of this blood was upon me, but I leave it to the Lord.

George Fox was what William James called "a once-born soul." He seemed to live all his life, and consciously from his eleventh year, in "pureness and righteousness." He never knew the dark despair and awful conviction of sin of his contemporary fellow-Puritan, the "twice-born" John Bunyan; nor the years under the law without the assurance of salvation of John Wesley, nor the reason's wrestle with doubt of his contemporary Pascal, who was only a year older than he. Although at a later period he passed through something corresponding to "the dark night of the soul," owing to the condition of the world and the persecution of the Quakers, there is very little evidence in his *Journal* of consciousness of sin on his own account. Indeed, in contrast to Bunyan, he is almost a humanist in his optimistic view of human nature. He believes there is "something of God in a man," a seed of God, an inward Light of heavenly origin that lighteth every man, at the apex of each man's soul where he may meet the divine. This spiritual principle in a man's soul is the basis of authority in religion, though erring man is never infallible. The individual must confirm his own leadings with the inspired group and with the Bible. Though Fox had a high view of the Scriptures, knew them by heart and used them skillfully in controversy, he stoutly refused to call the Bible "the Word of God" three centuries before our rationalistic higher critics, Dr. Harper and Schweitzer. Without church, or sacrament, or creed, he stands for the simplest, most immediate contact of the purified soul with the Living God. And he was sure that the revelation of God is an unending process. No sacred book was ever closed. Fox believed that his own halting discovery could not keep pace with God's initiative in continuous revelation.

In his psychology, Fox was about equally introvert and extrovert. Though much in silence, he was essentially keyed for action. Fox knows nothing of the Roman Catholic mystic's lonely ladder of purgation, illumination and union, though he passed through similiar experiences under another name. His inward experience rather resembled the transparent simplicity of Brother Lawrence. Like him he was an affirmative and practical mystic. When asked at Derby whether he was sanctified he says: "I answered, yes; for I was in the paradise of God. Then they asked me, if I had no sin? I answered 'Christ, my Savior, has taken away my sin, and in Him is no sin.' "

Thomas Carlyle counted George Fox "the greatest of the moderns," "one of those persons to whom the Divine Idea of the Universe is pleased to manifest itself"; and he adds that "the Quaker religion which he founded is something which it is impossible to over-praise. In a day of shams, it was a religion of veracity rooted in spiritual inwardness, and a return to something more like the gospel truth than men had ever known in England." Rufus Jones notes that Fox was not always inspired, but was often dull and tedious. He was an illiterate man, not intellectually qualified as were Luther, Calvin and Wesley to be a reformer of Christianity. The English Bible did not miraculously transform his style of writing in prison, as it seemed to do that of his contemporary, John Bunyan, in Bedford jail. Yet he had a certain majesty of personality that impressed both his friends and his foes. He dominated almost every group or assembly that he faced, and the piercing power of his eyes resembled that of the Apostle Paul or Wesley as they faced mobs thirsting for their blood. The overwhelming penetration of his personality might have become dogmatic or tyrannical had it not been for the humbling discipline of the almost superhuman sufferings which purged him like a refiner's fire, and gave him months for quiet meditation in prison. Sixty times Fox was brought before the courts and he was eight times imprisoned in verminous jails or castle dungeons. After the definite Quaker Act of 1662 his seventh term in prison lasted two years and eight months.

Though a mystic visionary, Fox was a practical organizer. After some years of travel as an itinerant shoemaker, he began to organize his separatist groups, for he was in complete revolt against the church of his day. His main instrument was the Monthly Meeting, superior to it was the Quarterly Meeting, and finally he organized the Yearly Meeting for the Friends of the whole country. These embodied a new type of group mysticism with a plan for democratic management, giving an equal place to women, arriving at spiritual unanimity and a "sense of the meeting," without any majority and minority vote.

Fox firmly believed that on occasions he was granted miraculous gifts and frequently the "wonderful power" "broke forth" when he was speaking. When he was struck such a blow that his hand seemed ruined and incapable of further use, he says: "I looked at it in the love of God and after a while the Lord's power sprang through me again, so that in a moment I recovered strength in my hand and arm in the sight of them all." Throughout his *Journal*, as in that of John Wesley, cases of physical healing and recovery that both men counted supernatural, were frequent. And as in the case of Francis of Assisi and many of our apostles, saints and mystics, Fox had prolonged trance states and the consciousness of voices and of sights when no external object was present.

Fox continues in his *Journal*:

When I came to Swarthmoor, I found the Friends there dressing the heads and hands of Friends and friendly people which had been broken or hurt. My body and arms were yellow, black, and blue with the blows and bruises I received amongst them that day. Now began the priests to prophesy again that within half a year we should be all put down and gone. There was a great rage in the country. I was moved of the Lord to write a paper "To the Protector Oliver Cromwell." After some time Captain Drury brought me before the Protector himself. I spake much to him of Truth, and much discourse I had with him about religion; wherein he carried himself very moderately. But he said we quarrelled with priests, whom he called ministers. As I spake, he several times said it was very good and it was truth. As I was turning, he caught me by the hand, and with tears in his eyes, said "Come again to my house, for if thou and I were but an hour of a day together, we should be nearer one to the other."

At Lanceston we settled in prison. The jailer put us down into Doomslale, a nasty, stinking place, where they used to put witches and murderers. The place was so noisome that it was said few that went in ever came out again alive. The excrements of the prisoners that from time to time had been put there, had not been carried out for many years. So that it was all like mire, and in some places to the top of the shoes in water. He would not let us cleanse it, nor suffer us to have beds or straw to lie on. We burnt a little straw to take away the stink. The smoke went up into the jailer's room, which put him into such a rage that he took the pots of excrements of the thieves, and poured them through a hole upon our heads whereby we were so bespattered that we could not touch ourselves or one another. In this manner were we fain to stand all night, for we could not sit down, the place was so full of filthy excrements. (Fox suffered more in prison than did the Apostle Paul yet he writes:) My imprisonment there was of the Lord, and for His service in those parts. A great convincement began in the country. In this year the Lord's truth was finely planted and many thousands were turned to the Lord; insomuch that there were seldom fewer than one thousand in prison in this nation for tithes, and not swearing, and not putting off their hats.

I went to Hampton Court, to speak with the Protector about the sufferings of Friends. I met him riding and before I came to him, as he rode at the head of his life-guard, I saw and felt a waft of death go forth against him; and when I came to him he looked like a dead man. After I had laid the sufferings of Friends before him, and had warned him he bid me come to his house. But when I came the doctors were not willing I should speak with him. So I passed away, and never saw him more. I had a sight and sense of the King's return a good while before, for I then foresaw the King's coming in again.

At the time of Fox's death, there were some sixty thousand Quakers in England who numbered more than all the Catholics, Presbyterians, Independents, and Baptists combined. But with a tendency to individualism and quietism, and lacking the aggressive evangelistic fervor of the Methodists and Baptists, this humane, idealistic and finally materially prosperous body never grew to become a popular mass movement in either England or America. Yet it has persisted, remained loyal to its principles, and has never grown old like most ecclesiastical bodies. Not only a few rare men like Penn and Woolman but the Society of Friends as a whole for three hundred years has carried out the principles and practices of their founder, George Fox, and of apostolic Christianity, as consistently as any religious body or denomination in the world. All this has been a monument not to George Fox but to his Master and to his discovery of God for himself and for all his fellow men who would pay the price of that discovery. At the end of his *Journal* we read:

After I had travelled through many countries, I returned to London. Long before this I had a vision wherein I saw the city lying in heaps, when it was burned. Another time I saw the angel of the Lord with a glittering drawn sword stretched southward. Not long after, the wars brake out with Holland, and the sickness brake forth, and afterwards the fire of London; so the Lord's sword was drawn indeed.

Now by reason of my long and close imprisonment I was grown very weak in body; but the Lord's power was over all. I lay all that winter, warring with the evil spirits of the world. It was a cruel, bloody, persecuting time. And whilst I was in my travails and sufferings I had a vision. They that can read these things must have the earthy, stony nature off them. Much I could speak of these things, but I leave them to the right eye and reader to see and read. It was now upon me from the Lord to go beyond the seas to visit the plantations of America in 1671 to 1673.

In 1690, the closing scenes in the earthly pilgrimage of George Fox are best described in the words of William Penn who was present at his death:

My beloved and dear Friend, George Fox, has finished his glorious testimony this night about half an hour after nine, being sensible to the last breath. Oh, he is gone and has left us in the storm that is over our heads. A prince indeed is fallen in Israel to-day. He died as he lived, a lamb, minding the things of God and His Church to the last in an universal spirit.

Penn continues, thus summing up his life:

When he was somewhat above twenty, he left his friends, and visited the most retired and religious people. Among them he sojourned till his more ample ministry came upon him. He was an example of silence, endeavouring to bring them from self-performances, turning to the

Light of Christ within them. In 1652 at the age of twenty-eight he being in retirement to the Lord upon a very high mountain, he had a vision of the great work of God in the earth, and of the way that he was to go forth to begin it. He saw people as thick as motes in the sun, that should in time be brought home to the Lord. His eye was directed northward, beholding a great people that should receive him and his message. He says: "The Lord opened unto me and let me see a great people in white raiment by a river side coming to the Lord." He was moved of the Lord to sound forth His great and notable day, as if he had been in a great auditory, and from thence went north, as the Lord had shown him, to feel and receive power from on high to speak in His name, to visit the public assemblies, to reprove, inform, and exhort them; sometimes in markets, fairs, streets, and by the highway-side, calling people to repentance. He was a man that God endued with a clear and wonderful depth, a discerner of others' spirits, and very much a master of his own, though the expression might sound uncouth and unfashionable to nice ears. In his testimony or ministry, he much laboured to bottom them upon Christ Jesus, the Light, by bringing them to something that was of God in themselves. He had an extraordinary gift in opening the Scriptures. But above all he excelled in prayer. The most awful, living, reverent frame I ever felt or beheld, I must say, was his in prayer. He knew and lived nearer to the Lord than other men.

We had hoped to include in this volume other representatives from the non-Christian religions such as the great Persian philosopher, theologian and Mohammedan Sufi mystic, al Ghazali (1058-1111), who says in his autobiography:

The science of the Sufis aims at detaching the heart from all that is not God, and at giving to it for sole occupation the meditation of the Divine Being. I recognized what no study can grasp, but only ecstasy, the transformation of the soul, and leading a pious life. I found I was impure before God. I repaired to God like a man in distress who has no more resources. My heart no longer felt any difficulty in renouncing glory, wealth, and my children. So I quitted Bagdad, and reserving from my fortune only what was indispensable for my subsistence, I distributed the rest. I went to Syria, where I remained about two years, with no other occupation than living in retreat and solitude, conquering my desires, combating my passions, training myself to purify my soul, to make my character perfect, to prepare my heart for meditating on God. I had never yet found myself completely in ecstasy, save in a few single hours; in this situation I spent ten years. During this solitary state things were revealed to me which it is impossible to describe.

I recognized that the Sufis are assuredly walking in the path of God. Both in their acts and in their inaction, they are illumined by the light which proceeds from the prophetic source. The first condition for a Sufi is to purge his heart entirely of all that is not God. The next key of the contemplative life consists in the humble prayers which escape from the fervent soul, and in the meditations on God, the end of Sufism being total absorption in God. God has brought prophetism near to men in giving them all a state analogous to it. In the prophetic the sight is illumined by a light which uncovers hidden things and objects which the intellect fails to reach. It is like an immediate perception, as if one touched the objects with one's hand.[6]

As we review the mystics discovery of God as the last of our Christian witnesses, George Fox is worthy of a place of honor among our adventurers and pathfinders. Lack of space limited us to the testimony of five prophets, five New Testament writers, five mystics, four reformers, four scientists, and six modern discoverers of God. Among the mystics who enjoyed the immediate experience of God all were different; and each was in some way unique and typical. Francis of Assisi stands out forever as the Christlike and childlike loving saint who reproduced perhaps more than any since the Apostle Paul the life of Jesus in the open Galilean sunshine. He enters the Kingdom like a little child, he retains the childlike spirit, he is a healthy extrovert, living in God's glad out of doors, touching the heart and affecting the conscience of Italy as Jesus did that of Galilee. He left us no teaching; only the priceless gift of life and of a loving character forever fragrant and winsome.

Thomas à Kempis, or whoever was the author of *The Imitation of Christ*, left us the teaching and technique of the saintly life. The *Imitation* is introvert not extrovert, a guide to meditation rather than to action, stimulating for character rather than for service, a manual of devotion for the cloister and for the inner chamber of the heart rather than a prophetic call for reformation. Yet in a materialistic age it has a message for us.

Somewhat similar but simpler and more appealing is Brother Lawrence and his practice of the presence of God. It carries its message from the cloister cell to the kitchen, from the so-called sacred to the secular world, to make all life sacred, in character and in service in the simple doing of the will of God. Brother

[6] William James, *Varieties of Religious Experience,* pp. 394-396.

Lawrence is the most single-hearted and simple of all our witnesses. We would hardly dream that there were any problems
in the world but one, even though that is the great essential.

Poles apart as were the two men at first sight, we passed from
Brother Lawrence to his contemporary Pascal, from the reduc-
tion of life to its first principles, moral and spiritual, in Brother
Lawrence, to a world of thought with its agonizing mental conflicts and its challenging unsolved problems. Yet Pascal fought
his doubts and gathered strength. His concluding words and
prayer are almost worthy of St. Francis or Brother Lawrence, and
Pascal, scientist and mathematician though he was, makes essentially the same discovery of God as they. He too enters the
Kingdom as a little child.

When we turn from this brilliant Frenchman, whose mind
resembled that of Descartes, to his contemporary, George Fox,
the Quaker mystic, we again pass from the complex to the
simple and essential. We turn from the Catholic churchman
and controversialist to the Quaker rebel and reformer. We pass
from one who was prevailingly a rationalist to the typical
mystic, from one who emphasized the historic, the external and
objective, to one who sought to find God in his own heart, from
the sacerdotal sacramentarian of the mass and creeds to the
unorthodox spiritual heretic and rebel without church, creed,
or sacrament. Few of our more than thirty witnesses so exclusively found the immediate experience of God, so dwelt upon the
Inner Light, or were so certain of their subjective experiences
that they assume an almost objective quality. In George Fox,
God is revealed and discovered in direct intuition in the native
monism of the child. In all of these mystics whether Christian
or non-Christian, personalistic or pantheistic there is no dualism to be overcome, for the child who is monistic dwells in one
simple world. Dualism is an affliction of the wise and prudent,
the curse of the sophisticated, the dreaded conclusion of the
philosopher. All that the greatest philosophy can do is to seal or
artificially bridge the rift created by the critical spirit. In our
most advanced spiritual maturity we return to the simple intuitions of childhood and youth, which George Fox as a once-born
soul never lost. Surely Fox and all our five mystics had immediately discovered God.

CHAPTER VII

THE DISCOVERY OF GOD DURING THE PROTESTANT REFORMATION

Both Catholics and Protestants are prejudiced inevitably concerning the volcanic Reformation which disrupted the church. The imperfect and divided Protestant churches were agreed upon three things: 1. The Roman Church was not the sole and infallible medium of God's authority in the world; 2. Protestants denied the miracle of transubstantiation whereby the grace of God was limited to the sacrament of the mass; and 3. They insisted that the reconciliation of man with God was the work of God and was not determined by merit or good works. Protestants held that the revolutionary religion of Jesus had become the reactionary religion of a sacerdotal hierarchy. As a totalitarian church under an infallible pope, medieval obscurantism had often regulated belief, directed the conscience, claimed to teach the only spiritual truth and mediated between God and man as the only authentic, supernatural means of salvation for lost humanity. The best Roman Catholics admit that official Rome had opposed almost every advance in science from Galileo to Copernicus and sometimes had burned its martyrs at the stake. They interpret Luther's outbreak as a divine judgment upon manifest moral and economic abuses. They admit that degrading superstitions and immoral practices had crept into the Roman Church as in the case of Tetzel's commercialized sale of indulgences in the time of Luther. However unauthorized, men were promised the forgiveness of sins past, present, and future and the deliverance of their relatives from the tortures of purgatory for certain cash payments, though originally indulgences did not apply to the remission of sin but only to the temporal penalties imposed by the church.

It was never Luther's original purpose either to found a new church or to undertake the thorough reformation of the Roman system, but only to save his own soul first and then to protest against certain specific abuses, corruptions, superstitions, and immoralities. When these were not admitted or corrected and

Luther was penalized by excommunication and his life threatened as that of John Huss and other martyrs had been, he was providentially driven on perforce, step by step, to see and boldly condemn the root causes and radical evils of the claims of papal infallibility, of medieval superstition, obscurantism and tyranny which were holding Europe in the bondage of moral slavery.

Just as the most enlightened Catholics admit the corruptions of the Roman Church, the most farsighted Protestants are the first to condemn the evils that afflicted the divided and ever multiplying Protestant sects which arose out of the inevitable conflict. The Reformation was an effort to return from the corruptions of the later Catholic Church to the primitive gospel of salvation by faith, with the direct access of each individual believer to God. But individuals, churches, nations and all society now became divided on a basis of extreme and dangerous individualism. Protestantism was a swinging of the pendulum from tyranny toward anarchy. The Reformation set free the individual but lost some of the social aspects of the original gospel of the Kingdom. The emphasis was now shifted from the coming of the Kingdom of God to the salvation of the individual soul. As Luther turned from the peasants to the princes so later Protestantism, and especially Puritanism and Calvinism, gradually and unconsciously came into alliance with the rising bourgeois capitalism and imperialism. Rome was bound up with medieval feudalism; Protestantism, all unconsciously, with modern capitalism and its monstrous economic injustice.

The Reformation with all its passions, errors and imperfections nevertheless made possible a vast emancipation of the human spirit. Luther's burning of the papal bull was a revolutionary act against the entire hierarchical system of Rome and all its "divine rights," against all formal external authority in religion, against the materialistic sacramentalism of the mass, the double standard of morality for clergy and laity, and the corrupt practices of the monasteries and the priesthood. The Reformation won potential freedom in religion over much of the world—the freedom which Christ once bestowed upon men. It led also to the restoration of the long neglected prophetic aspect of Christianity and to the Counter Reformation with its deeply needed reform and cleansing within the Church of Rome itself.

We are not studying in this chapter, however, the great theologians of the Reformation like John Calvin, Melanchthon, Zwingli, or Knox, but one or two who out of the Reformation to a marked degree discovered God. We include Luther, John Bunyan and John Wesley who were among the results of the Reformation in England, and Jonathan Edwards, from the later Puritan Reformation in America. This is not a history of movements, but a study of the movers of mankind, wherein we search for the source of their dynamic power.

MARTIN LUTHER, 1483-1546

The Renaissance with its wild license had partly broken the intellectual yoke of bondage of the Middle Ages; the Reformation was now to break its moral yoke, through assurance of personal salvation by faith, through Christ alone, with the right of private judgment. Luther's doctrine of the priesthood of all believers worked like dynamite for spiritual, intellectual and political liberty in the Old World and the New, and unwittingly laid the foundation of modern democracy.

Born of the free peasant class in the home of a humble miner, in poverty and piety, Luther was preparing for a worldly career in the study of law at the University of Erfurt. A friend's death and the fear of his own sudden death during a thunderstorm led him to enter the monastery of the Order of St. Augustine in Erfurt. His brilliant course in philosophy and law at the university and his later mastery of Latin, Greek and Hebrew laid a priceless foundation of wide culture for his future. He had taken the vows of poverty, chastity and obedience as he entered the monastery of mendicant and preaching friars. Here in agony of mind, by endless confession and ascetic practices, he vainly strove to attain righteousness, as Saul of Tarsus had done centuries before him. But constant dwelling upon his sins by daily confession, with incessant prayer and self-examination, led to morbid depression as he found that in the depths of his sinful heart he simply could not keep the burdensome monastic law. He fasted for days and spent nights without sleep until wakefulness became a confirmed habit and his health of both body and mind were endangered.

Luther was in his twentieth year when he first saw a complete copy of the Scriptures at the university. His first study in the monastery had led him to the morbid fear that he was reprobate and not of the elect. In his *Commentary on Galatians*, Luther says:

When I was a monk, I thought that I was utterly cast away, if at any time I felt the lust of the flesh: that is to say, if I felt any evil motion, fleshly lust, wrath, hatred, or envy. I assayed many ways to help to quiet my conscience, but it would not be, but was continually vexed with these thoughts: This or that sin thou hast committed: therefore thou art entered into this holy order in vain, and all thy good works are unprofitable. But if then I had rightly understood these sentences of Paul: "The flesh lusteth contrary to the Spirit, and the Spirit contrary to the flesh," I should not have so miserably tormented myself, but should have said to myself, "Martin, thou shalt not utterly be without sin, for thou hast flesh; thou shalt therefore feel the battle thereof." I remember that Staupitz was wont to say, "I have vowed unto God above a thousand times that I would become a better man: but I never performed that which I vowed. Hereafter I will make no such vow: for I have now learned by experience that I am not able to perform it. Unless, therefore, God be favorable and merciful unto me for Christ's sake, I shall not be able, with all my vows and all my good deeds, to stand before him."[1]

Said Luther: "When a fellow monk one day repeated the words of the Creed: 'I believe in the forgiveness of sins,' I saw the Scripture in an entirely new light; and straightway I felt as if I were born anew. It was as if I had found the door of Paradise thrown wide open." Almost beside himself after the long struggle of a tender conscience, at the age of twenty-nine he experienced what later would have been called conversion, as light began to dawn upon him. In Rom. 1:16-17, he saw the truth of justification by faith due solely to the grace of God, when all Europe was seeking justification by works.

Luther had begun to teach the logic and ethics of Aristotle but when he found him spiritually shallow and unsatisfying he won emancipation in Paul and Augustine. As able professor, popular preacher, administrator, subprior of the convent, and district vicar of his Augustinian order, Luther became one of the busiest men in Europe; uniting purity of character, sound

[1] Abridged from Luther's *Commentary on Galatians*, Philadelphia, 1891, pp. 510-514.

learning and keen judgment. As the greatest teacher of the Bible then in Germany, with newly opened eyes he now saw everywhere in the Old Testament and the New his "gospel" of the forgiving love of God revealed in Christ. Before he was forty he had become the popular lecturer in theology at the University of Wittenberg, and the flaming preacher in the castle church.

At this time the practice of indulgence had grown as an abuse out of the penitential system of Rome until in Luther's day John Tetzel was doing a thriving trade in the sale of these indulgences. The jealous princes were displeased that thrifty Germany was being drained by a steady stream of wealth flowing into the coffers of Rome. In 1517 Luther flamed and struck in protest against these superstitious abuses by boldly nailing his ninety-five theses against the sale of indulgences on the door of the castle church at Wittenberg, maintaining that God alone could remit the penalty for sin.

Step by step, Luther was led on from his attack on the abuse of indulgences to the evils of the system itself. He was now summoned to Rome by Leo X as a heretic and a rebel. Luther denied the divine right of the papacy and asserted the supreme authority of the Scriptures. Fearing that he would be put to death like Bruno or John Huss, Luther refused to go to Rome. He publicly burned the papal bull with a copy of the canon law, because the latter maintained the absolute supremacy of the pope over the Bible, the church, and the Christian conscience. Luther's debates and trials from Wittenberg to Augsburg, to Leipzig, and finally to Worms, coupled with his pamphleteering, inflamed all Germany. Of his writings he says characteristically: "I was born to fight with mobs and devils and so my books are very stormy and warlike." At Worms he took his famous stand before church and state and the whole world:

Unless I am convinced by the testimony of Scripture or by an evident reason—for I confide neither in the Pope nor in the councils alone, since it is certain that they have often erred and contradicted themselves—I am held fast by the Scriptures as adduced by me, and my conscience is taken captive by God's Word, and I neither can nor will revoke anything, seeing that it is not safe nor right to act against conscience. God help me. Amen.

The emperor's Spanish guards cried: "To the fire with him." But his courageous followers marched through their ranks with uplifted hands, after the old German manner of celebrating a victory. Luther rose to heroic heights in such a situation. He was joyous, smiling, and bold as a lion when in the midst of enemies who were seeking his life in order to strangle infant Protestantism at its birth. During the years in the early springtime of the Reformation, from 1519 to 1523, Luther was lifted above himself and gloriously reasserted the Pauline gospel of justification by faith as the basis of a new apostolic age of freedom. He discovered God by discovering the gospel.

Luther had gone to the monastery to propitiate the strict Judge by multiplied good works of merit and "get for himself a gracious God." Here he utterly failed and fell to the nethermost hell of the seventh chapter of Romans. But at last by bold faith alone he laid hold of the revelation of the God of grace in the gospel of the incarnated, crucified and risen Christ. The experience of Paul was now repeated in his life with the same power, with thousands of rejoicing converts in firm assurance of the Living God. Creative faith meant for him the certainty of the forgiveness of sins, in personal continuous surrender to God as the Father of Jesus Christ. This resulted in the complete freedom of the Christian man as a new creation in Christ. Luther, says Emerson, would have cut off his right hand rather than nail his theses to the door at Wittenberg, if he had supposed that they were destined to lead to the pale negations of Boston Unitarianism.

Though Luther criticized the Scriptures at his discretion, he was often inconsistent and confused in his thought. It was only the young Luther who wrote in his Preface to the New Testament in the 1522 edition:

You can now judge all the books and decide which are the best. John's Gospel and St. Paul's Epistles, especially that to the Romans and St. Peter's first Epistle are the true kernel and marrow of all the books. The Epistle to the Romans is really the chief part of the New Testament and the clearest of all the gospels, the daily bread of the soul. John's Gospel is the one tender, true chief Gospel, far, far to be preferred to the other three and placed high above them. St. James' Epistle is really an epistle of straw compared to them.

Luther's character is well described by Dr. McGiffert:

Medieval, conservative, intolerant, he introduced a régime of religious bigotry for a long time as narrow and as blighting to intellectual growth as Roman Catholicism at its worst. Full of faults he was, faults of temper and of taste,—passionate, domineering, obstinate, prejudiced, violent, vituperative and coarse. Nevertheless with all his medievalism the modern world owes more to him than to any other. He was a man through and through, a man of heroic mold, courageous, strong, masterful, frank, sincere and generous. Deadly in earnest and yet with the rare and saving grace of humor. Born to rule, a mere preacher and professor of theology in a small and out-of-the-way town, he dominated more than half the western world, and the whole of it is changed because he lived.[2]

It is one of the great moments of all history to see this man of lionlike mien, joyous and unafraid, as he faces at Worms the emperor and the representatives of the pope, as the tyranny most menacing to humanity's freedom in all the world. Every free man on earth owes him a debt of gratitude. His forced retirement in the castle of Wartburg was as providential as the Apostle Paul's imprisonment. Here began the constructive period of his work as a reformer. He completed in three months his translation of the New Testament and later turned to the Old Testament. He was the greatest of all popular biblical translators, and four centuries of German scholarship have never surpassed nor approached his living popular version. The German Bible became his greatest monument. At the pinnacle of his power he was probably the greatest moral leader in the world. As the major prophet of the Reformation he was to break the death grip of Rome over Europe. He was to win religious and intellectual liberty for the modern world.

Wholly apart from his work as a reformer, Luther is tremendous in the wrestle of his soul with God, as he beholds the goodness and the severity of God, God the All-terrible and God the All-merciful. Everything in Luther is dependent on his idea of God for he struggled about God and with God all his life. He experienced God as the wrathful Judge in his shrinking tender conscience, and he experienced him as the merciful God who has revealed his infinite love in the surrender of himself in

[2] A. C. McGiffert, *Martin Luther, the Man and His Work*, pp. 282, 287.

Christ. He asked: How can these two sides of God's character be united? Luther concluded that "God's own work is love, God's strange work is wrath." The latter is only the paradoxical way in which he does his own work. In Isa. 28:21, the prophet says: "To do his deed—strange is his deed. And to work his work—alien is his work," or as Luther interprets it, God destroys in order to save, as in Jer. 1:10. Luther says:

There are two kingdoms. The one is God's kingdom, the other is the kingdom of the world. God's kingdom is a realm of grace and mercy and not a realm of wrath or punishment. For in it is mere forgiving, saving, loving, serving, benevolence, peace and joy. But the kingdom of the world is a realm of wrath and severity. . . . Therefore it has and uses the sword. The Biblical words which speak of mercy belong to the Kingdom of God and the Christians, not to the earthly law. . . . But the kingdom of the world which is nothing more than the tool of the divine wrath over against the evildoers shall be severe. It looks after the evildoers in order to protect and to save the faithful. The earthly government might even be called a kingdom of God. For he wants it to last and wants us to live in obedience to it. But it is only the Kingdom of his left hand. In his right kingdom which he governs himself there is no father and mother, emperor and king, hangman and police, but where he is himself there the Gospel is preached to the poor. Although it does not seem that killing and despoiling is a work of love, and many simple-minded think it is no Christian work and should not be done by Christians, in reality it is a work of love—and if you see how it protects the faithful, wife and children, house and land, fortune and honor, and preserves and maintains peace by its doing you must find how precious and divine work it is.

Dr. Paul Tillich[3] in the *Protestant Digest*, October, 1941, thus interprets Luther at this point:

The mercy of God is more abundant because it is the true nature of God while wrath certainly is God's strange work. God acts through the contrast. He contradicts all human expectation. Only he who understands this understands the law that controls all life: The law of contrast. Condemning, deserting, destroying us is the way of saving, ac-

[3] Differing from the Protestant modernist portrayal of Luther by Harnack and McGiffert, Dr. Tillich represents in America the Neo-German view of Karl Holl, of Barth, and of Erich Seeberg in his *Luther's Theologie*. These seek to vindicate Luther from the aspersions of the modernist picture but some of them show the dichotomies in Luther's concepts of God.

cepting, fulfilling us. The affirmative side of the divine act is not manifest without the negative side.

. . . We had forgotten what Hegel had known, that history is not the soil for the happiness of the individual. Now we have learned this lesson once more and we will learn in the next years much more of it and the question will become urgent whether our idea of God and the Divine love is profound enough to be maintained in such a situation. He who does not understand that God acts through contrast, that his wrath is the tool of his love, cannot understand life and history. His faith will break down under the strain of the coming events.

The limitations of Luther's social ethics with respect to the present mass-society have been over emphasized. By a grotesque exaggeration the whole of German history, including militarism and Nazism has been derived from Luther's doctrine of the state. It is now time to ask for the truth in Luther's attitude over against Anglo-Saxon legalism on the one hand, and Nazi cynicism on the other hand. Our new understanding of the dynamic and irrational character of life and history, our new experience of the demonic forces in individuals and nations, their destructive and at the same time their creative character, make it possible to rediscover the profound doctrine of the reformer of the Christian Church: The doctrine of Love's strange work.

Not since the Apostle Paul wrote Galatians and Romans have we had as clear a statement on justification by faith as in Luther's *Concerning Christian Liberty*:[4]

Letter of Martin Luther to Pope Leo X. Among those monstrous evils of this age with which I have now for three years been waging war, I am sometimes compelled to look to you and to call you to mind, most blessed father Leo. I have been compelled by the causeless raging of your impious flatters against me to appeal from your seat to a future council—fearless of the futile decrees of your predecessors Pius and Julius, who in their foolish tyranny prohibited such an action. Your See, called the Court of Rome, neither you nor any man can deny to be more corrupt than any Babylon or Sodom. The Court of Rome stinks in the nostrils of the world, the papal authority is growing weak, and its notorious ignorance is evil spoken of. What indeed is such a vicar but antichrist and an idol?

Concerning Christian Liberty, though I know how poorly I am furnished, I have attained some little drop of faith. That I may open then an easier way for the ignorant—for these alone I am trying to

[4] Abbreviated from Luther's *Concerning Christian Liberty*, Harvard Classics ed., Vol. XXXVI, pp. 336-367.

serve—I first lay down these two propositions, concerning spiritual liberty and servitude:

A Christian man is the most free lord of all, and subject to none; a Christian man is the most dutiful servant of all, and subject to every one. They are both the statements of Paul himself. We may see by what means a man becomes justified, free, and a true Christian; that is, a spiritual, new, and inward man. One thing, and one alone, is necessary for life, justification, and Christian liberty; and that is the most holy word of God, the Gospel of Christ.

What is this word? I answer, the Gospel of God, concerning His Son, incarnate, suffering, risen, and glorified. For faith alone and the efficacious use of the word of God, bring salvation. The soul is justified by faith alone, and not by any works. Christ is full of grace, life, and salvation; the soul is full of sin, death, and condemnation. Let faith step in, and then sin, death, and hell will belong to Christ, and grace, life, and salvation to the soul. Thus the believing soul, by the pledge of its faith in Christ, becomes free from all sin, fearless of death, safe from hell, and endowed with the eternal righteousness, life, and salvation of its Husband Christ. Faith alone is the righteousness of a Christian man, and the fulfilling of all the commandments. Works, since they are irrational things, cannot glorify God, although they may be done to the glory of God, if faith be present.

Every Christian is by faith so exalted above all things that, in spiritual power, he is completely lord of all things. Nor are we only kings and the freest of all men, but also priests for ever, a dignity far higher than kingship. Those who are now boastfully called popes, bishops, and lords, Holy Scripture calls ministers, servants, and stewards, who are to serve the rest. We are all equally priests. Works of perfect freedom are done for no object but that of pleasing God, and not in order to obtain justification, which he already had to the full. Good works do not make a good man, but a good man does good works. As Christ says, "A good tree cannot bring forth evil fruit, neither can a corrupt tree bring forth good fruit." This leviathan, this perverted notion about works, is invincible when sincere faith is wanting. Here is the truly Christian life, here is faith really working by love, when a man applies himself with joy and love to the work of freest servitude. Lo! my God, without merit on my part, of His pure and free mercy, has given to me, an unworthy, condemned, and contemptible creature all the riches of justification and salvation in Christ.

Luther is a striking example of our thesis that man discovers God. Arising at the end of an epoch, out of the corruption of church and state from the almost unbroken tyranny of medieval absolutism, this man out of the struggle in his monk's cell feels himself seized by God's revelation of the forgiving grace of the gospel. He makes an epoch-making fresh discovery of God. As a result, notwithstanding all the shortcomings of Protestantism, for four centuries multitudes of men all over the world have sought immediate access to the divine and have made the mighty discovery of God for themselves.

JOHN BUNYAN, 1628-1688

John Bunyan followed his father's trade as a tinker, a maker and mender of pots and kettles in Bedford, England. He had been drafted as a soldier in the parliamentary army in the Civil War under Oliver Cromwell, but with the re-establishment of the monarchy under Charles the Second, all meetings such as those of the Baptists in Bedford became illegal, and the persecution and imprisonment of Nonconformists began. Bunyan had married a wife whose piety began to awaken him from his delight in rural sport and from his evil habits such as profane swearing. The quickening of his conscience in religion led to an agonizing spiritual conflict which lasted for some years. This struggle is vividly narrated in his *Grace Abounding to the Chief of Sinners.* It constitutes his spiritual autobiography of this period of terrific conflict. Bunyan no sooner seeks to reform his evil habits and finds comfort in some promise of Scripture, which he was now searching night and day, than he is plunged again and again into gloom and despair by the thought that he has committed the unpardonable sin, or that, like Esau, he can now find no place of repentance though he seeks it diligently and with tears.

Toward the close of this period of conflict, Bunyan joined the Baptist congregation at Bedford at the age of twenty-seven. Two years later he became a regular Nonconformist preacher while continuing to practice his trade. His fame as a preacher and writer spread widely, so that when he preached in London on but short notice, some twelve hundred would crowd his weekday morning meetings at seven o'clock, and some three thousand would eagerly gather on Sundays to hear him.

From 1660 to 1672, for a period of twelve years, he was confined to prison on account of his preaching during which time he wrote some of the most important of his sixty books. *Grace Abounding* was written in 1666 at the age of thirty-eight, and *Pilgrim's Progress* at the age of forty-seven. Later he wrote *The Life and Death of Mr. Badman*, which might be called the first modern English novel. As *Pilgrim's Progress* showed the ascent of the Christian to the Celestial City, *Mr. Badman* pictured a trader in a small town in his descent to destruction. Bunyan shows English Puritanism at its best though in him we see both its strength and its limitations. There is a psychic quality in Bunyan, as in George Fox in his early years, in the dramatic and vivid religious dreams of his childhood, in the visions he sees and the voices he hears. *Pilgrim's Progress* is one of the dozen greatest books in the English language. As *Mr. Badman* describes the temptations of the world and the flesh, *Grace Abounding* vividly recounts Bunyan's conflicts with the devil. An abbreviated statement thus tells the story of his spiritual autobiography in his own words:

GRACE ABOUNDING TO THE CHIEF OF SINNERS

*Or, a Brief Relation of the Exceeding Mercy of God
in Christ, to His Poor Servant, John Bunyan*

Children, I being taken from you in presence, (being in prison) I now once again, from the lions' dens, do look yet after you all. It is something of a relation of the work of God upon my own soul even from the very first till now. In this discourse you may see much of the grace of God towards me. I can remember my doubts, and sad months, my great sins, my great temptations, and my great fears of perishing for ever. God did not play in convincing me, the devil did not play in tempting me, neither did I play when I sunk as into a bottomless pit, when the pangs of hell caught hold upon me; wherefore I may not play in my relating of them, but be plain and simple.

It will not be amiss if I give you a hint of my pedigree; my father's house being of that rank that is meanest and most despised of all the families in the land. But yet it pleased God to put it into their hearts to put me to school, to learn both to read and write, though I did soon lose that little I learned. I was without God in the world, being taken captive by the devil. I had but few equals both for cursing, swearing, lying, and blaspheming the holy name of God, and they became as a second nature to me. These things when I was but a child nine or ten years old did so distress my soul that I was often much cast down, yet could I not let go my sins.

After this I changed my condition into a married state, and my mercy was to light upon a wife whose father was counted godly. We came together not having so much household stuff as a dish or spoon betwixt us both, yet she had *The Plain Man's Pathway to Heaven*, and *The Practice of Piety*, which her father had left her. These two books did beget within me some desires to religion. One day as I was in the midst of a game at cat, a voice did suddenly dart from heaven into my soul, which said, Wilt thou leave thy sins and go to heaven, or have thy sins and go to hell? At this I was put to an exceeding maze. I looked up to heaven as if I had seen the Lord Jesus looking down upon me as if he did severely threaten me. This conclusion was fastened on my spirit that I had been a great and grievous sinner, and that it was now too late for me to look after heaven; for Christ would not forgive me. I returned desperately to my sport again; and this kind of despair did possess my soul. I went on in sin with great greediness and I was the ungodliest fellow for swearing.

But quickly after this I betook me to my Bible, and began to take great pleasure in reading. Thus I continued about a year yet I knew not Christ. I was then never out of the Bible, either by reading or meditation; still crying out to God. One day betwixt Elstow and Bedford, the temptation was hot upon me to try if I had faith by doing of some miracle. I was tossed betwixt the devil and my own ignorance. Fearing I was not called, I cried to Christ to call me. About this time I began to break my mind to those poor people in Bedford, and to tell them my condition, of the vanity and inward wretchedness of my wicked heart. My conscience now was sore and I found myself as on a miry bog. The tempter would also much assault me. These things did sink me into very deep despair. This temptation lasted about a year. In prayer sometimes I have thought I should see the devil, nay, thought I have felt him, behind me, pull my clothes; he would be, also, continually at me in the time of prayer to have done.

At this time, also, I sat under the ministry of holy Mr. Gifford (of the Bedford Baptists). God did cast into my hand a book of Martin Luther; it was his comment on the Galatians. I found my condition so largely and profoundly handled, as if his book had been written out of my heart. Yet now again was I both a burden and a terror to myself. I came nearer to Judas. I could, for whole days together, feel my very body, as well as my mind, to shake and totter under the sense of the dreadful judgment of God. The tempter left me not and an hundred times did labour to break my peace. I could not be delivered, nor brought to peace again, until well-nigh two years and an half were completely finished. . . . Then these words did suddenly break in upon me, "My grace is sufficient for thee." I was as though I had seen the

Lord Jesus look down from heaven and direct these words unto me. The Scriptures now were wonderful things unto me; I saw that the truth and verity of them were the keys of the kingdom of heaven. O what did I now see in that blessed sixth of John, "And him that cometh to me I will in no wise cast out." The woman of Canaan that would not be daunted and the man that went to borrow bread at midnight were great encouragements unto me. I never saw those heights and depths in grace, and love, and mercy, as I saw after this temptation.

Now I shall go forward when I first did join in fellowship with the people of God in Bedford. . . . I was somewhat inclining to consumption, wherewith I was suddenly and violently seized insomuch that I thought I could not live. . . . When I had with comfort mused a while, that word fell with great weight upon my mind, "O death, where is thy sting? O grave, where is thy victory?" At this I became well both in body and mind at once, for my sickness did presently vanish, and I walked comfortably in my work for God again.

After I had been about five or six years awakened, the most able among the saints desired me that I would speak exhortation unto them. They came in to hear the Word by hundreds, and that from all parts. I went for the space of two years, crying out against men's sins, still preaching what I saw and felt. About the space of five years or more, I was caught in my present practice and cast into prison. When I went first to preach the Word abroad, the doctors and priests of the country did open wide against me with slanders and reproaches. It began therefore to be rumoured up and down among the people, that I was a witch, a Jesuit, a highwayman, and the like. Before I came to prison . . . the parting with my wife and poor children hath oft been to me in this place as the pulling the flesh from my bones because I should have often brought to my mind the many hardships, miseries and wants that my poor family was like to meet with, especially my poor blind child, who lay nearer my heart than all I had besides. Poor child, thought I, thou must be beaten, must beg, suffer hunger, cold, nakedness, and a thousand calamities. But I must venture you all with God, though it goeth to the quick to leave you. I had also this consideration, that if I should now venture all for God, I engaged God to take care of my concernments.

The Latin Catholic Church has been rich in its many types of piety which have spoken to us in St. Augustine, St. Francis, *The Imitation of Christ,* and Brother Lawrence. It is the emancipating Reformation that is voiced in Martin Luther in Germany and later in England in George Fox and in the universal language of John Bunyan. "We not only hail Bunyan as master of words, seer of visions and regnant in the realm of spiritual imagination; we know him as one who sought and struggled and attained, and so we reach out our hands across the years and hail him brother."[5] While *Pilgrim's Progress* may be read by un-prejudiced Catholics and high Anglicans, Bunyan is primarily English, Protestant, Puritan and Anabaptist. *Grace Abounding* and *Pilgrim's Progress* are the results of the Reformation, where the lonely soul without priest, confessional, or absolution, has to assume the responsibilities of its own salvation through Christ and walk alone with God. Salvation seems an arduous adventure on the straight, narrow and rugged way, battling with unseen principalities and powers of evil. An outcast from mother church, the solitary pilgrim must turn to the scroll in his bosom and meditate upon God's Word. Bunyan, whether he knew it or not, was the child of Paul, of Luther, and of Calvin. He shared their doctrine of justification by faith, the priesthood of all believers and, in place of priestly absolution, personal assurance of salvation. When Rome because of its corruptions became impossible, Calvin's genius created a closely federated church and gave it a courageous conviction of the absolute sovereignty of God, nerving the elect to dare the impossible. Great souls emerged like John Knox, unconquerable after eight years in the galleys, his back scarred by the scourge, William the Silent, and Oliver Cromwell; and Geneva became "the school of the martyrs." Later the Anabaptist movement in Germany, Britain and Europe was letting men loose upon the world with a revo-lutionary democracy that worked like dynamite.

The prisons of England were filled with Quakers and Baptists. It was the impact of this movement which launched the "May-flower" and sent Bunyan as a contemporary of George Fox, rejoicing to that "stinking jail" of Bedford. He had served briefly in the army, but for sixty stormy years he was Christ's militant soldier, and the trumpets were sounding in his soul throughout his burning pages. The Protestant Church lost much in its repudiation of all that was suspect in the ecclesiastical hierarchy, but the lonely agony of Bunyan's soul gave us *Pil-grim's Progress*. The Word of God became living and active and

[5] Gaius Glenn Atkins, *Pilgrims of the Lonely Road*, pp. 191-244.

sharper than a two-edged sword in Bunyan's hand, as he writes in *Grace Abounding*:

> Then fell with power that word of God upon me "See that ye refuse not Him that speaketh." This made a strange seizure upon my spirit; it brought light with it and commanded a silence in my heart of all those tumultuous thoughts that did like masterless hellhounds roar and bellow and make a hideous noise with me. It showed me also that Jesus Christ had yet a word of grace and mercy for me.

Froude reminds us that Bunyan signed an address to Cromwell "approving the dismissal of the Long Parliament, and recognizing Oliver himself as the Lord's instrument." But after the restoration of the monarchy, Baptists, Quakers and others were ruthlessly imprisoned: "Non-conformists refusing to attend worship in the parish churches were to be imprisoned. . . . Three months were allowed them to consider (then if obstinate) they were to be banished from the realm." The Bedford Baptists were the first to fall. The Anglican Tory magistrates seemed to themselves most tolerant in offering to release Bunyan if he would promise not to preach. He had only to be false to the compulsion of God upon his soul—"woe is me if I preach not" —and to return to the only thing for which he was lawfully fit, the tinkering of old kettles. They no more understood Bunyan than Nero could comprehend Paul. In Bunyan's English, Shakespeare and the King James Version were speaking; but in his soul the flaming Paul, Luther, Calvin and Fox's *Book of Martyrs* repeated their message.

The darker side of the picture of Bunyan's agonizing struggles with doubt and sin are given in *Grace Abounding*, the early part of which resembles the years in bondage of St. Augustine as recorded in his *Confessions*. It is only fair, however, to balance the dark description of his sinful heart with the brighter side of the picture as given in *Pilgrim's Progress*, from which limitations of space permit but the briefest excerpts:

> When at the first I took my Pen in hand
> Thus for to write; I did not understand
> That I at all should make a little Book
> In such a mode . . . nor did I intend
> But to divert myself in doing this

From worser thoughts which make me do amiss.
Thus I set Pen to Paper with delight,
And quickly had my thoughts in black and white.

As I walk'd through the wilderness of this world, I lighted on a certain place where was a Den, (the jail) and I laid me down in that place to sleep; and as I slept I dreamed a Dream. I dreamed, and behold I saw a Man cloathed with Rags, standing in a certain place, with his face from his own house, a Book in his hand, and a great Burden upon his back. I looked, and saw him open the Book, and read therein; and as he read, he wept and trembled; and not being able longer to contain, he brake out with a lamentable cry, saying *What shall I do?* . . . Then said *Evangelist*, pointing with his finger over a very wide field, Do you see yonder *Wicket-gate?* Do you see yonder shining Light? Then said *Evangelist*, Keep that Light in your eye, and go up directly thereto: so shalt thou see the Gate; at which, when thou knockest, it shall be told thee what thou shalt do. So I saw in my Dream that the Man began to run. . . . He ran thus till he came at a place somewhat ascending, and upon that place stood a Cross, and a little below in the bottom, a Sepulchre. So I saw in my Dream, that just as *Christian* came up with the *Cross*, his Burden loosed from his shoulders, and fell from off his back, and began to tumble, and so continued to do, till it came to the mouth of the Sepulchre, where it fell in, and I saw it no more. Then was *Christian* glad and lightsome, and said with a merry heart, *He hath given me rest by his sorrow, and life by his death.* . . . Then *Christian* gave three leaps for joy, and went on singing. . . .

And thus they came up to the Gate. The King then commanded to open the Gate. Now I saw in my Dream that these two men went in at the Gate; and lo, as they entered, they were transfigured, and they had Raiment put on that shone like Gold. All the Bells in the City rang again for joy, and it was said unto them, *Enter ye into the joy of your Lord.* I also heard the men themselves, that they sang with a loud voice, saying, *Blessing, Honour, Glory, and Power, be to him that sitteth upon the Throne, and to the Lamb for ever and ever.* . . . Then said *Valiant-for-truth*, "Though with great difficulty I am got hither, yet now I do not repent me of all the Trouble I have been at to arrive where I am. My sword I give to him that shall succeed me in my Pilgrimage, and my Courage and Skill to him that can get it. My Marks and Scars I carry with me, to be a witness for me that I have fought his Battles who now will be my Rewarder." As he went he said, *Death, where is thy Sting?* And as he went down deeper he said, *Grave, where is thy Victory?* So he passed over, and all the Trumpets sounded for him on the other side.

There can be no question that the writer of *Grace Abounding* and *Pilgrim's Progress* had discovered God. But each of our adventurers was a pathfinder for a multitude who were to follow. Though deprived of the comfort of the confessional and priestly counsel and absolution and all support of the Church Catholic, what countless thousands were to have their way lighted by Bunyan's lonely pilgrimage, to gather strength from his victories, sympathy from his sufferings and hope from the bright visions of the Celestial City.

JOHN WESLEY, 1703-1791

John Wesley's discovery of God is revealed not so much in the definitions of his theology or in his sermons, or even in the intimate experiences recorded in the twenty-six volumes of his *Journal*, as it is in his character, in the man himself. As in the case of his Master, we cannot separate his teaching from his life. His is one of the most consistently integrated and unified personalities recorded in this volume. His long life of eighty-eight years almost spanned the eighteenth century. This was a period of moral corruption and spiritual destitution, from the profligate king and prime minister down to the ignorant and brutalized masses; where every sixth shop in London was a public house, and where the poor were invited to get drunk for a penny or dead drunk for twopence; where a hundred and sixty crimes and minor offenses were punishable with death. Like our own, his age was a transitional period swept by the American, the French, and the industrial revolutions.

Wesley, who all his life bore the stamp of his Spartan mother, was the fifteenth of nineteen strong children as his mother was the twenty-fifth child of the great Dr. Annesley. We see Wesley as a frail boy, from the age of ten to seventeen in the Charterhouse School, systematically running thrice round the school yard each morning to train that wonderful mechanism of his body which was to carry him through titanic labors for eighty-eight years. From the age of seventeen to thirty, he was almost continuously at Oxford, where he was brilliant in the classics. Here he had the invaluable training of presiding at the daily student debates. He conversed for years with his brother Charles in Latin. Later he wrote a Greek grammar and began the conquest of German, French, Italian and Spanish. At Oxford he kindled that lifelong, insatiable intellectual curiosity which made him one of the best read men of his day, even though his reading had to be done mostly on horseback or, in later years, in a rattling coach. The fifty volumes of his Christian library which he wrote and edited for his followers were a worthy intellectual achievement.

It was at Oxford that he formed the Holy Club, with his brother Charles, George Whitefield, and four others, for the study and development of the higher religious life. And here at the age of twenty-two comes his spiritual awakening: He writes "I set out in earnest upon a new life. I set apart an hour or two a day for religious retirement; I communed every week; I watched against all sin, whether in word or deed."

The years from 1735 to 1738 Wesley spent in Georgia with the humanitarian philanthropist, Governor Oglethorpe. As an ascetic young Oxford scholar of thirty-two, looking on his own subjective soul rather than upon the world as his parish, Wesley writes as he starts for Georgia: "My chief motive is the hope of saving my own soul. I hope to learn the true sense of the gospel of Christianity by preaching it to the heathen. I am assured if I be once converted myself, God will then employ me." Later he writes: "I went to America to convert the Indians; but O! who shall convert me?" Wesley's *Journal* shows that during this "unconverted" period, he prayed from four to seven times a day; studied German, Latin, French, Italian, and labored incessantly for the colonists and the Indians. As in the case of Luther, Wesley's spiritual crisis was delayed by the erroneous teaching of the time and by the proud struggles of his own stubborn will. After he returned to England, what he regarded as his conversion occurred on May 24, 1738. He describes it in his *Journal*.[6]

[6] Wesley writes in his *Journal*: "In the evening I went very unwillingly to a society in Aldersgate Street, where one was reading Luther's preface to the Epistle to the Romans. About a quarter before nine, while he was describing the change which God works in the heart through faith in Christ, I felt my heart strangely warmed. I felt I did trust in Christ, Christ alone, for salvation; and an assurance was given me, that he had taken away *my* sins, even *mine*, and saved *me* from the law of sin and death. I began to pray with all my might for those who had in a more especial manner despitefully used me and persecuted me. I then testified openly to all there what I now felt in my heart."

This experience did not lead immediately to lasting assurance, stability and joy, for the entries in his diary during this year reveal recurring gloom and doubt, when he told his friends that he was not a Christian and never had been. Within a year, however, Wesley had found himself and instead of being a morbid introvert had become a healthy extrovert.

As soon as Wesley and Whitefield began to proclaim their message of a full gospel, all the churches in England were closed against them and they were driven to preach in the open air. On February 17, 1939, Whitefield spoke to two hundred colliers on a hillside, and soon he and Wesley were preaching to crowds estimated at from twenty thousand to sixty thousand. "Wesley preaching on his father's tombstone outside the Epworth Church made impossible the drunken vicar inside . . . made the empty churches forever intolerable." Soon a revival began to sweep England, Wales, Scotland, Ireland, and later America. As Wesley sent Francis Asbury and George Shadford to the colonies he said: "I let you loose on the great continent of America. Publish your message in the open face of the sun." At the very moment when David Hume was destroying the faith of many by his devastating skepticism Wesley was so transforming the characters of multitudes; his preaching changed the moral tone of English society and marked an epoch in British history.

At the foundation of his new organization, he wrote on May 1, 1738, in his *Journal*: "This evening our little society began, which afterward met in Fetter-lane." The society was divided into bands of five or ten persons each, to speak plainly to each other as to the "real state" of their hearts. These bands united in a conference every Wednesday evening. At the periodic love feast, Methodists come together to partake of water and biscuit or wafer as the sign of their spiritual fellowship. The class meeting began as an agency for collecting contributions and ended as a method of standardizing Methodist spiritual life. The conferences were organized to confer about the best ways of spreading holiness and ended as a powerful organism for the control of property and the guidance of preaching and worship. Somewhat autocratically, Wesley controlled almost everything until in 1784 he selected the Legal Hundred Ministers to exercise control after his death.

At his death there were only about seventy-five thousand avowed adherents, while today there are some thirty million Methodists and Wesleyans throughout the world. Wesley was a genius as a master organizer and wrote: "I know this is the peculiar talent God has given me." He was masterly also in the adaptation of the wisest means to reach his spiritual ends. In a remarkable way, he embodies all the habits and use of the means of grace which characterize the early disciples of Christianity. These were the systematic reading of the Bible, fervent prayer, tireless practical service for his fellow men, loyalty to the church and its sacraments, and finally the recognition of the necessity of rigorous discipline and the taking up of his daily cross.

Concerning prayer, on the first page of each of the twenty-six volumes of his *Journal* he wrote: "I resolve to devote one hour morning and evening to private prayer, no pretense or excuse whatever." It would take a large volume to describe his life of strenuous service. For over fifty years he traveled as an itinerant preacher, chiefly on horseback, a distance of two hundred and fifty thousand miles, or ten times around the world. He daily rose at four and preached from two to five times a day. He wrote two hundred and thirty-three books or pamphlets in the course of his crowded life, printed over four hundred and fifty publications for wide circulation, wrote handbooks on medicine, chemistry, physics, politics, poetry, and religion, and preached forty thousand sermons, many of which were published. He poured out his life for the poor, organized schools, promoted popular education, corresponded with the organizer of the first Sunday schools, devised a loan fund, was a pioneer in many forms of social service, and flamed against "American slavery, the vilest that ever saw the sun."

Finally, like his Master, Wesley was "made perfect by suffering." Wesley mastered himself, trained his mind, buffeted his body, and deeply influenced his generation. At the age of eighty-eight, he was still powerful. At his death on March 9, 1791, Wesley's worn body was carried by six poor men; he left behind him "a good library of books, a well-worn clergyman's gown, a much-abused reputation, and—the Methodist Church."

With all his faults, his many-sided spiritual character towers above his century like a vast Himalayan peak. With Goethe,

Kant, Rousseau, Napoleon; in the century of Marlborough, Pitt, Clive, Warren H'astings, Frederick the Great, and George Washington, he was a giant among giants. Wesley was rational, logical, warmhearted, forgiving, humble, yet a man of iron will and a born leader of men. He was fearless and courageous, calmly facing raging mobs. He was sane, tranquil and well poised, a man of quiet dignity. Like Cromwell, he was a "practical mystic." He was transparently honest and frank, a man of deep moral earnestness. He seemed an embodied conscience to his age. Added to all this was the drive and dynamic of a boundless devotion and sacrifice, coupled with a tireless patience. It was the balance of these qualities that made him the great preacher, writer, organizer, statesman, reformer, educator, social servant, evangelist and dominant leader of the evangelical revival of the eighteenth century. He was the director of a religious crusade which changed England, awakened his century and helped to uplift mankind. "No man lived nearer the center than John Wesley."

Seldom do we find a man of such inexhaustible energy who achieves such a harmonious integration of character, such tolerance and such poise. Master organizer though he was, he always gave precedence to the primary spiritual demands over all matters of discipline. Through fifty years of controversy, the three foes within Christianity which Wesley feared and fought the most were a harsh Calvinism that believed in the damnation of unbaptized infants and those who were not "called," the antinomianism that depreciated moral conduct, character, and all use of means of grace save only the passive quietism of miraculously saving faith; and an extreme, impractical mysticism which blindly sought for ends without an intelligent use of means.

Though Wesley shared something of the eighteenth century's exaggerated reliance upon reason, he made provision for the emotional life of his converts, but his chief reliance was upon a religion of the will. He believed in immediate contact of the soul with God, as the means of adjusting his total life to the will of God; but he always combined this with uncommon "common sense." To an extraordinary degree, he was both an idealist and a realist. For forty years, he preached the undimmed ideal of sinless perfection, but he never professed to have attained it for a single hour. Like the Apostle Paul, Wesley was a little giant, five feet five inches in height, never weighing over a hundred and twenty pounds; but no man ever gained a more superb mental control of himself or used his body for eighty-eight years as a more perfect instrument of his mighty spiritual purpose.[7]

Like St. Augustine, with profound self-knowledge, Wesley was a great psychologist; he had followed the command of early philosophy "know thyself," but his one absorbing, lifelong quest and adventure was the discovery of God. Seldom does one who sets out in such desperate earnest to save his own soul so lose himself in the redemption of his fellow men, until at last he can say "I look on all the world as my parish." At the very end, he cries with all his failing strength: "The best of all is, God is with us." The twenty-six volumes of his *Journal*[8] were intended for the edification of his faithful followers. He shares with them his wide reading and his most intimate personal spiritual experiences, though always with a genuine humble disparagement of himself. He kept a faithful daily account of his financial expenditures through seventy years. Bishop McConnell, who has written the best life of John Wesley that we have, shows that if we read his remarkable *Journal* noting its straightforward English style, its sound practical sense, and its deep devotion, "the effect becomes massive." The limitations of space will permit but a few excerpts from the *Journal* of John Wesley, which he kept for over fifty years:[9]

[7] On next to the last year of his life, on January 1, 1790, he writes: "I am now an old man, decayed from head to foot. My eyes are dim; my right hand shakes much; my mouth is hot and dry every morning. I have a lingering fever almost every day; my motion is weak and slow. However, blessed be God, I do not slack my labor. I can preach and work still." Of all our witnesses in this volume the men who achieved or had the gift of this almost superhuman capacity for work were the Apostle Paul, John Wesley, and among our moderns, President Harper and Albert Schweitzer.

[8] Now published in four volumes in Everyman's Library in 2145 pages of fine print.

[9] A series of necessarily fragmentary quotations from Wesley's *Journal*, 4 vols. (Everyman's Library ed.); Vol. I, pp. 1, 4, 9, 97; Vol. II, pp. 2, 57, 72, 107, 133, 255, 352, 387, 421.

It was in pursuance of an advice given by Bishop Taylor, in his *Rules for Holy Living and Dying*, that, about fifteen years ago, I began to take a more exact account than I had done before, of the manner wherein I spent my time, writing down how I had employed every hour. Of this journal thus occasionally compiled, the following is a short extract: I had no design or desire to trouble the world with any of my little affairs, had not an obligation been laid upon me, to do what in me lies, in obedience to that command of God "Let not the good which is in you be evil spoken of."

In November 1729, at which time I came to reside at Oxford, Mr. Morgan, my brother, myself, and one more agreed to spend three or four evenings in a week together. Our design was to read over the classics, which we had before read in private, on common nights, and on Sunday some book in divinity. Some of the men of wit in Christ Church made reflections upon the Sacramentarians, as they were pleased to call us, styling us, The Holy Club. When I was about twenty-two, my father pressed me to enter into Holy Orders. At the same time the providence of God directing me to Kempis's *Christian Pattern*, I set apart an hour or two a day for religious retirement. I began to aim at, and pray for inward holiness.

. . . Our main doctrines which include all the rest, are repentance, faith and holiness. The first of these we account, as it were, the porch of religion; the next, the door; the third, religion itself. My doctrines are simply the common fundamental principles of Christianity.

For admission to the society of Methodists, Wesley says:

They do not impose in order to their admission any opinions whatever. They think and let think. One condition and only one, is required—a real desire to save the soul. They lay stress upon nothing else. I will not quarrel with you about any opinion. Only see that your heart be right toward God, that you know and love the Lord Jesus Christ; that you love your neighbor, and walk as your Master walked; and I desire no more. I am sick of opinions. I am weary to bear them. My soul loathes this frothy food. Give me solid and substantial religion; give me an humble, quiet love of God and man. Man is not a clod of earth, a lump of clay without sense or understanding, but a spirit like his Creator; a spirit endowed with a free will, the power of choosing good or evil.

By faith man experiences an inward change of nature, called "regeneration," and an outward change in his relationship, called "justification." By this faith we are saved from all uneasiness of mind, from the anguish of a wounded spirit, from discontent, from fear and sorrow of heart, and from that inexpressible listlessness and weariness, both of the world and ourselves, which we had so helplessly labored under for many years. In this we find that love of God and of all mankind which we had elsewhere sought in vain. This results in "assurance," releasing a man from the spirit of the servant or slave who is seeking to work out his salvation by his own merit, and setting him free as a son, at leisure from himself, for a joyous life of service for God and his fellowmen. This life of faith in glad sonship results in personal holiness, striving to live in the moral "perfection."

Regarding the means of spiritual growth in the reading of the Bible and prayer, Wesley says:

I want to know one thing. God himself has condescended to teach the way; for this end he came down from heaven. He hath written it down in a book. O give me that book! At any price give me that book of God. I have it: here is knowledge for me. Let me be a man of one book. Here then I am, far from the busy ways of men. I sit down alone; only God is here. In his presence I open, I read the book.

Regarding outdoor preaching when the churches were closed, Wesley writes:

I reached Bristol and met Mr. Whitefield there. I could scarce reconcile myself at first to this strange way of preaching in the fields, of which he set me an example on Sunday. At four in the afternoon, I submitted to be more vile, and proclaimed in the highways the glad tidings of salvation, speaking from a little eminence in a ground adjoining to the city to about three thousand people, (among them) the colliers of Kingswood neither fearing God nor regarding man: so ignorant of the things of God, that they seemed but one remove from the beasts.

For a decade Wesley faced the violence of mobs and for twenty years the opposition of the churches. He always faced a mob in person and feared not the face of man. Again and again he preached in the midst of showers of stones or tiles or rotten eggs. Repeatedly one finds in Wesley's *Journal* entries like the following at Falmouth:

The house was beset on all sides by an innumerable multitude. Away went all the things and the door fell back into the room. I stepped forward at once into the midst of them and said, "here I am; which of you has anything to say to me?" I came bareheaded as I was into the middle of the street, and then raising my voice said, "Neighbors, countrymen, do you desire to hear me speak?" They cried vehemently, "Yes, yes. He shall speak. He shall."

At Walsall I received some blows, lost part of my clothes, and was covered with dirt. Here, although the hands of perhaps some hundreds of people seemed lifted up to strike or throw, yet they were one and all stopped in some way so that no man touched me.

April, 1740. Not only the court and the alleys, but all the street, upwards and downwards, was filled with people, shouting, cursing and swearing, and ready to swallow the ground with fierceness and rage.

October, 1743. Two years ago a piece of brick grazed my shoulders. It was a year after that the stone struck me between the eyes. Last month I received one blow, and this evening two; one before we came into the town and one after we were gone out. But both were as nothing; for though one man struck me on the breast with all his might, and the other on the mouth with such a force that the blood gushed out immediately, I felt no more pain from either of the blows, than if they had touched me with a straw.

1743. . . . While I was speaking, a gentleman rode up very drunk; and, after many unseemly and bitter words, laboured much to ride over some of the people. I was surprised to hear he was a neighboring clergyman. And this, too, is a man zealous for the Church! Ah, poor Church, if it stood in need of such defenders.

October, 1749. Such rage and bitterness I scarcely ever saw before, in any creatures that bore the form of men. They followed us in full cry. My heart was filled with love, my eyes with tears, and my mouth with arguments. They were amazed, they were ashamed, they were melted down, they devoured every word.

Wesley was surprisingly modern in some of his views. He accepted the idea of evolution. Many decades before Darwin, Wesley wrote:

All is metamorphosis in the physical world. Forms are continually changing. By what degree does nature raise herself up to man? The ape is this rough draught of man; the last creature that serves to display the admirable progression of the works of God.

In December 1746, I resumed my vegetable diet, which I had now discontinued for several years, and found it of use both to my soul and body. I read today the most correct history of St. Patrick. The whole smells strong of romance. His success staggers me. Thousands are converted, without any opposition: twelve thousand at one sermon. If these things were so, either there was then no Devil in the world, or St. Patrick did not preach the Gospel of Christ.

In riding to Newcastle, I finished the tenth Iliad of Homer. What an amazing genius had this man! And what a vein of piety runs through his whole work.

I finished the translation of Martin Luther's Life. Doubtless he was a man highly favoured of God, and a blessed instrument in his hand. But O! what pity that he had no faithful friend! None that would, at all hazards, rebuke him plainly and sharply, for his rough, untractable spirit, and bitter zeal for opinions, so greatly obstructive of the work of God. I preached, as usual, at five, at ten, and at five in the evening; besides meeting the Leaders, the Bands, the Preachers. But I felt no faintness or weariness either of body or mind. Preaching thrice in the day, and riding upward of fifty miles, would be work enough. But they would take no denial. So I preached at three to a great multitude. It rained almost all the time; but none went away.

Mr. Whitefield preached. How wise is God, in giving different talents to different Preachers! Even the little improprieties both of his language and manner were a means of profiting many.

I revised Grecian Antiquities. I revised Mr. Lewis's Hebrew Antiquities. I prepared a short History of England and a short Roman History. I read over Mr. Holmes's Latin Grammar. It is now about eighteen years since I began writing and printing books. I found that on March 1, 1756, I had gained by printing and preaching together, a debt of twelve hundred and thirty-six pounds.

I was not able to sit up above two or three hours together. However, I preached in the morning and evening, and spoke severally to the Members. I do indeed live by preaching! I was extremely hoarse. Tuesday morning I began spitting blood. I rested another day.

At Newcastle. I was extremely weary when we came in, having preached four times on Saturday. But my strength soon returned.

JONATHAN EDWARDS, 1703-1758

Jonathan Edwards, greatest of the Puritans, was America's original philosopher, and one of the noblest saints and evangelists that this country ever produced. He helped to fulfill and terminate the mission of rigid Calvinism which, although it was to make a contribution to the future of America that was incalculably great, as a separate authoritarian system had served its day. English rationalism under Milton and Locke had turned from Calvinism to Arminianism, which was only a modified

Calvinism, and this later developed into Arianism, deism and Unitarianism. Already the tides were flowing from the struggles of Puritan absolutism toward both the French and American revolutions, and Edwards was powerless to stay them.

John Calvin's secular son, James Madison, became the "father of the Constitution," developing the checks and balances between the President, Congress, Supreme Court, and the people— all of whom Madison and the founding fathers distrusted. Calvin's great spiritual son, Jonathan Edwards, became a watershed in the life of New England and America. In making the last effort to establish the sovereignty of God in American life where the theocracy of Massachusetts Bay had finally failed, Edwards was only opening the door to domesticating God. In asserting the depravity of man, by a strange irony of fate he was causing a reaction which paved the way for the more optimistic anthropology of Unitarianism. In his bold use of reason, his pietistic individualism and, as the father of American evangelism, in his treating men as free, he was unconsciously hastening the decay of Calvinism. Richard Niebuhr says: "A single line of development leads from Jonathan Edwards and his great system of God-centered faith through the Arminianism of the Evangelical revival, the Unitarianism of Channing and Parker, and the humanism of transcendental philosophy, to the man-centered, this-worldly, lift-yourself-by-your-own-bootstraps doctrine of New Thought and Christian Science."

Jonathan Edwards, as a son of the manse, was born of four generations of Puritan religious enthusiasts. Even in his childhood he enjoyed his religion with every other natural good. Religiously, he had been moved at the age of ten by a revival in his father's church and by another just before he entered college, but he was perplexed that he never had a clear experience of conversion which so many realized later under his own preaching. He began reading Latin in his father's study at the age of six, and entered Yale at thirteen with a reading knowledge of Latin, Greek, and Hebrew. At the age of fifteen he was captivated and fired by John Locke. Soon he was outlining massive volumes that he hoped to write in philosophy. As one who was to become the keenest and most original philosopher in America, with a wrench he had torn himself from the study of science to philosophy, and from that in turn finally to theology.

In Edwards' *Personal Narrative* written in 1739, at the age of thirty-six, he vividly describes his early spiritual experience in language that reminds us of St. Augustine in his *Confessions*:

I had a variety of concerns and exercises about my soul from my childhood; but had two remarkable seasons of awakening, before I met with that change by which I was brought to those new dispositions, and that new sense of things, that I have since had. The first time was when I was a boy, some years before I went to college, at a time of awakening in my father's congregation, I was then very much affected for many months, and concerned about the things of religion, and my soul's salvation. I used to pray five times a day in secret, and to spend much time in religious talk with other boys; and used to meet with them to pray together. I experienced I know not what kind of delight in religion. My mind was much engaged in it, and had much self righteous pleasure; and it was my delight to abound in religious duties. I with some of my schoolmates joined together, and built a booth in a swamp, in a very retired spot, for a place of prayer. And besides, I had particular secret places of my own in the woods, where I used to retire by myself; and was from time to time much affected.

But in process of time, my convictions and affections wore off; and I entirely lost all those affections and went on in the ways of sin. Indeed I was at times very uneasy, especially towards the latter part of my time at college; when it pleased God, to seize me with a pleurisy. I had great and violent inward struggles, till, after many conflicts with wicked inclinations, I was brought wholly to break off all former wicked ways, and all ways of known outward sin. I made seeking my salvation the main business of my life. I felt a spirit to part with all things in the world, for an interest in Christ.

From my childhood up, my mind had been full of objections against the doctrine of God's sovereignty, in choosing whom he would to eternal life, and rejecting whom he pleased. It used to appear like a horrible doctrine to me. But I remember the time very well, when I seemed to be convinced, and fully satisfied, as to this sovereignty of God. My mind rested in it; and it put an end to all those cavils and objections. And there has been a wonderful alteration in my mind, in respect to the doctrine of God's sovereignty, from that day to this. The doctrine has very often appeared exceeding pleasant, bright, and sweet. Absolute sovereignty is what I love to ascribe to God. I thought with myself, how excellent a Being that was, and how happy I should be, if I might enjoy that God, and be wrapt up to him in heaven, and be as it were swallowed up in him for ever! I kept saying, and as it were singing over these words of scripture to myself; and went to pray to God that I might enjoy him.

I began to have a new kind of apprehension and idea of Christ, and the work of redemption, and the glorious way of salvation by him. An inward, sweet sense of these things, at times, came into my heart; and my soul was led away in pleasant views and contemplations of them. And my mind was greatly engaged to spend my time in reading and meditating on Christ, on the beauty and excellency of his person, and the lovely way of salvation by free grace in him. This I know not how to express otherwise, than by a calm, sweet abstraction of soul from all the concerns of this world; and sometimes a kind of vision, or fixed ideas and imaginations, of being alone in the mountains, or some solitary wilderness, far from all mankind, sweetly conversing with Christ, and wrapt and swallowed up in God. The sense I had of divine things would often of a sudden kindle up, as it were, a sweet burning in my heart; an ardor of soul, that I know not how to express.

The appearance of every thing was altered; there seemed to be, as it were, a calm, sweet cast, or appearance of divine glory, in almost every thing. God's excellency, his wisdom, his purity and love, seemed to appear in every thing; in the sun, moon, and stars; in the clouds, and blue sky; in the grass, flowers, trees; in the water, and all nature; which used greatly to fix my mind. I often used to sit and view the moon for continuance; and in the day, spent much time in viewing the clouds and sky, to behold the sweet glory of God in these things; in the mean time, singing forth, with a low voice my contemplations of the Creator and Redeemer.

And scarce any thing, among all the works of nature, was so sweet to me as thunder and lightning; formerly, nothing had been so terrible to me. I felt God, so to speak, at the first appearance of a thunder storm leading me to sweet contemplations of my great and glorious God. While thus engaged, it always seemed natural to me to sing, or chant for my meditations; or, to speak my thoughts in soliloquies with a singing voice. I often felt a mourning and lamenting in my heart, that I had not turned to God sooner, that I might have had more time to grow in grace. I spent most of my time in thinking of divine things, year after year; often walking alone in the woods, and solitary places, for meditation, soliloquy, and prayer, and converse with God; and it was always my manner, at such times, to sing forth my contemplations. I was almost constantly in ejaculatory prayer, wherever I was. Prayer seemed to be natural to me, as the breath by which the inward burnings of my heart had vent. My sense of divine things seemed gradually to increase, until I went to preach at New York in 1722, at the age of nineteen.[10]

In Yale, Edwards found his intimate friends not in his class-mates but in Isaac Newton and John Locke. Like Plato he always lived with the great. When pastor of the little Scotch Presbyterian church in New York, in 1722, near the corner of Wall Street and Broadway, he used to walk in the woods near by alone with God. Strange to think: Edwards was a contemporary of Benjamin Franklin. They were the two great representative intellects and writers of America. Both were scientists and philosophers, both rationalists, both leaders of men. They never came together nor could they have understood each other had they met upon Boston Common, for they were poles apart, living in different worlds. They represented the two strangely contrasted religious movements which developed almost simultaneously during the eighteenth century both in England and in the American colonies. One took the form of deism, or rational natural religion on the theological left wing, the other on the right wing, the pietism and evangelism of the Great Awakening led by Jonathan Edwards and George Whitefield in America and by John Wesley in England.

The first overemphasized cold reason, and the second emotion; the first was too exclusively Hellenic, the second too narrowly Hebraic; while both suffered from a warped and one-sided development. Franklin depersonalized God, and Edwards dehumanized man. Franklin was broad but morally and spiritually shallow; Edwards was narrow, characterized by depth and single-mindedness. Franklin was for all his breadth, with his cold, prudential morality, the embodiment of a shallow deistic gospel of enlightened self-interest: "Early to bed and early to rise, makes a man healthy, wealthy and wise." Edwards suffered from his narrow Calvinism; he took no interest in the politics of the wicked world and would probably have had as little sympathy with the American Revolution as had John Wesley.

In 1724, at the age of twenty-one, he was virtually in charge

[10] These abbreviated quotations are from his own *Personal Narrative* in the volume on *Jonathan Edwards* by Faust and Johnson, American Writers Series, pp. 57-72.

of Yale University when it had less than a hundred students.[11] Despite the intellectual storms that raged about him at the college and during most of his life, almost nothing was able to break his inward peace of mind, though we read in his diary of June 6, 1724, at Yale: "I have now abundant reason to be convinced of the troublesomeness and vexation of the world and that it will never be another kind of world."

In 1727, at the age of twenty-three, he was called to succeed his grandfather, Solomon Stoddard, as pastor of the church at Northampton, on the frontier west of Boston.

Edwards made his first public impact when he preached in Boston in 1731 on "God Glorified in Man's Dependence." It was "like the first booming of a solitary gun upon the opening of a great battle." As Edwards was preaching to his own congregation on the text: "That every mouth may be stopped," conviction fell upon his people. That was the beginning of the Great Awakening in New England. It was desperately needed there where the theocracy had passed from Puritan asceticism to an almost dead formal Pharisaism.

Space will permit only an abbreviated statement of Edwards' account of this revival in his own words:

The town of Northampton has now about two hundred families of rational and intelligent people. After a time of extraordinary dullness in religion and of licentiousness and frivolity among the youth, a new spirit and a remarkable religious concern began to appear in 1733. After the death of several of the young people and a series of group meetings, the Spirit of God began extraordinarily to work among us and a number were savingly converted. An earnest concern about religion and the eternal world became universal in the town among persons of all degrees and all ages. Other discourse than of the things of religion would scarcely be tolerated in any company. The temptation was now rather to neglect worldly affairs too much. Everyone appeared to be pressing into the Kingdom. It then seemed to be a dreadful thing to be out of Christ, in danger every day of dropping into hell. Souls came as it were by blocks to Christ and daily sinners were delivered. This soon made a glorious alteration in the town; it seemed to be full of the presence of God, full of love and joy. The work in this town and some others about us has been extraordinary in affecting all

[11] See the best life of *Jonathan Edwards*, by Ola Elizabeth Winslow, pp. 54-59, 70-72, 81-84.

classes, sober and vicious, high and low, rich and poor, wise and unwise. It has had a saving effect on about six hundred and twenty communicants, including almost all our adult persons; more than three hundred souls were savingly brought home to Christ within half a year.[12]

During the high tide of the revival, persons under deep conviction of sin, after sleepless nights poured into Edwards' parsonage seeking peace; first the youth and then the elders of the congregation. The flame of the revival sprang up wherever Edwards preached over New England. Although there were emotional excesses that were bitterly denounced, and although reaction often followed the revival, Edwards rightly defended it because it produced "a remarkable and general alteration of the face of New England." The upheaval of the Great Awakening was the most potent force in America in the mid-eighteenth century. Jonathan Edwards, though he held that the will is not free to supply the necessary motive for conversion, probably never realized that he was himself overthrowing the cast-iron Calvinistic system by his practical emphasis on the fact of conversion held by Methodist Arminianism, and his appeal to men as though they were free.

Whatever the theory, the results changed the lives of individuals and of society, and finally even the theological climate. The warm glow of the religious revival not only corrected and supplemented the cold deism and skepticism of the eighteenth century, but it increased the membership of the rapidly multiplying popular churches—Methodist, Baptist, Congregational, Presbyterian, and others. These churches contributed to the movement for popular education, the rise of political democracy, and the social revolution which transformed the colonies. The Great Awakening in America became part of a world-wide movement which included the Methodist revival in the British Empire and the pietist movement from Germany. For good or ill from the days of Edwards, Whitefield, and Wesley, to Finney and Moody, America has ever been the land of revivals and of the awakenings of evangelical religion.

Edwards as a man was better than his Calvinistic creed with "a God-consciousness as passionate as that of Spinoza." Combining

[12] *Works of President Edwards* (New York ed.), Vol. III, pp. 231-267; from *A Narrative of the Surprising Work of God.*

the mystical and logical, he was a Platonist lover of perfection and of beauty. He was by nature full of sweetness and light, though always counting himself the chief of sinners. He derived his teaching chiefly from his open Bible, from Locke, and English critical rationalism, though he became the bulwark of declining Calvinism in New England after the fall of the theocracy. He writes: "I should not take it at all amiss to be called a Calvinist for distinction's sake, though I utterly disclaim a dependence on Calvin . . . and cannot be charged with believing in everything just as he taught."

It is not easy for us moderns to understand Edwards. His mental climate is so different; the moral altitude of the rarefied atmosphere of his thought is harder to breathe for men who habitually live in the heavier air of the materialistic lowlands. Jonathan Edwards was the Karl Barth of his day, but he meant far more to America than did Barth to the Europe of our time. Because of his profound personal experience, his high philosophy and theology centered in his sublime vision of God. His message and his gift to America were nothing less than the God-centered life. Edwards traces everything back to the fountainhead where all of life was of God, by God, and for God, in whom we live and more and have our being. To the godless man, however cultured, or to the utopian humanist, Edwards is not only incomprehensible but anathema. We cast the first stone if we seize upon the manifest shortcomings of a stern Calvinism and a rigid Puritanism but never rise to see the real Edwards, the latchet of whose shoes most of us are unworthy to loosen. Everywhere and in everything he saw God's glory and in this ineffable glory and sweetness he found salvation for his own soul. This meant the beginning of a new age following the harsh theocracy of New England.

We will not quote here from Edwards' famous "Sinners in the Hands of an Angry God." That series of imprecatory sermons sank deep into the mind of New England, and the Unitarians Emerson, Channing and Theodore Parker, never forgave Edwards for them. We must remember, however, that John Calvin and the century that followed him must share with Edwards in the blame. All were the prisoners of their time and of its theological background. Of the more than a thousand sermons which Edwards has left us, which are on a higher intellectual plane than Wesley's more practical sermons, and which cover the whole gamut of theology, Scripture and practical life, very few are of this nature. It is amazing, nevertheless, what contradictory views men can hold of a loving God.

When Edwards objected to the "halfway covenant" which provided for an associate, unconverted, "worldly" membership in his local church at Northampton, he was opposed by influential members of the congregation and heartlessly dismissed after twenty-three years in its pastorate. In his farewell sermon, without bitterness he says:

The prophet Jeremiah puts the people in mind how long he had laboured among them; that is, three and twenty years. I have spoken the word of God to you, unto the three and twentieth year, rising early and speaking. My work is finished. You have publicly rejected me.

After six months in perplexity and threatened with poverty, America's most brilliant philosopher went as a missionary to the savage Indians in the little village of Stockbridge. In 1757, after six years in poverty, he was called to the presidency of Princeton, then known as the College of New Jersey, to succeed the second president, the Reverend Aaron Burr, who was Edwards' son-in-law and the father of the notorious duelist and Vice-President of the United States. After two months in Princeton, Edwards died suddenly as the result of an anti-smallpox inoculation. He had initiated and directed a popular movement of far-reaching consequences and he had laid the foundation for a new system of religious thought in America. He was a great evangelist and a thinker, a compelling preacher and master logician. As a philosopher, he was on the side of the "New Light," but he never broke from his prison of Calvinism. His biographer, Ola Elizabeth Winslow, concludes: "As a shaping force in American culture, the man himself has been more important than anything he ever did or said or wrote. As an achievement in human living, the whole seems greater than the sum of its parts. He became the bright symbol of what he called a thousand times and more, 'the things of religion,' " Most of us today are compelled to disagree with both the harsh Calvinism of Edwards and the rationalistic deism of Benjamin Franklin, but there can be no question that in a unique way, Jonathan Edwards had certainly discovered God.

As truly as Benjamin Franklin, as surely as Washington or Jefferson, Jonathan Edwards was one of the builders of the new world. Through him a modified Puritanism was to make its spiritual contribution to a country whose boundless wealth might easily develop into a materialistic plutocracy ever in danger of forgetting God. Thus throughout the emancipating Protestant Reformation, through Luther in Germany and Continental Europe, through John Bunyan and John Wesley in Puritan England and the broad sweep of the Evangelical Revival, and through Jonathan Edwards in the greater liberties and greater dangers of the new world, these pathfinders were to lead the way for a great multitude which no man could number who would be privileged to make the discovery of God for themselves.

CHAPTER VIII

THE SCIENTISTS' DISCOVERY OF GOD

AT FIRST sight, it will not appear that the great scientists made as deep a discovery of God as the early prophets, saints, mystics, and reformers, but the significance of their very real experience and their invaluable contribution to our time can only be realized against the background of our modern age of skepticism and materialism. Materialism as a theory of the nature of the world held that all existence depended entirely upon matter and motion, matter being the fundamental and final reality. As early as the fourth century B.C., Democritus believed that all reality could be accounted for by atoms and their motions in space, and the later Epicureans and Stoics also thought that the real was corporeal or material in its nature. There have been recurring periods in history marked by strong materialistic tendencies. These were often in association with advances in science, as in the eighteenth rationalistic century of the Enlightenment, and in the nineteenth century, proud of its brilliant scientific discoveries.

Naturalistic and sensualistic philosophy were neighbors of this materialism. The industrial revolution had led to the rapid mechanizing of work and thought. The growth of machine industry and the concentration of material wealth under laissez-faire economics had left congested urban slums and masses of impoverished humanity robbed of all opportunity for abundant life whether material, intellectual, or spiritual. The machine age was accompanied by the apparent triumphs of mechanistic natural science, by deterministic biology, behavioristic and physiological psychology, philosophic positivism and the self-sufficient social sciences which, all combined, seemed on the surface to leave out God and religion as needless hypotheses if not gross superstitions.

The work of Newton—which seemed to some to prove a mechanistic closed universe under inexorable law—of Darwin —with apparently triumphant evolution working automatically by natural selection—the influence of Herbert Spencer, Huxley, Haeckel, David Strauss, Karl Marx, and scores of scientists, philosophers, and writers, seemed to involve a philosophy which left no room for God's creation, or man's soul, and which repudiated the fundamental postulates of Christianity. Yet it was the Christian religion, with its Jewish and Graeco-Roman background, that had been the chief factor in the very birth of modern science and in creating and maintaining Western civilization and culture for centuries.

Nietzsche had, however, attacked both Christian theology and morality. John Draper brought out his *History of the Conflict between Religion and Science*, Andrew D. White his *History of the Warfare of Science with Theology in Christendom*, Bradlaugh preached atheism to the masses in England, while Robert Ingersoll triumphantly orated for thirty years on the "scientific" grounds for disbelief in God and in the inspiration of the Bible. Later, Marxian Communism, Fascism, and Nazism were to make their assaults upon all vital religion that maintained that man must obey God rather than man. All these movements gathered headway between 1870 and 1939, at the outbreak of World War II, until masses of men began to feel that they had entered upon a period of volcanic revolution, where all areas of man's life would be affected—religious, moral, intellectual, economic, political and social.

We understand science as ordered knowledge of natural phenomena and of the relations between these phenomena. It arose much later than religion, art and primitive philosophy. Thales and the Ionian philosophers began to break from mythology about 580 B.C., then Pythagoras and his followers made great advances in mathematics and astronomy. Aristotle made the first synthesis of the scientific knowledge of his day and mapped out the fields of the respective sciences. Thomas Aquinas made the next great synthesis of religion, philosophy and science based on the authority of Aristotle and this held sway over Europe for the next three centuries. The Renaissance began the assertion of the autonomous human intellect against the authority of medievalism, through such pioneers as Leonardo da Vinci, Copernicus, and Galileo.

Modern science, however, had its birth in monotheism, as the basis of the uniformity of nature. It was Christianity with its original heritage of freedom that gave birth to the empirical method with its appeal to experience on which the modern world was based. Jesus was hounded to death for his realistic empirical naturalism by the harsh religious traditionalists of his day. The same spirit of medieval dogmatic authority opposed or persecuted each autonomous modern science as it arose, including the science of biblical historical criticism. Robert H. Murray in his *Science and Scientists of the Nineteenth Century* shows that not only ecclesiastics but repeatedly dogmatic scientists in their new orthodoxy shut their minds against new truth in their own fields.

Dr. William Ernest Hocking shows in his recent book, *What Man Can Do For Man,* that science was itself an outgrowth of the religious strivings of the Middle Ages and that the ceaseless search by science for verifiable truth is one of the noblest human inspirations and itself is an aspect of God. But science tried to exclude religion and ethics from the universe. Its progressive secularization in the modern period of four centuries from 1540 to 1940, has at last made a meaningless jumping jack of a universe of purposeless change, and modern man as a result has missed the mark and is tired of himself. The sick soul and the psychiatrist are twin features of the modern era. The psychiatrist is the embodiment of applied science endeavoring to deal with the ravages of the mistakes of science. Man has become meaningless. Dr. Hocking shows that this desiccated picture of a world without values is "a damnable lie." The self-awareness of the scientist and the genuineness of that aspect of God must be incorporated into the body of science itself. As John Locke said: "We are all the workmanship of one Maker, we are sent into the world by his order, and about his business, we are made to last during his and not one another's pleasure." Science alone is not enough—nothing is enough without the rediscovery of God. Dr. Hocking concludes: "It is truth that the world, like the human self, has its own unity in a living purpose: it is the truth of the existence of God."

It was no accident, therefore, that practically all the great empirical pathfinders and discoverers of the new world of modern science were devout Christians. These included the courageous, persecuted Franciscan saint and scholar, Roger Bacon; Copernicus, the bold heliocentric astronomer and canon of the cathedral; Tycho Brahe, Kepler and the great experimenter, Galileo, who believed that the stars in their courses fight for Christ "our Crucified." He passed on the torch to Newton, greatest of them all, who was born the year Galileo died. All of these could have cried with the devout Kepler: "These are thy thoughts I am thinking after Thee." These great pathfinders are brilliantly described by the contemporary Christian poet, Alfred Noyes, in his *Watchers of the Skies*. Newton's discovery that all the movements of the heavens could be included under one simple law was the first great physical synthesis and probably represents the highest achievement yet made in the history of science. Our space will permit only a brief study of the faith and experience of four men selected out of hundreds of believing modern scientists: Newton, Pasteur, Michael Pupin and Arthur Compton.

SIR ISAAC NEWTON, 1642-1727

All his life Newton needed some external stimulus to rouse his latent powers. As a boy in the Grantham grammar school, he neglected his studies and stood last in the lowest form but one. When the boy above him, who was a bully, kicked him in the stomach, Newton was roused first to thrash him with his fists and then in emulation to pass him in his studies until he stood first in the school. When he left the school he tried farming and failed. In Cambridge, where his poverty forced him to earn his way by performing menial duties, he was at first deficient in mathematics, as Pasteur later was in chemistry. But he was soon tackling Euclid, Kepler's optics, the binomial theorem and differential calculus. When driven from Cambridge by the great plague at the age of twenty-two, in his enforced solitude he solved a major problem of the ages. Observing the fall of an apple in his garden, he was led on to formulate the universal theory of gravitation, discerning in the secret of the heavens the unity of God's universe.

For three decades he won victory after victory; during the first decade in light and color in his discovery of the spectrum, in the second decade on gravitation and optics, in the third decade in astronomy and pure mathematics. Absorbed in deep concentration, he often forgot to eat, neglected his health, and worked almost all night. He had made the greatest of all scientific generalizations up to that time in his theory of universal gravitation, his three laws of motion published in his great *Principia*, and his extension of the order of nature to show that the law of the heavens was also the law of the earth, that the moon and the falling stone are bound by one common law.

Newton had been religious from his youth and counted the study of the Scriptures and reading theology his noblest occupation. He was a firm believer in God's revelation. There was a vein of the mystic as well as of the rationalist in him, and he spent hours in studying and copying passages from Jacob Boehme, the mystical shoemaker. He demanded freedom in thought as in science and was not supposed to be quite orthodox on the trinity; he was accused of being an Arian or Unitarian. Newton said however: "The Father is God, creating and a person; the Son is God, created and a person; the Holy Ghost is God, preceding and a person." Though Newton withstood the attacks of the deists and attempted to prove the existence of God he was undoubtedly influenced by the chilling deism which made the intellectual climate of the day. He almost believed the universe was a vast machine created by a personal and spiritual God who needed now to do little more than keep it in repair.

He was a devout Christian himself, feeling: "like a boy playing on the seashore . . . while the great ocean of truth lay all undiscovered before me." Bishop Burnet speaks of him as the "whitest soul" he ever knew. De Morgan, his severest biographer, says: "It is enough that Newton is the greatest philosopher, and one of the best of men: We cannot find in his character an acquired failing . . . He remains an object of unqualified wonder, and all but unqualified respect." Laplace placed his *Principia* above all other productions of the human intellect. Voltaire, present at his funeral, said: "If all the geniuses of the universe assembled, he should lead the band." Newton never realized that the very laws that he had discovered would be used by others to support the mechanistic naturalism of a closed material universe which seemed to require no God. Both Newton and Descartes thought that they had rendered the highest service to religion as well as to science. Both believed in God's Word and in his world; in his two revelations in the Scriptures and in nature. They believed their science had reclaimed nature from the superstition of black magic and the devil and restored it to God. John Locke, Newton's contemporary, could say: "The works of nature everywhere sufficiently evidence a Deity."

It amazes us, however, to realize that Newton's scholarship was not modern save in science. With the other scientists of his day he believed in and practiced alchemy to transmute metals. He and his contemporaries believed that disease was the act of God or of demons. Newton had scarcely the faintest conception of modern historical criticism, or the bringing of reason to bear upon his faith. He accepted the chronology of Archbishop Usher in dating the creation in 4004 B.C. Though he was devoutly religious, God's revelation to him was not in the field of religion but in science. He died at the age of eighty-five, full of days and honors and was buried in Westminster Abbey. A bibliography of his works together with a list of books illustrating his life contains four hundred and twelve entries.

There can be no question that Newton had made the discovery of God in his own life, and that his researches were laying the foundation for a wider synthesis of reason and faith and of science and religion in the future. He made his own partial contribution toward bridging the gulf between an unscientific belief and an unbelieving science. In Newton, man's religious discovery of God and God's revelation in the natural world met. In the humble room in which he was born appears Pope's celebrated epitaph: "Nature and nature's laws lay hid in night: God said 'let Newton be' and all was light."

Newton never attributed his great discoveries to his own genius. The statement ascribed to him is: "If I saw further, 'twas because I stood on giant shoulders." Alfred Noyes thus paraphrases Newton's *Principia*:

> Whence arises all
> This order, this unbroken chain of law . . .
> Whence, but from some divine transcendent Power . . . .
> And Newton, from a height above all worlds
> Answered and answers still: "This universe
> Exists, and by that one impossible fact

Declares itself a miracle; postulates
An infinite Power within itself, a Whole
Greater than any part, a Unity
Sustaining all, binding all worlds in one . . . .
'Tis not the lack of links within the chain
From cause to cause, but that the chain exists.
That's the unfathomable mystery,
The one unquestioned miracle that we know,
Implying every attribute of God."[1]

LOUIS PASTEUR, 1822-1895

Sir William Osler paid tribute to Pasteur for three great discoveries—a knowledge of the true nature of the processes of fermentation, with their wide-reaching implications; a knowledge of the chief maladies which have scourged man and animals; and a knowledge of the measures by which the human body may be protected against these diseases, or their poison neutralized when once within the body. Dr. Osler praises alike the lofty character of Pasteur and the method and the success of his scientific and humanitarian work.

Ancient physicians from Hippocrates to Galen had accurately described many diseases but of their cure they knew little, and of their causes almost nothing. In Pasteur's youth science had as yet learned little more of the causes of the great scourges of the human race—its plagues, fevers and pestilences—than had the Greeks. Before Pasteur man's sickness was obscured almost in Egyptian darkness; from him the first dawn of a new day of the scientific conquest of disease in surgery and medicine begins to break.

As the son of a humble tanner, Louis Pasteur entered school in the Latin Quarter of Paris, but his frail health soon gave way. When at the age of twenty he won his baccalaureate in science, attached to his diploma were the words "mediocre in chemistry"! He never was a genius and his beginning was little more promising than that of Newton. Indomitable, however, he wrote to his parents "will, work, and success between them fill human existence." He had the infinite capacity for taking pains, enthusiastic concentration upon a great objective, and the gift of imagination. Pasteur began work in his laboratory on the rotary

[1] Noyes, *Watchers of the Sky*.

polarization of liquids and then upon crystallography. His first startling piece of research was done upon racemic acid. When he made this discovery he rushed from his laboratory, like Archimedes in his new found joy, and embraced the curator as he realized the consequences of his experiment. He had found the hidden secret of racemic acid, to the joy and pride of his professors, who said "he throws light upon everything he touches." They soon said "in chemistry you are in the front rank of inventors." Already his work was reflecting "glory on French chemistry."

Pasteur early became professor of physics at Dijon and then in Strassburg. Enthusiastic over his laboratory discoveries, he writes characteristically: "I am on the verge of mysteries, and the veil which covers them is getting thinner and thinner." At the age of thirty, he pursued his crystals and their hidden secrets to the laboratories of Leipzig, Trieste, Vienna and Prague, and returned with the red ribbon of the Legion of Honor and a financial award for his "splendid discoveries." His studies in molecular dissymmetry gave rise, two decades later, to a new science of the chemistry of space.

When Pasteur was then promoted to the deanship of the new Faculty of Sciences at Lille, he was soon upon the trail of the germinal source of disease. At the age of forty-three he was acknowledged to be the leading chemist of his day and honors were showered upon him from his own country and abroad. The distinguished English surgeon, Lord Lister, president of the British Royal Society, utilizing and acknowledging the discoveries of Pasteur, was the first to reform surgical operations so as to obviate bacterial infections. It was he who banished hospital gangrene and suppurating wounds from his hospital in Glasgow. The suppuration and septic poisoning which had raged like the plague in surgical wards of hospitals and in dressing stations on all the battlefields of the world, were now to be eliminated and wounds were to be healed "by first intention."

From this time (1860-1870) dates the beginning of modern surgery. Pasteur sought to utilize the healing of his Master's seamless robe beside humanity's beds of pain through the instrumentality of science consecrated to religious ends. As Sir William Osler says: "The first outcome of the researches of

Pasteur upon fermentation and spontaneous generation represents a transformation in the practice of surgery, which, it is not too much to say, has been one of the greatest boons ever conferred upon humanity." Lord Lister said in the *Lancet* in 1867: "A flood of light has been thrown upon this most important subject by the philosophic researches of Pasteur who has demonstrated that it is minute particles suspended in the air which are the germs of various low forms of life, now shown by Pasteur to be the essential cause of putrescence." As Newton had seen the connection between the falling apple and the moon, Pasteur had seen the relation between fermentation, putrefaction and infectious diseases. He had found both the cause and cure of certain germinal maladies.

The national tragedy of the defeat of France by Germany nearly killed Pasteur and he suffered from a stroke of paralysis. But undaunted he heroically labored on for twenty-seven years more. After he had revolutionized the production of alcohols and saved the silk industry, Pasteur turned his attention to France's fatal cattle scourge known as anthrax. This had killed from twenty-five to thirty per cent of the nation's sheep and cattle, destroying both man and beast in other parts of Europe. Supplementing the labors of Koch in Germany, Pasteur discovered the cause and cure of the disease by inoculation, just as Jenner had learned to vaccinate and cure smallpox by cowpox. The financial values of these discoveries were estimated by T. H. Huxley to be more than the billion dollar war indemnity paid by France to Germany in 1870. Yet Pasteur chose to remain poor and live almost the simple life of a penitent monk.

Pasteur had as much of a scientific passion for truth as Newton, Darwin or Huxley, as when he said: "Worship the spirit of criticism. If reduced to itself, it is not an awakener of ideas or a stimulant to great things, but, without it, everything is fallible." Yet reason and faith, science and religion were well balanced in his life. Pasteur wrote to his sisters: "If you should falter in life's journey, a hand will be there to support you. If that should be wanting, God who alone could take that hand from you, would himself accomplish its work." As a devout, practicing Catholic, one of the saints of science, Pasteur never felt alone in his laboratory. He took time for prayer and devotional reading even during his busy days, that he might be a better scientist and servant of man. Science for him was but a means, a technique of life. He did not, like Darwin, allow his higher capacities and spiritual potentialities to atrophy or wither away from neglect, until his mind became a mere machine for the discovery and utilization of natural laws.

As a scientist and humble follower of the Nazarene Pasteur believed he was God's child, redeemed by his grace, in God's world of human suffering which he hoped to allay by his service to man. Science and religion were not to him two separate compartments of life; there was no division between the sacred and secular. His work in the laboratory like that of Brother Lawrence in his kitchen, was as sacred as that of the priest before the high altar. Like Pascal he had tried to learn the lesson of his frequent breakdowns in health and with utter consecration. As a means to his great end of the glory of God and the utmost service to man he was ever seeking to perfect himself in character, "conforming to the very highest religious ideals." Pasteur had found in individual experience, free from all intolerance and controversy, a personal religion of love, peace, devotion and service, with instinctive sympathy for the sorrows of others.

The practical results of Pasteur's researches have placed in our hands the successful prophylactic treatment of one disease after another, thus advancing the frontiers of life and pushing back the boundaries of death. Pasteur's address at the inauguration of the first Institute for the treatment of hydrophobia shows his spiritual background and the philosophy of his life which was identical with the motivation of the ministry of healing of the Galilean whom he counted Lord and Master:

Two opposing laws seem to be now in contest. The one, a law of blood and death, opening out each day new modes of destruction, forces nations to be always ready for battle. The other a law of peace, work and health whose only aim is to deliver man from the calamities which beset him. The one seeks violent conquests, the other the relief of mankind. The one places a single life above all victories, the other sacrifices hundreds of thousands of lives to the ambition of a single individual. (In the contrast between Pasteur and Hitler, how much truer this is today, fifty years after it was uttered.) The law of which we are the instruments strives even through the carnage to cure the wounds due to the law of war. Treatment by our antiseptic methods may preserve the lives of thousands of soldiers. Which of those two laws will prevail, God only knows. But of this we may be sure, that science, in obeying the law of humanity, will always labor to enlarge the frontiers of life.

Science as represented by such men as Newton, Pasteur, Michael Pupin and Arthur Compton has been doing just that. But Hitler's National Socialist scientists with their anti-Semitic racial theories and their laboratories of destruction have been serving the other law of life. Scientists of the first type have discovered God and have sought to allow their science and all its applications to be motivated by the love of God and man. Scientists of the second type, serving a totalitarian order under a superman, super-race, superstate, supermorality and super-religion of godless paganism, have often served the stream of evil influence described by two great Catholic Christians, St. Augustine and Louis Pasteur. It is evident that godless modern science cannot save the world, but a science, like Pasteur's, that, consciously or unconsciously, is motivated by the discovery of God can serve all humanity. At the very end of his life Pasteur was working for the conquest of diphtheria and plague, but for the unconquered regions beyond he had to pass on the torch to younger hands. After twenty-seven years of work, suffering from the effects of his earlier paralysis, he still felt that he was just beginning his course. He believed there were yet endless reaches of personal life beyond the portal which men wrongly call death. The best was yet to be. Concerning personal immortality, he had not the shadow of a doubt.

Dr. Osler points out that the last great lesson for us of Pasteur's life was his humility before the unsolved problems of the universe. Pasteur thus voices his own creed in his eulogy upon Littre:

He who proclaims the existence of the Infinite—and none can avoid it—accumulates in that affirmation more of the supernatural than is to be found in all the miracles of all the religions; for the notion of the Infinite presents that double character, that it forces itself upon us and yet is incomprehensible. When this notion seizes upon our understanding we can but kneel . . . I see everywhere the inevitable expression of the Infinite in the world; through it the supernatural is at the bottom of every heart. The idea of God is a form of the idea of the Infinite. As long as the mystery of the Infinite weighs on human thought, temples will be erected for the worship of the Infinite . . . Men will be seen kneeling, prostrated in the thought of the Infinite . . . Blessed is he who carries within himself God, an ideal, and who obeys it: ideal of art, ideal of science, ideal of the gospel virtues, therein lie the springs of great thoughts and great actions; they all reflect light from the Infinite.

Dr. Osler concluded:

After reading for the third or fourth time the *Life of Louis Pasteur,* I am of the opinion expressed recently by the anonymous writer of a beautiful tribute in the *Spectator,* "that Pasteur was the most perfect man who has entered the kingdom of Science."

If this was so, was it not because Pasteur, without philosophy or dogma, had by simple faith entered the Kingdom of God like a little child? Can anyone save an atheist, or an anti-theistic humanist who believes there is no objective reality corresponding to man's subjective word "God," deny that Pasteur as well as his fellow countrymen, Pascal and Brother Lawrence, had made the great discovery of God? Pasteur believed, as he had said so often, that this was the one essential determinative thing about his life.

At the end:

Rich in years and in honors, this simple and devout Catholic, this great human benefactor, whose scientific acumen and profound sagacity enabled him to solve the problems of the world of the infinitely small (as he called it), passed quietly away on September 28, 1895: One of his hands rested in that of his wife, Mme. Pasteur, the other held a crucifix.

MICHAEL PUPIN, 1859-1935

When Michael Pupin first went away to the high school in Serbia and heard from his teacher of Benjamin Franklin and his kite, he began to ask fundamental questions: What is light? What is electricity? What is magnetism? What is matter? What is life? And he gave the rest of his life seeking to answer those questions. He never lost the "poetry of science" in delving into its later prose, nor the high idealism which saw God everywhere when he worked day and night in the fields of peasant Serbia or later in the laboratories of England, Germany, and America.

The Serbian boy of fifteen who landed at Castle Garden with five cents in his pocket and rose, as he recounts in his autobiography, *From Immigrant to Inventor,* had as a scientist almost the simplest faith of anyone described in this volume. From the time he knelt before the icons of the saints in the little village Greek Orthodox Church with his devout peasant mother, throughout his studies in the universities of Europe and America, and in the midst of his brilliant discoveries in science, his child-like faith and his robust piety were unbroken. He never knew the doubts, the agonies and remorse of an Augustine or a "twice-born" soul. And he owed almost everything to his remarkable peasant mother.

Though, like his father, she could neither read nor write, it was she who not only taught him of God but who insisted upon his higher education, sending him, in her poverty and illiteracy, from his Serbian village to the great schools and universities of Prague, Columbia, Cambridge and Berlin, saying: "I am illiterate and blind myself and cannot venture beyond the village, but you, my son, must provide yourself with another pair of eyes. Knowledge is the golden ladder over which we climb to heaven." It was she who taught him the lives of the saints, especially of St. Sava, the great educator, first archbishop of an autonomous Serbian church, seven centuries before. And with equal devotion she almost worshiped the great saints of modern science when her son shared his enthusiasms with her on each vacation, as he slept by night on the ground under the stars of God and by day read Faraday, Clerk Maxwell, Lagrange, or Helmholtz.

It was his mother who would not let him marry and settle down as a Serbian peasant, but sternly sent him back to Cambridge and Berlin saying:

I go to church, my son, not so much because I expect the priest to reveal to me some new divine truth, but because I wish to look at the ikons of the saints. That reminds me of their saintly work, and through the contemplation of their work I communicate with God. Cambridge is a great temple consecrated to the eternal truth. It is filled with ikons of the great saints of science. The contemplation of their saintly work will enable you to communicate with the spirit of eternal truth

. . . God sends sunlight . . . If all is done by the same heavenly force which hurls the lightning across the sombre summer clouds and also carries the humble human voice over the wires between distant peoples, then I see in it a new proof of God's infinite wisdom. Who can fathom the power of God! I include all knowledge which brings me nearer to God; and this new knowledge certainly does.

There was never any conflict between the mother's religion and the son's science, for the son was as devout as his mother and the mother had faith in science as had her son. Would that there had never been the fatal divorce between science and religion; between an unbelieving science and an unscientific faith!

When Michael first landed as a penniless immigrant in America, he knew of nobody save Benjamin Franklin, Abraham Lincoln, and Harriet Beecher Stowe, but he was filled with what was for him a holy dream of liberty and democracy, and was avid in his search for truth. Nine years he worked on farms and in factories till he was ready for what seemed to him the sacredness of citizenship in the land of the free. Working as a poor boy in the priceless library of Cooper Union and in its night classes, he fitted himself to enter Columbia, especially inspired with religious fervor by the lives of the great scientists and inventors. Overcoming a thousand handicaps, he mastered several languages, brilliantly entered Columbia on a free scholarship, and won honors in literature—Greek, Latin, and English—in mathematics, and in science. His simple faith never wavered, whether worshiping before the icons in the Serbian village church; or listening eagerly to Henry Ward Beecher every Sunday in Plymouth Church, Brooklyn; or worshiping in the college chapel at Cambridge where the great Isaac Newton had worshiped two centuries before him with equal devotion; or in the lecture room and laboratory of Germany's greatest scientist, Helmholtz. Michael Pupin always seemed to feel: "God, God everywhere, and underneath the everlasting arms." There was for him no dualism between spirit and matter, the sacred and the secular, religion and science, God and his universe.

When, in 1889, he became a teacher of mathematical physics in the Department of Electrical Engineering at Columbia, in his first lectures he told the students that "No electrical generator generates electricity, because electricity was made by God and, according to Faraday, its quantity in the universe is constant." It merely generates the *motion* of electricity which works for us through the telegraph, telephone, electric lighting, radio, etc.

It was Michael Pupin who obtained the first X-ray photograph in America in 1896, two weeks after the discovery was announced in Germany. His invention of the electrical resonator for practicing harmonic telegraphy, the "Pupin coil," and his high-inductance wave conductors were purchased by the American Telephone and Telegraph Company and helped to make possible the achievements of the long-distance telephone. The invention saved that company more than a hundred million dollars and was worth to them at least ten times what they paid Pupin for it. Later the Marconi Company of America bought his inventions relating to electrical tuning and rectification in wireless telegraphy. After receiving degrees, gold medals, honors, and prizes from various institutes and academies in America and Europe, he left a foundation for scholarships for the education of poor Serbian boys. And his contagious belief and radiant experience in the discovery of God had helped a whole generation of his students.

At the close of his autobiography, *From Immigrant to Inventor*, after seeing beyond science the vision of God, Michael Pupin also sees beyond man's strife and war to at least the beginnings of a new social order of justice and peace that man may yet build in some dim likeness to the Kingdom of God on earth. He writes:

The physical facts of science are not cold, unless your soul and your heart are cold. There is white heat somewhere in every physical fact when we decipher correctly the message which it conveys to us. Fifty years ago, when as a member of a herdsman's squad of boys I watched the stars on the black background of a summer midnight sky, I felt that their light was a language proclaiming the glory of God. Has science changed that vision of the early childhood days? Fifty years ago, instructed by David's psalms, I found in the light of the stars a heavenly language which proclaims the glory of God, but I did not know how that language reached me, and I hoped that some day I might find out. That hope was in my soul when I landed at Castle Garden. Today science tells me that the stars themselves bring it to me. The light of the stars is a part of the life-giving breath of God. I never look now upon the starlit vault of the heaven without feeling this divine breath and its quickening action upon my soul.

We feel intuitively that science will never penetrate the mysteries beyond physical phenomena, but our faith encourages us in the belief that there behind the impenetrable veil of this eternal background is the throne of a Divine power, the soul of the physical world. Does not all our experience teach us that progress means more complete coordination of all natural activities, the activities of the atoms in the burning stars as well as of the cells in our terrestrial bodies? The most nearly perfect product of these coordinating instrumentalities is man. There certainly is something in the evolutionary progress of the world which favors the view that the coordinating instrumentalities which guide the activities of every organism, and which are very powerful in man, may enable us some day to find a way of coordinating the non-coordinated activities of the many millions of individuals, and thus of creating an ideal democracy.

During a postgraduate year of study in New York at Union Theological Seminary and Columbia, the writer had the privilege of belonging to a group of graduate students and faculty members who formed a seminar for a study of religious experience, especially on the discovery of God in human life. At that time we heard both from Michael Pupin and John Dewey and the contrast was striking. We held Dewey in high admiration and affection as an educator, a philosopher, a great humanist, and a fearless social prophet, but it was almost pathetic to hear him speak of religion. He could neither affirm nor deny God, nor could he testify that he had ever discovered him in experience. This is not to say that John Dewey was not known and used by God, or that he will not go on in the great adventure of the discovery of God in the endless reaches of eternity. But in the field of religion, at least, he had not only failed to find God himself, but he had increased the paralyzing doubt and agnosticism of many in our generation.

In contrast to this the simple faith and radiant assurance of Michael Pupin was a spiritual stimulus. He had done good and only good. He had discovered God as Creator, as Father and a. Friend. He worshiped him alike in his transcendence, in his immanence in nature revealed in the laws which science was increasingly discovering, and in his work of redemption in Christ as Saviour and Lord. As Kepler and Newton would have said, in the discovery of all these laws of science he was only thinking God's thoughts after him. And this simple Serbian peasant boy was following, not unworthily, in the footsteps of the great Newton and the devout Pasteur.

ARTHUR COMPTON, 1892-

Arthur Compton, physicist and Nobel prize winner, is a radiant Christian, leading a well-balanced life devoted both to science and religion. He was born fifty years ago in Wooster, Ohio, where his father was professor of philosophy and dean of the College of Wooster. At family prayers, all the three sons, who later distinguished themselves in the fields of science and education, took part in prayer. In adolescence, Arthur quite naturally joined the church. At the same age, he was fascinated by his study of the stars with his little telescope. Even today he has an amazing knowledge of the heavens, and an hour with him in the open air at night is an unforgettable experience. During his college course at Wooster, when other students were volunteering for service on the foreign mission field, Compton, with equal devotion, dedicated his life to Christ in the cause of science.

After study in the College of Wooster and at Princeton, Arthur Compton was in turn instructor in physics at the University of Minnesota and professor in Washington University, St. Louis, and since 1923 professor of physics in the University of Chicago. He directed the World Survey of Cosmic Rays, he was chairman of the Committee on X rays, he won the Rumford gold medal of the American Academy of Sciences in 1926, and the Nobel Prize in physics in 1927. He has worked on specific heats and the earth's rotation, on X rays, and is now conducting experiments on cosmic rays, working with helpers on the high mountains of Peru. The "Compton effect" first observed by him is explained as a scattering of the energy quanta, which are supposed to make up X rays, upon collision with free or loosely bound electrons with a resulting loss of momentum and a corresponding increase in wave length.

Busy as he is in his laboratory, he almost does a full man's work in the field of religion as well. He loves to teach a Bible class in the Baptist Church at the University of Chicago. He is a deacon and active member of the church and tireless in his Christian activity in connection with the Laymen's Missionary Movement, the National Conference of Christians and Jews and other organizations. He is a profoundly religious man. He sees God in everything, God in nature, God in history, God in the human heart, and finally "the glory of God in the face of Jesus Christ." In his personal life he has extraordinary insight into the spiritual significance of everything to which he gives his attention. One of his intimate friends says, "His home is a praying home. Above all his life is joyously, radiantly religious, minute by minute."

Arthur Compton agrees with Robert A. Millikan that there is no conflict whatever between science and religion when each is correctly understood: "The purpose of science is to develop a knowledge of the facts, the laws and the processes of nature. The even more important task of religion is to develop the consciences, the ideals, and the aspirations of mankind." Both agree with Galileo that we should go to the Bible not as a scientific authority but as a moral and spiritual guide. Both would agree with Lord Kelvin, a lifelong member of the church, who found vital religion in the first chapter of Genesis, "In the beginning God created the heaven and the earth," but who scientifically computed the age of the earth at approximately a hundred million years. And they would agree with Lord Kelvin again when he said: "If you think strongly enough you will be forced by science to the belief in God, which is the foundation of all religion. You will find it not antagonistic but helpful to religion." And all these scientific Christians agree with Pasteur in the words inscribed on his tomb at the Pasteur Institute, "Happy is he who carries God within him."

In his Garvin Lecture on "The Idea of God as Affected by Modern Knowledge,"[2] Dr. Compton says:

I am a man of science, to whom the interpretation of the world comes primarily from the study of nature's laws. Never was it as clear

[2] The following much-abbreviated statement is from Dr. Arthur Compton's lecture on "The Idea of God as Affected by Modern Knowledge," given in Lancaster, Pennsylvania, in 1940.

as it is today that this world has not made itself. In these days of knowledge of the gradual evolution of life, it would be ludicrous to suppose that our coming into being was the result of any dimly formed plan conceived by our invertebrate ancestors. Rather it is clear that forces operating in nature over which we have no control have been responsible for the gradual development of life until man appears on the scene. What are these powers? Scientists try to describe their action by formulating "natural laws." For our present purpose we may follow the theologians' nomenclature and call these higher powers "God." Science, in its efforts to learn the laws of nature, is in theological language seeking to understand the way in which God acts. But action implies an actor, and theology is concerned with the actor. In this sense of the actor in all world events, there can be no question of God's existence. The real problem comes when we begin to consider His attributes. Is the Actor intelligent? Does He have a plan? Is He interested in the welfare of men and women? Can He be described as morally good?

Such questions can be answered only by inference from His observed actions. If we mean by God's actions the events that occur in the world of nature, including the acts of men as being a part of nature, the study of natural science is the primary source of the raw material for building our idea of God. I am convinced that the most fundamental answer to this question is that which considers the value of life. What are we here for? Do we not feel that life is most worth while when we know that we are doing something of lasting value for someone we love? As we view our evolution from life's primitive beginnings, we can see, though dimly, the outline of a great plan. If this is true, are we not of value to the Planner? I doubt whether there is any objective for life that is ultimately more satisfying than trying to live the life that one comes to feel God wants him to live. This is why Jesus placed "Love the Lord thy God with all thy heart" as the first commandment. For if that love is present, living a life according to His plan will be one's greatest joy. The writer of the Westminster Catechism expressed the idea simply: "Man's chief end is to glorify God and enjoy Him forever." Such a view of life worth living implies, however, that we can look to our God for understanding and sympathy. Otherwise there would be no reason for our love and loyalty and a supreme effort to do our part. Some fortunate persons have an immediate awareness of God's presence and comradeship, a religious experience which gives a satisfying basis for love and loyalty.

. . . First among the attributes of God that we must consider is that of His intelligence. We are to approach this question on the basis of what we see happening in the world. If we see in nature evidence of a plan, this will imply intelligence. The alternative to an intelligent plan for the world is that things have happened to be as they are through chance. Consider the physicist's problem of accounting for the way atoms are formed. Next consider biological evolution. One well known aspect of this process is that at each stage of evolution, organisms arise having new characteristics. Thus each of the senses, smell, sight, etc., is a property that could never have been inferred from the properties of more primitive forms such as plants. Life itself, purposive action, and reason, all represent new inventions of nature, whose possibility had previously been hidden. To this phenomenon is given the descriptive name, "emergent evolution." Equally remarkable is an observation of the paleontologists. They have shown that changes occur for ages in a single direction, as if a definite experiment were being tried. Instead of variations at random, as Darwin had supposed, this means progress along the same line, generation after generation.

. . . We should note that the theory of evolution is in no sense an explanation of why these things happen. One is reminded of Huxley's comment, "How it is that anything so remarkable as a state of consciousness comes about as a result of irritating nervous tissue, is just as unaccountable as the appearance of the Djin when Aladdin rubbed his lamp." Is it reasonable to suppose that the Powers that made us endowed us with the mystery of consciousness and purposive action, gave us sight and hearing, taught us to enjoy music and the beauties of nature, made it possible for us to understand something of our setting in the world, opened to us the mystery of companionship and love—can it be that these Powers are themselves unconscious of what goes on? Such considerations have led Jeans in his interpretation of astronomy to conclude that God is the Master Mathematician. The chance of a world such as ours occurring without intelligent design becomes more and more remote as we learn of its wonders.

Concerning God's relation to man, might we not reasonably assume that an intelligent Creator would find His intelligent creatures of especial interest? . . . Let us ask ourselves then whether the evidence indicates that God is friendly toward man. As was perhaps first seen clearly by Pythagoras, if we live in accord with nature's rules, we and our fellows have a fuller and a happier life. At each stage of development there has been tragic suffering. This has been nature's method of forcing slowly developing humanity to search for and follow the better way.

It would be hard to imagine a process for achieving adaptation to environment that would be more certainly effective than the one we see now working in nature. Without any kind of partiality, the laws of nature bring into being only those creatures to which nature's laws are on the whole friendly. Is nature then friendly to us? Assuredly, if we

will learn her laws and discipline ourselves to live accordingly. . . .
Is the God thus revealed by nature severe? Certainly no more so than the
God of the Bible. "All things work together for good" for him who
serves the Lord. This is the exact parallel of nature's laws that are
friendly to the well-adapted organism. On the other hand, nature's
uncompromising attitude is accurately caught in Paul's proverb, "The
wages of sin is death." Jesus himself pictures the Father as adamant
in removing from among His children those who will not accept His
principles of love as the guide for life.

Is God good? There are certain theological difficulties raised by this
view of the relationship between God and man. The first is God's un-
doubted responsibility for permitting evil to be present in the world.
It would indeed seem that from the very nature of the evolutionary
method such evils must be present in order that man's moral character
shall develop. The second problem is that of God's mercy toward men,
so confidently taught by Jesus. My impression is that this mercy is very
real, but is to be found in the psychological rather than the physical
realm. Here it is that a sane, well-balanced religion, which helps men
to feel the understanding and sympathetic presence of their Creator,
offers the solace for which all yearn.

We find then that through a period of a billion years life has gradually developed on this planet. . . . Now we can feel that we are sharing
with our Creator the great task which He has undertaken. We can truly
say, "My Father worketh hitherto, and I work." Science can have no
quarrel with a religion which postulates a God to whom men are as
His children. It is possible to see the whole great drama of evolution as
leading toward the goal of the making of persons, with free, intelligent
wills, capable of learning nature's laws, of seeing dimly God's purpose
in nature, and of working with Him to make that purpose effective.
A group of leading American scientific men in fact recently expressed
just such a view.

It is a sublime conception of God which is furnished by science, and
one wholly consonant with the highest ideals of religion, when it represents Him as revealed through countless ages in the development of
the earth as an abode for man, and in the age-long inbreathing of life
into its constituent matter, culminating in man with his spiritual
nature and all his God-like powers.

Science has thus helped us to appreciate the inspiring setting in which
we find ourselves. If the creation of intelligent persons is a major objective of the Creator of the Universe, and if, as we have reason to
surmise, mankind is his highest development in this direction, the opportunity and responsibility of working as God's partners in his great
task should inspire us to the highest achievement of which we are able.

What nobler ambition can one have than to cooperate with his Maker in bringing about a better world in which to live?

In his lecture on "The Human Meaning of Science" given at the University of North Carolina in 1940, Dr. Compton said:

In bringing about a spirit of love of one's fellows no agency has appeared that is comparable in effectiveness with the Christian religion. Such a spirit was the very heart of Jesus' teaching. . . . It is Jesus' answer in his parable of the Good Samaritan which seems to have emphasized for the first time that the neighbor to be loved is everyone with whom one has dealings. The great objective in Jesus' mind is to win the love of the Father, whose companionship is the great sustaining and motivating power. Jesus thought of God as loving those who try to do His will as a father loves his children. Such fatherhood of God implies brotherhood of all men of good will.

Not only did Jesus make this "love" or "good will" the essence of His teaching, but He made of Himself a living example of how that spirit could be expressed in action. For those who would understand and share His spirit, however, this point is most important: it was His feeling of close partnership with God that gave Him the faith and courage to live His life of sacrifice. . . . The history of civilization has revealed no other agency comparable in effectiveness in molding attitudes.

. . . Faith in an intelligent God may be a thoroughly scientific attitude. . . . The resulting attitude after each "revolution" in science and religion is almost inevitably more adequate and satisfying than the earlier view around which the faith was originally formed. The scientist who recognizes God knows the God of Newton. He feels that God is in nature, that the orderly ways in which nature works are themselves the manifestations of God's will and purpose. . . . The physicist finds the world built, as far as he can now tell, of a few different elemental units, which he calls protons, electrons, neutrons, and photons. From the protons, electrons, and neutrons the atoms and molecules are built, and from the molecules, the ordinary things with which we are acquainted. Streams of photons make up rays of light and heat, carrying signals from one atom to another. Can it be a matter of chance that protons and photons and electrons have that particular set of characteristics that is necessary for development into a world of infinite variety and life? My late colleague, Dr. Breasted, placed "The Dawn of Conscience" at five or six thousand years ago. For the preceding thousand million years of the earth's history, God held in His own hands the whole responsibility for evolution of life upon this planet. Consciously sharing God's great task, men may now fairly be called His children. If we follow the thought that we have been developing to a reasoned conclusion, we are led to see that a surprisingly large share of the responsibility for carrying through a major program of the God of the Universe rests upon the shoulders of men. We feel that we are a vital part of a great enterprise in which a mighty Intelligence is working out His hidden plan. If indeed the creation of intelligent persons is a major objective of the Creator of the Universe, and if, as we have reason to surmise, mankind is now His highest development in this direction, the opportunity and responsibility of working as God's partners in His great task are almost overwhelming. What nobler ambition can one have than to cooperate with his Maker in bringing about a better world in which to live? "My Father worketh hitherto, and I work."[1]

As we recall the life and testimony of these four typical scientists, Isaac Newton, Louis Pasteur, Michael Pupin, and Arthur Compton, we do not claim that they rank spiritually with the great prophets, apostles, mystic saints and reformers previously studied in this volume. However distinguished they were as scientists they were not great spiritual adventurers and discoverers, as the faith of each was somewhat conventional and traditional. Their very vocation was perhaps a handicap. Prophets, apostles, missionaries, priests, ministers, medieval saints who devoted their whole lives to this great quest, the great reformers who battled for religious freedom, and modern social reformers, have had the advantage of a calling which spiritually developed all the best that was in them. The statesman, the politician, the lawyer, the businessman, the scientist, is sometimes immersed in the material universe, or in the "godless world" of a human society of greed and strife and war, surrounded by all the manifold temptations of his calling.

The importance of the true Christian or spiritual idealist in each of these callings is evident and the spiritual opportunity of the believing scientist is strategic as we have seen in Newton, Pasteur, Pupin and Compton. We have maintained that in science as well as in art and religion God reveals himself in all the true, the beautiful and the good. It is all one world and it

---

[1] Excerpts from Dr. Compton's lecture on "The Human Meaning of Science" are quoted by permission of the University of North Carolina Press, Chapel Hill, N. C.

is God's world. Here, especially in a materialistic and worldly age and in the transitional period at the end of an epoch in the great world crisis, we have need of spiritual discoverers and pathfinders in all callings who will redeem the whole of human experience for spiritual ends. We need men who will lead us beyond the false antithesis of an unbelieving science and an unscientific belief, beyond a nontheistic humanism and a bigoted, ignorant fundamentalism, in order that the whole of life and society may be brought within the purpose of the spiritual creation, redemption and the realized will of God. It is in the hope that all men may have all man-made obstacles removed and may make the discovery of God for themselves that we have cited these scientists who confirm our universal thesis that man discovers God.

CHAPTER IX

THE MODERN DISCOVERY OF GOD

THE introduction to the chapter on the scientists' discovery of God will apply equally to this one. Whatever else it is, this is not an "age of faith." Rather it is a period of sophistication, materialism, worldliness and skepticism. Never was it harder to believe in God than under the present poignant realization of the unsolved problem of evil. Most of the discoverers whom we have chosen as representative of this period believed that we were living at the end of an age, that we were entering a transitional period of crisis, that we were witnessing the breakdown of a basically unjust economic order whose criminal greed and blindness were driving our "immoral society" toward class war at home and world war abroad. They saw that war was but the symptom and result of the sickness of our selfish acquisitive society, and that worldly Christians had not proved to be the salt of the earth, but were themselves God's chief problems.

Of modern men we have chosen Tolstoy first, because he undoubtedly discovered God in his life, but also because of the fundamental mistake in his philosophy, his theology and his experience which proved his undoing, and which may serve as a warning to many today who are in grave danger of repeating his error.

Though a minor prophet we have selected William Rainey Harper, partly because of his unmistakable discovery of God, but mainly because he made it possible for numbers of modern men to make the necessary synthesis between science and religion, to apply reason to faith and the scientific method to religion in such a way as to deliver many from the clinging grave clothes of superstition, and from unworthy and erroneous views of the nature of God.

We have chosen Booker T. Washington as our third witness, not only for himself, but as a representative of his race which we have not yet emancipated from economic slavery. We fear that America's treatment of the Negro, like Hitler's treatment of the

Jew, is symptomatic of a deeper malady which may obstruct our own discovery of God.

For our fourth modernist and liberal, our choice lay between William Temple, Archbishop of Canterbury, and Reinhold Niebuhr. We chose the latter because he is an American, familiar with our pressing problems, and because, even though he is of necessity a prophet in his own country, misunderstood as every radical and courageous prophet has been in his own age, it is more important that we should understand him, who as mercilessly as Amos lays bare the evils of our age and their painful solution.

We have chosen the unorthodox non-Christian, Gandhi, as one of the greatest modern discoverers of God. And we have given the place of honor, to the last of our thirty-four pathfinders—to Albert Schweitzer, adventurer in science, art and religion; philosopher, theologian, musician, missionary and "suffering servant," who as much as any of our discoverers comes to grips with the stark problem of evil in the darkest continent of our agonizing world.

Let us then retrace the path of these explorers.

COUNT LEO TOLSTOY, 1828-1910

Tolstoy, as a son of the Russian aristocracy, inherited his "peer and peasant" view of life in the last period of serfdom. At Kazan University he lazily developed a contempt for academic learning but came under the "tremendous influence" of Rousseau, and, like him, idealized a return to nature. At Moscow he plunged into the dissipated life of a young officer, but even at this time started his diary which is a remarkable work of psychological self-study and self-criticism. He was gay in society but quarreled with the fellow members of his literary circle, and returned from a tour abroad with disgust for materialistic plutocratic Western civilization. His genius reached its climax in his greatest novels—his Iliad of *War and Peace* and *Anna Karenina* —in which the modern realistic novel probably attained its highest point. With piercing insight he intuitively sees and feels the world around and within him, and then is able dramatically to embody it in lifelike images and artistic shape. He tries to lay bare the mechanism of consciousness but early sees the conflict between the spontaneous unreflecting life of nature and the claims of reason and moral law. All during his later years he sought the inner meaning and ultimate unity and reality of what lies behind human existence, with a passionate craving for a religious justification for his life.

His conversion came late in life. During an eight-year period between his forty-ninth and fifty-seventh year he passed through a transitional stage of mental agony and strife, which he describes with imaginative sincerity and rhetorical power in *A Confession*. The merciless laying bare of his soul with piercing and relentless psychological insight reminds us of St. Augustine's volume by the same name. Tolstoy writes: "I only lived at those times when I believed in God. To know God and to live is one and the same thing." He devoted his last thirty years to the condemnation of civilized industrial, political, national and ecclesiastical life which seemed to him doomed to destruction. In *A Confession*, he vividly states his own experience as follows:

I was baptized and brought up in the Orthodox Christian faith. But when I abandoned the second course of the University at the age of eighteen I no longer believed any of the things I had been taught. As from the age of fifteen I began to read philosophical works, my rejection of the doctrine became a conscious one. From the time I was sixteen I ceased to say my prayers and ceased to go to church or to fast, but I believed in something. . . . My only real faith, that which gave impulse to my life, was a belief in perfecting myself. I tried to perfect my will, I drew up rules I tried to follow; I perfectly myself physically. Very soon this effort again changed into a desire to be stronger than others: to be more famous, more important and richer than others. With all my soul I wished to be good, but I was young, passionate and alone. I cannot think of these years without horror, loathing and heartache. I killed men in war and challenged men to duels in order to kill them. Lying, robbery, adultery of all kinds, drunkenness, violence, murder—there was no crime I did not commit. So I lived for ten years. I began to write from vanity. To get fame and money it was necessary to hide the good and to display the evil.

At twenty-six years of age I returned to Petersburg after the war, and met the writers. Our vocation was to teach mankind. And lest the simple question should suggest itself: What do I know, and what can I teach? it was explained on this theory that this need not be known. In the third year of this life I began to doubt the infallibility of this (orthodox) religion and to examine it. Almost all the writers were immoral, but they were self-confident and self-satisfied. I became revolting to myself, and I realized that that faith was a fraud. This was just as in a lunatic asylum. I simply called all men lunatics except myself. I should perhaps then have come to the state of despair I reached fifteen years later had there not been one side of life still unexplored; that was marriage. Family life completely diverted me from all search for the general meaning of life. But five years ago something very strange began to happen to me. Moments of perplexity began to recur oftener and oftener, expressed by the questions: What is it for? What does it lead to? My life came to a standstill; it was meaningless. I was not yet fifty; my name was famous; yet I could not live and feared death.

There is an Eastern fable of a traveller overtaken by an enraged beast. Escaping from the beast he gets into a dry well, but sees at the bottom of the well a dragon that has opened its jaws to swallow him. He seizes a twig and clings to it. Then he sees that two mice, a black and a white one gnaw at it. So I too clung to the twig of life, knowing that the dragon of death was inevitably awaiting me, and the white and black mice of day and night gnawed at the branch by which I hung. This is not a fable but the real unanswerable truth intelligible to all. I sought in all the sciences, but found nothing. I sought everywhere in philosophy. Why do I exist, and why does the universe exist? Philosophy not merely does not reply, but is itself only asking that question. There is no answer. In that which Schopenhauer calls "professorial philosophy" the reply is always one and the same—the reply given by Socrates, Schopenhauer, Solomon, and Buddha. What remains after the complete annihilation of the will is, of course, nothing. All is vanity. So said Solomon and this is what the Indian wisdom tells through Sakya Muni; life is the greatest of evils.

Not finding an explanation in science I began to seek for it in life, hoping to find it among the people around me. For people of my circle there were four ways out of the terrible position: ignorance, epicureanism, strength and energy in destroying life when one has understood that it is an evil; and the way of weakness, seeing the truth yet clinging to life, knowing that nothing can come of it. If I did not kill myself it was due to some dim consciousness of the invalidity of my thoughts. I long lived in this state of lunacy characteristic of us very liberal and learned people. I understood that it was not possible to seek in rational knowledge for a reply to my question.

What meaning has life that death does not destroy?—Union with the eternal God. Faith makes it possible to live. It alone gives mankind a reply. Faith is knowledge of the meaning of human life. Faith is the strength of life. I studied Buddhism and Mohammedanism from books, and most of all I studied Christianity both from books and from the people around me. But I could not accept the faith of these people. Their lives were like my own, they did not correspond to the principles they expounded.

Then I began to draw near to the believers among the poor, simple, unlettered folk: pilgrims, monks, sectarians, and peasants. The whole life of the working-folk believers was a confirmation of the meaning of life which their faith gave them. And I learnt to love these people. Though I was quite convinced of the impossibility of proving the existence of a Deity as Kant had shown, I yet sought for God and hoped that I should find Him. "He exists," said I, and at once life rose within me, and I felt the possibility and joy of being. I returned to the belief in that Will which produced me and desires something of me. I returned to the belief that the chief and only aim of my life is to be better, i.e., to live in accord with that Will.

. . . Yesterday I hardly slept all night. Having posted up my diary, I prayed to God. It is impossible to convey the sweetness of the feeling I experienced during my prayer. . . . I wished to merge into the Universal Being. I asked him to pardon my crimes; yet, no, I did not ask for that, for I felt that if he had given me this blissful moment, he had pardoned me. I asked, and at the same time felt that I had nothing to ask; and that I cannot and do not know how to ask: I thanked him, but not with words or thought. I combined in one feeling both petition and gratitude. Fear quite vanished. I could not have separated any one emotion—faith, hope, or love—from the general feeling. No, this was what I experienced yesterday; it was love of God, lofty love, uniting in itself all that is good, excluding all that is bad.[1]

In *What I Believe* Tolstoy says:

I was for thirty-five years a nihilist in the sense of an absence of any belief. Five years ago I came to believe in Christ's teaching, and my life suddenly changed. I, like that thief on the cross, have believed Christ's teaching and have been saved. I was nailed by some force to that life of suffering like the thief to the cross. Suddenly I heard the words of Christ and understood them and instead of despair I experienced happiness and the joy of life undisturbed by death. Surely it can harm no one if I tell how this befell me? Christ's teaching of love, meekness, humility, self-sacrifice, and repayment of good for evil was for me the essence of Christianity. Christ's words *"Resist not him that is evil"* were for me truly a key opening everything else. Christ repeatedly says that only he can be his disciple who is ready to endure all consequences that

[1] Aylmer Maude, *Life of Tolstoy*, Vol. I, pp. 63-64.

result from the fulfilment of the law of non-resistance to evil. He himself dies forbidding resistance to evil. It is impossible at one and the same time to confess Christ as God, the basis of whose teaching is non-resistance to him that is evil, and consciously and calmly to work for the establishment of property, law-courts, government, and military forces, to establish a life contrary to the teaching of Christ. The command of non-resistance to him that is evil is one that makes a complete whole of all the teaching, an obligatory rule—a law to be fulfilled, a key which opens everything. It is clearly said: "Do not go to law; Do not condemn to punishment in the courts." Temptation consists in the delusion that my life can be secured by defending myself and my property from other people. I cannot take part in any Governmental activity that has for its aim the defence of people and their property by violence; I cannot be a judge or take part in trials, or be an official, or serve in any Government office.[2]

During the last ten years of his life Tolstoy's position as the greatest living writer in the world was unchallenged. His works were eventually translated into some fifty languages. In his *Memoirs* he divides his life into four periods: The innocent, joyous, poetic time of childhood, up to the age of fourteen; his "terrible twenties" obsessed by his besetting sins of ambition, vanity, gambling and licentiousness, lasting till his marriage at the age of thirty-four; the third period of eighteen years when he was honest, pure and tolerably happy in his family life, but always a thorough egoist; the fourth period which he hoped would be the last, dating from his Christian conversion, during which in cold rationalism he tried to shape his life in literal accordance with the Sermon on the Mount. At the surprisingly early age of twenty-seven he had recorded his ambition in his diary: "My conversations on divinity and faith have led me to a great idea, for the realization of which I am ready to devote my whole life. The idea is the founding of a new religion (Tolstoyanism), corresponding to the level of human development, the religion of Christ, but purified of all dogmas and mysteries, a practical religion not promising a blessed future life, but bestowing happiness here on earth."

Characteristically Russian, he carried his ideas to the last extreme. If they conflicted with the whole experience of humanity, then humanity must be wrong. The three greatest novelists of

[2] Abbreviated from Tolstoy's *What I Believe.*

the day—Turgenev, Dostoevski and Tolstoy—all were geniuses. Turgenev excelled as an artist, Tolstoy as a moralist and the greatest literary genius of them all, while Dostoevski was by far the most spiritual, the most lovable, the most Christian, "one of the most profound thinkers of modern times, who found in the Christian religion the only solution of the riddle of existence." Professor Phelps is regretfully compelled to add regarding Tolstoy: "His satanic pride made frank friendship with him almost an impossibility. Despite our immense respect for his literary power, despite the enormous influence for good that his later books have effected, it must be said that of all the great Russian writers, Tolstoy was the most unlovely."

In *My Religion* Tolstoy frankly states his creed:

I believe in God, who is for me spirit, love, the principle of all things. I believe that God is in me, as I am in Him. I believe that the true welfare of man consists in fulfilling the will of God. I believe that from the fulfillment of the will of God there can follow nothing but that which is good for me and for all men. I believe that the will of God is that every man should love his fellow-men, and should act toward others as he desires that they should act toward him. I believe that the reason of life is for each of us simply to grow in love. I believe that this growth in love will contribute more than any other force to establish the Kingdom of God on earth. To replace a social life in which division, falsehood and violence are all-powerful, with a new order in which humanity, truth and brotherhood will reign. I believe that the will of God has never been more clearly, more freely, expressed than in the teaching of the man Jesus. I believe that this teaching will give welfare to all humanity, save men from destruction, and give this world the greatest happiness.

. . . Jesus showed me that resort to violence for the resistance of evil is destructive of my welfare. I know now that a great portion of the evils that afflict mankind is due to the erroneous belief that life can be made secure by violence. I am obliged to renounce violence, and abstain from it altogether. I know that all men everywhere are brothers and equals, and that my true welfare is found in my unity with the whole world. I believe that the fulfillment of the teaching of Jesus is possible. I believe that even if I should be the only one, there is nothing else for me to do but to fulfill it.

In the case of Tolstoy, as with Plato, we are equally amazed at what he found in his discovery of God and what he failed to find; and surprised at how high he reached, yet also at how far he fell short. Like Plato he groped, he wavered, he rose to great moral heights, and then fell to discouraging depths, but never reached an adequate faith in God nor in personal immortality. His pale subjective definition of God in *The Christian Teaching* is: "The desire for universal welfare is that which gives life to all that does exist; it is that which we call God." Elsewhere he says: "A God-Creator there is not." "With certainty He is not a person." He thinks of man pantheistically as a particle of the impersonal divine. But God is *"not* Creator, Trinity, Redeemer, or Ruler."

We may learn in our study not only positively from what men found of God but negatively from their mistakes in what they failed to find. We must observe where they took what seems to us the wrong path, and where they suffered as a result of it. Tolstoy as a Christian anarchist was typically Russian in many ways. He was a rationalist, an absolutist, and a humanist who plunged to extremes. He was a scathing critic but not a reformer. Unconsciously he came to destroy but not to fulfill. He would destroy the church by his rationalism, the state by philosophical anarchy, the race by the ideal of absolute celibacy. Dr. E. J. Dillon in his long conversations with him, recorded in his *Count Leo Tolstoy*, found that he had for the most part an austere, ascetic, antisocial rule of life. He had little respect for science or history. Though a great moralist and psychologist, as a critic he had but a smattering of Greek, of Hebrew, of theology, or philosophy.

He confessed: "I am a finger post which points the way but does not follow it." He was rigid in theory but elastic in practice; and his life was a bundle of painful contradictions. A titan physically, mentally and morally, he never mastered himself nor achieved integration of character, nor peace in his heart, in his home or in society. Unlike St. Francis he preached poverty, chastity and obedience but realized none of them in experience. He says frankly: "Yes, I am a sinful man. I came into the world with an ardent temperament which I cannot master." His diary reveals his agonizing struggles and moral lapses even in old age. Tolstoy compared himself to Buddha, Solomon and Schopenhauer. Like Nietzsche he was ever the self-conscious center of his own system. He never sought anonymity like St. Francis. He called his new religion Tolstoyanism and he wanted the whole world to watch him. He could not be a joyous pagan like Thoreau at Walden. He fled from the world but never found solitude or rest.

The unresolved conflicts of his life were traceable in part to the contradictions in his philosophy. There can be but one sun in a solar system. The central sun in the ethics of Christianity is love. Christians are to love God, their neighbor and their enemy. But this constraining and consuming love Tolstoy never found. Instead he introduces a second absolute into his system in what he conceives to be the new and absolute *"law"* of nonresistance. He believed that no one must be coerced to do anything against his will and the evil man must not be restrained. For Tolstoy almost everything except nonresistance became sin. The state itself, organized society, all property, police, prisons, military service, law courts, taxes and government service were evil. There is no center but the rational ego for his philosophical anarchy. As an ascetic he condemned all wine, tobacco and coffee. Yet he himself often lacked mental discipline, perseverance, balance and sane common sense. After he had excommunicated the Russian Church—because there was "no truth in this religion but only hypocrisy"—naturally the church excommunicated him. Even sex and all physical love were sinful. For him love and sex "never attain any worthy end but always impede" the soul.

Marriage, he held, is "a fall, a sin." The contradictions of his system are revealed in his character, his home and in the sect of Tolstoyans who became his followers. His own moral struggle increased to the very end. Almost the last act of his life was to flee from his unhappy home. But for him there was now no refuge, no monk's cell, no solitude, no peace; for there was no union, communion or fellowship with God as Father.

WILLIAM RAINEY HARPER, 1856-1906

Out of the depths of scientific agnosticism, this great modernist discovered God. What was more important, in a scientific and materialistic age of skepticism, he enabled thousands of modern students, including the writer, to find a rational, empirical faith and a spiritually satisfying yet intellectually stimulating experience of God. It is for this reason that we include Dr. Harper here with the prophets, saints and sages in this volume when some might be tempted to ask, "Is Saul also among the prophets?"

Primitive religion always springs up spontaneously as one of man's first responses to his environment, his first groping quest for reality. Later, religion develops into theology, under the reflective form of religious consciousness. Then there arises the inevitable conflict between theology and religion, reason and faith, science and tradition; for there must ever be strife between an unscientific belief and an unbelieving science. As between the two contending parties of realists and idealists, of radicals and reactionaries, of modernists and traditionalists, perhaps each possesses a priceless half-truth and is viewing one side of the shield of reality. It is then that the prophetic mediator, who has experimentally known the reality of both religion and science, must lead both parties as far as possible to realize the all-embracing truths of life as a whole. The man who has gone from simple faith to reason, who has mastered both the thesis of religion and the antithesis of science can lead others to the dialectic synthesis of the more abundant and all-embracing life.

With Professor Briggs Dr. Harper helped to introduce in America the application of science to religion and of historical criticism to the Bible, in what was then counted the heresy of higher criticism. Uneducated fundamentalists believe unquestioningly in an inerrant, verbally inspired Bible, in a world created in six days and that the theory of evolution was an atheistic invention of the devil. On the other hand, thousands of men educated in a naturalistic period of modern science, and multitudes among the masses in a materialistic industrial age had lost their religious heritage and experience. It was now that the prophet was needed to apply reason to faith, modern thought to agelong experience, the scientific method to the eternal truth of religion. William Rainey Harper was such a prophet.

The story of Dr. Harper's life is soon told. He was born in a log cabin which is still standing in New Concord, Ohio. This precocious genius could read at three. He entered Muskingum College at ten and graduated at fourteen, delivering the salutatory commencement address in Hebrew. He taught Hebrew at sixteen, and took his Ph.D. degree at Yale at eighteen. Then followed three brief decades of titanic activity of this human dynamo. After teaching in Tennessee and at Dennison University in Ohio he taught in the Baptist Union Theological Seminary in Chicago, and was called to Yale in 1886. Here he taught Hebrew, Old Testament exegesis, Chaldean and Sanskrit. He offered weekly eight-hour courses in Hebrew, four hours in Assyrian, four in Arabic, and one each in Aramaic and Syriac. This would be work enough for several ordinary men, but not for Dr. Harper. He began issuing a stream of more than thirty textbooks—*A Hebrew Manual, An Inductive Latin Method, An Inductive Greek Method, Inductive Studies in English,* etc., etc. —as well as writing scores of articles in various magazines. For rest, "during the Christmas vacation one of his classes read the Hebrew Bible at sight eight hours per day for ten days." He was the only living human who could enthuse and excite throngs of eager students over Hebrew and Sanskrit! "It was a vision that would have filled with satisfaction the heart of Plato or Socrates or Arnold of Rugby to see the young professor with his audience of eager students held spellbound by his enthusiasm." Possibly his fellow student President Thompson exaggerates when he says "he could read a German grammar about twice, and take the whole thing in just like a sponge."

He created nationwide correspondence schools in Hebrew and other languages and in the English Bible; he was the principal of the Chautauqua College of Liberal Arts and played in the band there for relaxation; he launched and personally attended six simultaneous summer schools; he inaugurated and edited two journals and lectured all over the Continent. The writer watched him working a basic sixteen-hour day at Yale and often much longer. At the sound of the first bell for a class, he would throw himself upon a couch, sleep soundly for eight minutes, wake himself by his automatic brain alarm clock, and enter the class with youthful exuberance.

When Mr. Rockefeller suggested a million dollar college, Dr. Harper was not interested, but there was born in his mind the creative idea of "the great university"—great "to begin with," as he wrote: "I have a plan which I am persuaded will revolutionize University study in this country." When asked how much it would cost to establish it, Dr. Harper replied: "When the University has fifty million dollars, the first step will have been taken." When his annual deficits mounted to over two hundred thousand dollars a year, Dr. Harper was joyfully undismayed—whatever were the misgivings of Mr. Rockefeller and his board

Dr. Harper began work in the University of Chicago in 1891, giving fifteen years of his life to this project. For his faculty, he called about him leading professors from two continents, including eight former college presidents. He believed that the university, which had its birth in the democracy of a group of medieval scholars, must become the leader of modern democracy. Each teacher should be an investigator and all the faculty should have the right of self-government, freedom from church, or financial, or political control, and the right of free utterance. The university should be in continuous operation, it should control all games, eliminating the professionalism that was rife in other universities, and its professional schools in divinity, law, medicine, and education should not be mere trade schools to find employment for materialistic students, but should produce leaders in thought and national life. Harper taught his students and faculty not what to think but how to think. To create, finance and father a university which within five years should rival Yale or Harvard, Oxford or Cambridge, would have been a colossal work for a score of men—but not for Dr. Harper. As chairman of the Educational Commission and member of the Board of Education of Chicago, he felt he must completely reorganize the corrupt politician-controlled school system of the great gangster metropolis, as well as take a leading part in a score of different national and international organizations and movements.

Undoubtedly, he undertook to do too much; he had too many irons in the fire. He could not build a thousand-year-old university, like those of Europe, in a few years. Neither he nor the university had the ripe culture of Oxford or Cambridge. There was an almost boyish and immature vein in him up to the last. But in his wide and varied interests and relationships, in the titanic energy of his life as scholar, teacher, writer, organizer, and even prophet, in his very attempting of the impossible, there was in him an element of the divine. He was, with all his human frailties and shortcomings, a man made in the image of God. He was always reaching out into the infinite.

As to his religious life, there was a time when young Harper not only passed through a devastating period of doubt and unbelief in his own experience, but when, as he confessed to us students at Yale, he led others astray from the faith. Of this period he writes:

Let me tell you, out of my own experience, that during several years before personally accepting the Christian faith I studied the Bible earnestly and carefully for the purpose of discovering that which would enable me to convince others that it was only an ordinary book, and very ordinary at that. I could not, if I would, here tell you of the work of those years—years spent in finding, not in settling difficulties. After a while, I began to see some faint rays of coming light. And as the light grew brighter the difficulties did not diminish in number or in character. I desired to be a Christian, but no man told me what I now know, and what I beg you to hear from me, that I could first become a Christian and settle the difficulties later. I went forward; yet the difficulties remained. What could I do with them? Only one thing: take up again the study of the Bible, this time going deep, and working from a different point of view; and it was not long until I discovered that the difficulties were in some cases altogether imaginary; and that from the new point of view, and with the more scientific study, principles could be found which, if followed out, gave to the whole case a different aspect.[3]

To retrace his religious life, we note that at the age of twenty in Dennison, Ohio, to the surprise of all his friends, young Harper rose in the Baptist prayer meeting and said: "I want to be a Christian. I don't know what it is to be a Christian, but I know I am not a Christian and I want to be one." President Andrews says, "He accepted joyfully the law of service to God and man, with the creed naturally accompanying—Christ, the church, the primacy of the spiritual and the endurance of our immaterial part after bodily death. From that creed he never swerved in any iota." For fifteen years he was a member of the Hyde Park Baptist Church near the university in Chicago; in

[3] W. R. Harper, *Religion and the Higher Life,* p. 107. University of Chicago Press.

1897 he became superintendent of the Sunday school, and conducted a university Bible class at 8:30 Sunday mornings, as Dr. Arthur Compton does today.

When about to undergo a sudden operation for appendicitis, he wrote to a friend, "I shall 'step into the dark' tomorrow with the strong conviction that somehow I shall come out again. If not, you and I know that there is a Divine plan which works for the good of the universe whatever it may have for each of us." Shortly after, in 1905, Dr. Harper called Dr. Goodspeed and another friend to say that he had just received his "death sentence" in the discovery that he was suffering from an incurable malignant cancer. He never wavered in his faith and continued not only the direction of the university but to teach his classes of freshmen and upper classmen in bed up to the last. Just at the end he said to Dr. Goodspeed that his faith was *infinitely* stronger and sweeter than ever before." Still a comparatively young man, at the age of fifty he passed over and, as for Valiant-for-truth, "All the trumpets sounded for him on the other side."

In the much-abbreviated statement which follows, this great scientist, modernist and rationalist tells us of his simple faith in his *Religion and the Higher Life*. In speaking of "America as a Missionary Field," Dr. Harper says:

The world has had sixty centuries of history. These fall quite naturally into three divisions of about twenty centuries each. During the first twenty the great civilizing forces came from Babylonia and Egypt. Babylonia was the great power in the first twenty centuries, Syria in the second. The close of the first saw the coming of the Hebrew tribe under Abraham's leadership; the close of the second was marked by the coming of the Son of man, the ideal Hebrew, to whom Syria, with sore travail, at last gave birth. The work of centuries of Greek and Roman history was but a contribution to this, the crowning event of forty centuries. The third period of twenty centuries is but now drawing to its close. In this third period the central figure has been England.

. . . The Babylonian, Syrian, and English periods are passed. The American is coming. Will there be new revelations of God in this period? . . . Does not the world know God in a new way because of the discoveries made by science in these latest years—discoveries which teach us nothing, if they do not teach of God and of his laws? . . . It has taken centuries for most of these revelations to gain recognition as divine. In Christ the Son we are accustomed to say, and we believe, that

God the Father revealed himself. . . . Christianity cannot be said to have achieved final success until her founder Jesus Christ has been everywhere recognized. The arena in which the great trial shall be conducted is America. If America is to do the work of evangelizing the world, she must first Christianize herself. She is to be the leader of the world's influence and thought during the next twenty centuries, just as Babylonia, Syria, and England, each in turn, has been leader during the past centuries. But, more than this, she is to be the arena of an intellectual, social, and spiritual conflict, in which Christianity must vindicate itself against all opposing forces. Centuries will pass; and gradually humanity will come to recognize the significance of love; gradually Jesus the Christ will come to reign in the hearts of men.[4]

In urging upon the students of the University of Chicago to study the original Scriptures, each man for himself, Dr. Harper said:[5]

I have come with the sincere feeling that I have for you a message. The positions suggested are those which I have tested by my own personal experience of more than twenty-five years in Bible study and Bible teaching.

He said to the students in Chicago just what he said to us at Yale more than fifty years ago:

The religious experience must invariably include a consciousness of sin. In every true experience there must likewise be found a sense of fellowship with God. There has come to some the experience of love for God—not fear, nor merely reverence, but a love represented to be like that of son for father. Was not God a Father, and his true followers sons? One's conception of God, one's attitude toward him, is the fundamental thing in life.

The writer must ask leave to speak in the first person regarding his debt to Dr. Harper. It is now more than fifty years since I sat at the feet of this man at Yale, who was the most inspiring teacher I had ever known, and was led to form the most important habit of my life—the daily study of this great religious library called the Bible. I might have formed the habit of devotional study through Moody at Northfield, but after hearing Harper the study had to be both critical and devotional, in the

---

[4] *Religion and the Higher Life,* pp. 173-184.
[5] *Ibid.,* pp. 146-172.

application of reason to faith and the scientific method to religion. Dr. Harper furnished us with "the acids of modernity" as a solvent which could in time cut away the last vestiges of superstition from our lives.

Like Jeremiah, his work was both negative and positive, "to root up and pull down, to build and to plant." Under him, we found both a divine and a human element running parallel throughout the Scriptures. There was evidence of divine inspiration from the first verse of Genesis "In the beginning God . . ." to the close of Revelation. But there was also from first to last a human element, for the Bible was the most gloriously human book in the world. Dr. Harper's pupils saw in the stories in the early chapters of Genesis, which were similar to and sometimes borrowed from those of the surrounding nations, that they must be studied in the light of historical criticism.

For illustration, if in any other ancient book like *Aesop's Fables* we read of a serpent holding a conversation with a woman, we would take it not as serious history but as beautiful folklore from the period of the childhood of the race. It sounded like Homer to read of angels or the sons of God having intercourse with the daughters of men and giving birth to giants and heroes (Gen. 6:1-4). If we read the imprecatory Psalms, historically interpreted, with their moral evil corrected by the later love of Christ, they did not disturb us. A simple mistake, which was noticed even by John Wesley, where the writer of the First Gospel ascribes a quotation to Jeremiah which is actually found in Zechariah, was only one of hundreds of such insignificant details in a glorious human document.[6] Much more serious was the portrayal of a Moloch-like God who would endlessly torture his helpless victims when there was no hope of reformation or redemption. As we have said this would of course be infinitely worse than the *Gestapo* of Hitler and Himmler when for a few days or weeks they torture their prisoners for the purpose of the forced confession of truth or falsehood.

Much more important than Dr. Harper's critical scholarship in delivering his students from being victims of error and superstition was his creative and constructive faith and inspiration which led us each to make his own discovery of God. Espe-

[6] Matt. 27:7-10 and Zech. 11:13.

cially noteworthy in the light of his own affliction are his remarks about suffering:

The religion of Jesus Christ is a religion capable of adjustment to any and every individual. Its simplicity, as the Master himself presented it, is marvelous; and it appeals as strongly to the reason as to the heart. It is a religion that says: "Come unto me all ye that labor and are heavy laden, and I will give you rest." The greatest minds of nineteen centuries have found this religion helpful. Accept this unique, wonderful character, Jesus Christ, as your leader and guide. He is within your reach, within the reach of everyone who will stretch his hands out after him. Accept him, if you have not already done so, and try him. To whom else will you go?

Some of us are wondering what is ahead. There are times in every man's life when, as he regards the world, it seems to be as a "great battlefield heaped with the slain, an inferno of infinite suffering, a slaughterhouse resounding with the cries of a ceaseles agony." Suffering is everywhere, and will come sooner or later in every experience. At times it will be something which one must carry quite alone. What preparation shall we make for the sorrows and agonies of life which, soon or late, we must suffer? My answer to the first is: Face to face, just as you would meet an enemy, face to face, as you would meet a friend, face to face as you would meet God himself. If God has to do with mortal man, his messages are delivered in the events which make up life's experience. That man has not learned to live who does not recognize in every event of life the hand of God stretched forth to guide and lift him up. Begin at once to suffer. Make earnest and continuous effort to obtain a vision of God. The heart must see God, if the intellect would understand him. And, finally, hold relationship with that unique character in the world's history who suffered as no man ever suffered before or since—alone in the agony of Gethsemane, upon the cross, in the face of all the world. Hold relationship with this man, Jesus, for in so doing you at once begin to suffer with him and with the world for which he suffered. This, above all things else, was his mission, to make God known to man; Jesus, the brother, through whom the Father might be revealed. To see Jesus is to have the sight of God. In fellowship, then, with Jesus the sufferer; in companionship with Jesus the friend and brother; and in obedience to Jesus the Lord, one is best prepared for the battle of life.

BOOKER T. WASHINGTON, 1858-1915

We include Booker Washington among our pathfinders not

only because of the discovery of God which he made for himself and his race, but because we believe that we in America need to discover the Negro as man—brother man—lest the judgment of God fall upon us. In an hour when demonic falsehood and hate is murdering and robbing the Jew and hounding him across Europe, we cannot afford, if we would win both the war and the peace, to be guilty of a like sin in our denial of human justice to the Negro. As the acid test of Britain's demand for free democracy for herself is her treatment of India, so the acid test of American democracy is our treatment of the Negro.

We take Booker Washington as a type of his race. Though not a genius like Tolstoy, he was a greater spirit than he, and is worthy to stand beside the adventurers in this volume. Booker Washington was born as a slave, and was about seven years old when the Civil War ended. The formative years of his life were, therefore, spent in the atmosphere of war and terrible days of reconstruction which followed. The Thirteenth Amendment had completed the abolition of slavery and promised personal freedom to the Negroes. The Fourteenth Amendment guaranteed their rights of citizenship, while the Fifteenth Amendment was intended to safeguard their right of suffrage. These rights were guaranteed *on paper* but the Negro was soon cheated out of many of them. By poll tax, educational and electoral restrictions, the bulk of the Negroes and even poor whites in many states were and still are barred from the polls. The Fourteenth Amendment, which had been violently forced into the Constitution by the armed North, and which provided that *persons* should not be deprived of life, liberty or property *"without due process of law,"* was so twisted by the Supreme Court that rich *corporations* were removed from control by state law. Under this amendment which was intended to protect the Negro, nearly a thousand cases were so decided that, in the words of Senator Borah, the court became the "economic dictator of the United States," corporations were given free license, and the Negro was kept in economic slavery.

The life of Booker Washington marks the heroic struggle of the Negro for economic freedom and racial uplift. As we are fortunate in possessing his autobiography, we shall as far as possible let him tell his own story.[7]

I was born a slave on a plantation in Franklin County, Virginia, in 1858 or 1859. My life had its beginning in the midst of the most miserable, desolate, and discouraging surroundings. I was born in a typical log cabin where I lived with my mother and a brother and sister. In the slave quarters, and even later, I heard whispered conversations of the tortures which the slaves suffered in the slave ship while being conveyed from Africa to America. Of my father I know even less than of my mother. I do not even know his name. Whoever he was, I never heard of his taking the least interest in me or providing in any way for my rearing. There was no wooden floor in our cabin, the naked earth being used as a floor. I cannot remember having slept in a bed until after our family was declared free by the Emancipation Proclamation. Three children slept in a bundle of filthy rags laid upon the dirt floor. There was no period of my life that was devoted to play. From the time that I can remember anything, almost every day of my life has been occupied in some kind of labor. I had no schooling whatever while I was a slave. One day, while at work in a coal mine, I happened to overhear two miners talking about a great school for colored people. I noiselessly crept as close as I could. It seemed to me that it must be the greatest place on earth, and not even Heaven presented more attractions for me at that time than did the Hampton Normal and Agricultural Institute.

In order to save money to attend this school he began to work for a spartan New England woman at five dollars a month. Here for a year and a half he learned the lessons of industry, cleanliness, punctuality, orderliness and honesty, upon which his character and work were afterward founded. Finally the great day came, and he tells us how he started for Hampton on foot, on this long journey of five hundred miles:

As soon as possible after reaching the grounds of the Hampton Institute, I presented myself before the head teacher. After some hours, the teacher said to me, "The adjoining recitation-room needs sweeping. Take the broom and sweep it." It occurred to me at once that here was my chance. I swept the recitation-room three times. Then I got a dust-

[7] We are chiefly indebted for the account of Mr. Washington's early life to his *Up From Slavery*, and for his later life to *Booker T. Washington, Builder of a Civilization*, by Emmett J. Scott and Lyman Beecher Stowe, as well as to *Makers of Freedom*.

ing cloth and I dusted it four times. All the woodwork around the walls, every bench, table and desk, I went over four times with my dusting-cloth. When I was through, I reported to the head teacher. She went into the room and inspected the floor and closets; then she took her handkerchief and rubbed it on the woodwork about the walls and quietly remarked, "I guess you will do to enter this institution." I was one of the happiest souls on earth. The sweeping of that room was my college examination.

Life at Hampton was a revelation to me, and was constantly taking me into a new world. The matter of having meals at regular hours, of eating on a tablecloth, using a napkin, the use of the bathtub and of the toothbrush, as well as the use of sheets on the bed, were all new to me. The greatest benefits that I got out of my life at the Hampton Institute were contact with a great man, General S. C. Armstrong, who was, in my opinion, the rarest, strongest, and most beautiful character that it has ever been my privilege to meet, and learning what education was expected to do for an individual. I learned to love labor and I got my first taste of what it means to live a life of unselfishness. The great and prevailing idea that seemed to take possession of every one was to prepare himself to lift up his people at home. No one seemed to think of himself. Perhaps the most valuable thing that I got out of my second year was an understanding of the use and value of the Bible. At the present time, when I am at home, no matter how busy I am, I always make it a rule to read a chapter or a portion of a chapter in the morning, before beginning the work of the day.

After graduation and serving as a teacher, there soon came the great opportunity of his life, to open a new institution at Tuskegee. It did not seem very promising to begin a school with thirty poor colored students, without land, buildings, or teachers, on a deserted plantation, equipped with a kitchen, a stable and a henhouse which had to serve as classrooms. Later they found an old abandoned plantation of a thousand acres for sale at five hundred dollars, or about fifty cents an acre on an old barren hill of sand and clay. Booker borrowed $250 and took possession.

The old stable and henhouse were used as recitation rooms. The president shouldered his own ax, and by working every afternoon with the entire school, finally cleared some twenty acres and planted a crop. He was at first met with suspicion and almost universal opposition from both races. Many of the white men believed he was "spoiling the niggers by education." The

Negroes, however, began "to learn by doing." The industrial work finally became as popular as the academic branches. In order to raise funds, Booker Washington made a tour of the North. He walked two miles in a storm to spend three hours with a gentleman in New England who gave him nothing, but later, unasked, sent him $10,000. Collis P. Huntington first gave him two dollars, but on his last visit he gave $50,000. Andrew Carnegie seemed to take little interest in the school at first, but afterwards he gave the money for a library building and $600,000 for the endowment fund. These men were human and rose above race prejudice, as did John D. Rockefeller and Julius Rosenwald. The latter alone gave directly, or through the Julius Rosenwald Fund, $4,366,519 toward the construction of 4,977 Negro schools, 217 teachers' homes, and 163 shops. The total cost of these buildings exceeded $28,000,000. This was but a small fraction of what Rosenwald and Rockefeller did for the two persecuted races of the earth, the Jew and the Negro. These two races in turn have had to be the Suffering Servant for all humanity.

Booker Washington finally developed not only as a financier and executive, but as a really great American orator. At the Atlanta Exposition in 1895 for the first time in history a Negro had been asked to speak on the same platform with a southern white man. Mr. Washington thus tells the story:

Almost the first thing that I heard from an old colored man was: "Dat's de man of my race what's gwine to make a speech at de Exposition tomorrow. I'se sho' gwine to hear him." I did not sleep much that night. The next morning, before day, I kneeled down and asked God's blessing upon my effort. I make it a rule never to go before an audience, on any occasion, without asking the blessing of God upon what I want to say. The first thing that I remember, after I had finished speaking, was that Governor Bullock rushed across the platform and took me by the hand, and that others did the same. The editor of the *Atlanta Constitution* telegraphed to a New York paper: "Professor Booker T. Washington's address yesterday was one of the most notable ever delivered to a southern audience. The address was a revelation. The whole speech is a platform upon which blacks and whites can stand with full justice to each other."

A Negro Moses, as the South itself now called him, delivered an oration that marked a new epoch in racial history. Clark Howell said, "That man's speech was the beginning of a moral revolution in America. The whole audience was on its feet in a delirium of applause. I have heard the great orators of many countries, but not even Gladstone himself could have pleaded a cause with more consummate power than did this angular Negro. Most of the Negroes in the audience were crying." Upon the publication of his book *Up From Slavery* in 1900, 10,000 copies were soon sold. One anonymous donor upon reading the book contributed $250,000 toward the building fund. Twenty years after beginning in a broken-down shanty, Booker Washington had built up at Tuskegee a great institution of 66 buildings and 2,300 acres of land. The property and endowment were valued at $1,700,000. The number of students had grown from 30 to 1,400, drawn from 27 states. Tuskegee was a masterpiece of administration, and has furnished a model for hundreds of institutions among white people and in other lands. Visitors from Oxford and Cambridge, educators from Europe and Asia, often visit the school. President Eliot stated that under Booker Washington the institution had achieved in two decades what it had taken Harvard two centuries to accomplish.

Mr. Washington and his teachers went weekly to the churches, schools, farms and homes of the people to show them "how they could make their farms more productive, their homes more comfortable, their schools more useful and their church services more inspiring." The extension work of Tuskegee began even before that of the demonstration agents of the United States Department of Agriculture. The agents of Tuskegee from their model farm were soon introducing better breeds of cattle, hogs and chickens and a higher standard of living for their race. Next came the summer school for teachers, attended by some five hundred Negro educators gathered from over fifteen states. Mr. Washington made long tours through nine of the southern states to widen his work for the race. He founded the Teachers' Institute, the Ministers' Night School, the Building and Loan Association, the town library and reading rooms, and the National Negro Business League. Booker Washington concluded the last volume of his *Story of the Negro* as follows:

In slavery the progress of the Negro was a menace to the white man. In freedom the security and happiness of each race depends, to a very large extent, on the education and the progress of the other. The problem of slavery was to keep the Negro down; the problem of freedom is to raise him up. One cannot hold another in a ditch without himself staying in a ditch. The time will come when the Negro in the South will be accorded all the political rights which his ability, character, and material possessions entitle him to.

For nothing was Mr. Washington so bitterly attacked as when he was invited to dinner with President Theodore Roosevelt at the White House. Feeling was so deeply stirred over this incident that both the President and Mr. Washington received many threats against their lives. Mr. Washington said:

The public interest aroused by this dinner seemed all the more extraordinary because I had taken tea with Queen Victoria at Windsor Castle; I had dined with the governors of nearly every state in the North; I had taken dinner in the same room with President McKinley at Chicago and I had dined with ex-President Harrison in Paris.

On one occasion he wrote:

It is now long ago that I resolved that I would permit no man to narrow and degrade my soul by making me hate him. With God's help, I believe that I have completely rid myself of any ill feeling. It is a pleasure to add that in all my contact with the white people of the South I have never received a single personal insult.

His was a great soul in which no bitterness or littleness could even find a lurking place. His was the great heart of Lincoln, with malice toward none and charity for all. He loved all men and all men loved him. His jaded body finally collapsed under the domination of his great will and indomitable spirit. When he was seriously ill at St. Luke's Hospital, New York, and told that he had but a few hours to live, he insisted on leaving at once for home, saying: "I was born in the South, I have lived and labored in the South, and I expect to die and be buried in the South."

Booker Washington's projected influence was revealed in many of his students like Professor George W. Carver, the eminent agricultural chemist, a full-blooded African who also was born as a slave. Mr. Washington found him as a promising boy in the Agricultural Department of the Iowa State College. He asked him to tackle with his laboratory the barren old hill of sand and clay on which Tuskegee stands. Out of that sand, Professor Carver developed some eighty-five chemical and commercial products. From the common clay he has discovered more than two hundred. That thin sandy soil, purchased at fifty cents an acre, would yield at first only peanuts and sweet potatoes. Out of the peanuts Professor Carver has made over three hundred products, and from the sweet potato a hundred and twelve. Several of these have commercial and financial possibilities. The parable is plain. Booker Washington saw more in that barren hill, more in the boy Carver, more in every boy of his race, and more in the Negro as man than did `multitudes about him, blinded by race prejudice.

We chose Booker Washington as one of our witnesses to the discovery of God because the human rights of free democracy, the constitutional guarantees of American citizenship and the basic principles of the Christian religion are being denied today in our present treatment of the Negro in America. In the three and a quarter centuries since the first cargo of Negroes was captured, dragged here from Africa and sold into slavery, there has never been such bitterness and such a feeling of hopeless despair among American Negroes as at present. These thirteen million Negroes, constituting a tenth of our population, are not only the largest minority group but are the only group for which a double standard of personal treatment and citizenship is observed. While Chinese and even some Japanese, with Filipinos, Mexicans and Indians are often free to become integrated along with whites into any arm of the fighting services for which they qualify, it is only the Negroes who are absolutely and completely segregated into units of their own on a basis of inferiority.

Most of the peoples of the earth and the majority of our Allies in the war are colored people. Japan is now able to say to these races that they will never be given complete freedom, equality, and justice by Americans who deny to their own colored citizens the things for which they fight themselves. Every American lynching and race riot gives joy in Japan. During his last series of meetings held to proclaim a gospel of love to non-Christian students in Asia, the writer witnessed in Tokyo the gloating publication of the account of our last lynching in the United States. Even the photograph of this Negro being burned at the stake was placarded on the front page of Japan's greatest daily, and America was held up to scorn as the only nation on earth which descended to the barbarity of lynching its own citizens.

If Soviet Russia can rise superior to race prejudice and give equal treatment to all, and if all Mohammedans do likewise, Americans may well ask themselves whether Anglo-Saxon Christians are the only ones who cannot do so. Is there then something defective in our religion or in ourselves that we will not practice racial brotherhood? Up to the date of writing this chapter Negroes have been resolutely segregated in the army. Such prejudice and *discrimination* on the part of most of the armed forces against soldiers and sailors, and all other forms of social *differentiation* give aid and comfort to our enemy Japan and give the lie both to our profession of Christianity and of democracy. In the typical action of refusing the use of Negro blood to save human life in the war, we place ourselves on the same degraded level as the Nazis in their theories of race, blood and soil. Pearl Buck has dared to say that in our racial attitudes to the Negro we belong with Hitler in this war.

Basic to all our discrimination and injustice is our denial of economic opportunity to the Negro to earn a living. Negroes are still frozen on lessening relief rolls while other citizens are rushing into the wide-open doors of industry. This is the lengthening shadow which darkens the path of Negro progress. From most callings and many defense industries, the Negro is still excluded. He is the last to be hired, the first to be fired in industry; we pay him less for doing the same job, and charge him more for renting the same house. We imprison him in American ghettos like Harlem where the Negro is helpless against the high rents and miserable housing in the segregation to which race prejudice dooms him. Caught in a vicious circle as the Negro always is this results in fresh outbreaks of crime. When hope is taken away from any people, moral degeneration swiftly follows. We shut out the Negro from the polls, from the protection of most trade unions, from the opportunities of equal education, and often from equal justice in the courts and outside of them.

After persistent discrimination practiced against Negroes by industries receiving defense contracts, the President issued an executive order announcing that industries discriminating against persons on account of race, creed, color or national origin would be denied government contracts. This was the first executive order affecting the welfare of Negroes on a large scale issued since Lincoln's Emancipation Proclamation of January 1, 1863. There has been, however, widespread and shameless violation of the President's order and of the action of Governor Lehman's committee by employers and labor unions alike. When the ship-owners refused to allow Negroes in their crews, President Roosevelt wired his warning to them, and Joseph Curran, president of the National Maritime Union, stated that the ships should not sail with exclusively white crews. The result was that mixed crews have manned most of our ships since that time and Negroes have been among the rescued crews. This shows that the case is not hopeless if the rest of us who call ourselves Christians or Americans will do likewise.

Hitlerism makes no pretense of loving its fellow men and wanting all people to be free and equal. Ought we not to decide in America whether we are going to stand for the totalitarian principle of a white ruler race and a subject colored race, or be consistent with our own democratic and Christian principles? Let us not be hypocrites or allow the specter of the fear of inter-marriage to poison everything we do. As Pearl Buck says, we should not deny the rights and privileges of American democracy and the principles of Christian brotherhood to some thirteen million Americans, and risk our very democracy itself by main-taining a determined ruler-subject relationship between white and colored, because some day a few white and colored indi-viduals may choose to marry each other. "Is democracy right or is it wrong? If it is right then let us dare to make it true."

The Negro is the symbol of the all too large proportion of our people ill-fed, ill-clad, and ill-housed in inexcusable slums, urban and rural. He is the representative, or the Suffering Servant, who must bear the monstrous injustice resulting from the sickness of our acquisitive society. The judgments of God lie heavily upon us in this world catastrophe. Have not Abraham Lincoln and Booker Washington both a message for America in this hour of judgment? An abbreviation of Lincoln's message to America during the Civil War, may have an application also to the present world crisis:

> Fervently do we pray that this mighty scourge of war may speedily pass away. Yet if God will that it continue until every drop of blood drawn with the lash shall be paid by another drawn with the sword, still it must be said, "The judgments of the Lord are true and righteous altogether." Both (sides) may be, and one must be wrong. I am almost ready to say that God wills that the war shall not end yet. He could either have saved or destroyed the Union without a human contest. He could give the victory to either side any day. Yet the contest continues. The Almighty has his own purposes. If we shall suppose that American slavery is one of those offences which, having continued through his appointed time, he now wills to remove, and that he gives to both this terrible war, shall we discern any departure from those divine attributes which the believers in a loving God always ascribe to him? With malice toward none; with charity for all, let us strive to finish the work we are in, to do all which may achieve *a just and lasting peace* among ourselves, and with all nations.[8]

Finally, Lincoln said, *We* shall nobly save or meanly lose the last best hope of earth.

If we could fully understand and appropriate the message of both Lincoln and Booker Washington in our attitude to the Negro, might it not remove a great barrier to our own fuller discovery of God? For we would then first go and be reconciled to our Negro brother, if our treatment of him is a fundamental denial of the fatherhood of God, the brotherhood of man and the priceless worth of the individual brother for whom Christ died. Booker Washington's whole life was a witness to his discovery of God for himself and his race. And he being dead yet speaketh. Could his message be better stated than in that great Negro spiritual through the mouth of this "Moses" calling us to end the economic slavery of his people:

Let *My* people go!

[8] From Lincoln's second inaugural address and from a fragment he wrote during the War Between the States, intended for no eye but his own.

REINHOLD NIEBUHR, 1892-

When Professor John Baillie suggested that Reinhold Niebuhr deliver the Gifford Lectures[9] in 1939, he made the exaggerated statement, "Intellectually Niebuhr is head and shoulders, he is legs and ankles above any other American." Replying to Professor Baillie's statement regarding Niebuhr, a score of men may be named, each more brilliant and distinguished in his special field, but Niebuhr is unique in that he invades the fields of philosophy, theology, economics, politics, sociology, literature and practical life all at once, in both English and German. It is therefore difficult to capture his thought, and any statement of it by him or another seems less than the whole, and fails to convey its richness and complexity.

In *Who's Who* and other sources the story of Niebuhr's short fifty years is soon told. He was born in Wright City, Missouri, in 1892, the son of a humble German pastor of the Evangelical Synod of North America, who strove to rear and educate a large family on a slender salary of less than a hundred dollars a month. Niebuhr came of a long line of German farmers, pastors, theologians and philosophers, with the distinctive type of German philosophic mind which is in marked contrast to the more pragmatic and superficial Anglo-Saxon type; yet he is completely American. Educated at his denominational Elmhurst College and the Eden Theological Seminary, and later at Yale Divinity School, he was for thirteen years, from 1915 to 1928, the pastor of a poor workers' church in Detroit, where he was exposed to all the grim realities and unsolved problems of our industrial civilization. Since 1928, he has occupied the chair in Applied Christianity and Christian Ethics in the Union Theological Seminary which gave him a national platform as a leader of thought in speaking and writing. Niebuhr is dismissed by those who do not understand him as a "pessimist" or as an uncomfort-

[9] Lord Gifford established this theological lectureship in 1888, to be delivered in four Scottish universities. In 1899, Josiah Royce lectured on "The World and the Individual," at Aberdeen; at Edinburgh in 1901, William James gave his "Varieties of Religious Experience"; Professor Hocking delivered his lectures in 1937; in 1929, John Dewey delivered his disappointing "Quest for Certainty"; and in 1939, Reinhold Niebuhr gave his series on "The Nature and Destiny of Man."

able critic of their familiar assumptions and their most cherished sins, but so were most of the prophets and reformers from Amos to the present day. The publication of his *Moral Man and Immoral Society* in 1932 marked the beginning of a change in the climate of American religious opinion.

There are four main strands in Reinhold Niebuhr's thought, or four sources from which he derives his own position, though each of these is highly complex. These are: 1. Christian orthodoxy, from which he derives, through St. Paul, Augustine, Lutheran and Reformed sources, his emphases upon sin and grace. Consciously or unconsciously he derives much from John Calvin, also, as does American activism and optimism. The American spirit, which Niebuhr so well embodies, is in part a synthesis of Calvinism and the enthusiasm engendered by the discovery of a new continent and a long-open pioneering frontier. 2. Modern liberalism as the result of the scientific spirit and historical criticism, derived in part from the Renaissance and the Enlightenment. Niebuhr is a thorough liberal, yet one of the most merciless critics of the futilities of modern liberalism both in dealing with the present world crisis and in understanding the permanent human problem. Niebuhr's own position is a synthesis between the liberal and humanistic tendencies of the Renaissance and the theologically darker views associated with the Reformation. 3. In his social theory, Niebuhr has been influenced by Marx, but he is severely critical of Marxism as a total interpretation of life. 4. In his social gospel, Niebuhr is not a naïve optimist like some of the disciples of Rauschenbush whose aim was "to re-establish the idea of the Kingdom of God in the thought of the church and *to assist in its practical realization in the world.*" He believes that the Kingdom of God will be realized not within history but beyond history. He keeps a complete balance between an individual and social emphasis in Christianity, and between optimism and pessimism.

These are the sources from which Niebuhr derives his thought, yet, as we have seen, he is a most vigorous critic of all four of them. He does not accept the whole of any one of them, nor does he attempt a compromising synthesis to unite all that is true in each; much less does he seek to make an eclectic mosaic of fragments of each in one artificial whole. Rather he holds them all in dialectic tension. After severe criticism he leaves the opposites to stand in their extreme form and allows his constructive thought to be influenced by the tensions between them. Niebuhr uses the word dialectic not as synonymous with logic, nor in the Hegelian or Marxian sense, but as *the preservation of opposite tendencies in a state of tension.* In his preface to *Beyond Tragedy,* he refers to Christianity's dialectical conception of the relation of time and eternity, of God and the world, of nature and grace. He holds that the biblical view of life is dialectical because it affirms the meaning of history and of man's natural existence on the one hand, and on the other insists that the center, source and fulfillment of history lie beyond history. Christianity's view of history is tragic in so far as it recognizes evil as an inevitable concomitant of even the highest spiritual attainments. It is beyond tragedy in so far as it does not regard evil as inherent in existence itself but as finally under the dominion of a good God.[10]

In Niebuhr's view of the sinfulness of the human heart and man's absolute dependence upon the grace of God, he reaffirms the message of the Apostle Paul, Augustine and the Reformation. His thought is never sentimental nor idealistic but realistic in seeing the stubbornness of evil in every human situation. He tears the masks from modern life. He reaffirms the tragic element in life, but he sees "beyond tragedy" to the ultimate triumph of the good. He sees generous elements of good in all men, but in "immoral society" the evils of sinful individual men are compounded and multiplied in group egoism so that nations, classes and races fall below the average individual members of these groups. This results in the blindness of each class in its own interests, all looking upon their judgments as objective and impartial, and identifying the interests of their group with universal interests, whether bourgeois, proletarian, or Christian. Sin "lies at the juncture of nature and spirit," in contrast to all views which locate sin in the body or in matter. It is not merely

[10] The writer has here rewritten several paragraphs from *The Kingdom of God and the American Dream,* pp. 268-272. Although he is an intimate friend, this is written without the knowledge or consent of Reinhold Niebuhr. The writer, however, is indebted to several mutual friends, especially to John Bennett for his "Contribution of Reinhold Niebuhr" in the Spring number, 1937, of *Religion in Life.*

ignorance of atavism, and it reappears in all individuals and in all societies upon every level of life.

Niebuhr makes constant attack upon optimistic liberals like John Dewey, who seem to think that by a little more education, or writing, or preaching, they can construct a satisfactory society. What seemed his catastrophic pessimism in 1932 is now proved to be a true diagnosis of the evils of our society in the present world crisis. Niebuhr holds that the Christian ethic of love is relevant to every social situation but fully applicable to none. The absolute ethic of Jesus must be maintained as a frame of reference by which every individual and society must continually be judged, but it is an "impossible possibility," and it becomes a false perfectionism when it is set up as a law to be applied to all concrete situations.

Niebuhr's view of human nature in *The Nature and Destiny of Man* may be stated as follows:[11]

The Christian view of man, which modern culture ostensibly rejects, is that God, as the source of all existence, creates the world which is "good." Man, created and finite, both body and spirit, understood primarily from the standpoint of God, is made in "the image of God," and capable of fellowship with him. The homelessness of the human spirit is the ground of all religion, for man cannot find the meaning of life in himself or the world, but only in God. God, as will and personality, is the only possible ground of real individuality in man, and reveals himself to man. The Christian faith in God's self-disclosure, culminating in the revelation of Christ, is the basis of the Christian concept of personality and individuality. Man as a unity of will is known and loved of God and can find his end only in the will of God, without whom he is lost and undone.

Man, who refuses to admit his creaturely dependence, is a sinner, in rebellion against God, his evil residing in the will in the very center of his personality. Man's essence is free self-determination but the wrong use of his freedom results in its self-destruction. Consequently as a sinner, man is ever under the judgment of the eternal and holy God. The law of man's nature is love, a harmonious relation of life to life, in obedience to the divine center and source of his life, which is love. This law is violated by man falsely making himself the center and source of his own life, in selfishness and pride. Standing at the junction of nature and spirit, man wilfully breaks the harmonies of nature. His

[11] Abbreviated from *The Nature and Destiny of Man*, Vol. I, pp. 12-25.

sin is spiritual though the infection of rebellion spreads from the spirit to the body. In his ignorance man's will-to-power overreaches his dependence in overweaning pride. Man's sin, while essentially rebellion against God, results in moral and social injustice in his relation to man. As a selfish sinner, he supremely loves neither God nor his neighbor but himself and his self-centered world.

Man's initial sin is pride and his initial return to God must be through humble repentance. All men have sinned. They may see, however, in the record of Jesus, imperfectly recorded, one who as a Son perfectly obeyed the Father, voluntarily suffered the results of the sins of the other sons of men, and in self-sacrificing love called all prodigal humanity to repent and return to God as Father. That is the human side of the picture; but there is a corresponding and antecedent Divine reality. Those who have faith see Jesus not only as truly human, limited and fallible, but as the unique and adequate revelation of God himself. Jesus is thus not only truly son of man, but as truly Son of God, who reveals the very heart of the Father as forgiving and redeeming love.

. . . The God whom Jesus revealed takes sin seriously; it is not merely wiped out by sentimental love. God is always a God of righteous judgment as well as of love. In the epic and mystery of the cross is revealed both God's "wrath" and his mercy which is ultimately supreme. In the cross God takes the consequences of sin upon himself as symbolic of his bearing sin in all history. Mercy does not cancel out judgment, but vicariously as the Suffering Servant of all humanity Christ bears our sins in his own body upon the tree. For in fullest measure God was in Christ reconciling the world unto himself. In the fallible human Jesus is thus the full and final revelation of God in history. Through Jesus, men discover God, see the self-revelation of God in Christ, and are moved to return to God as repentant sons. . . . They share Jesus' vision of the Kingdom of God, which though it is to be realized only beyond history, becomes the pattern from which they seek to build their ever-imperfect social life amid the relativities of history, according to this perfect frame of reference. Christians are forgiven, ever-imperfect sons, who seek the Kingdom of God by the doing of God's will on earth. Thus Niebuhr takes a full or orthodox view of the person and work of Christ, of the incarnation, the atonement and of the Triune God. This will doubtless be stated as fully and clearly in his second volume of the Gifford Lectures on *The Destiny of Man* as was his belief in sin and grace in the first volume on *The Nature of Man*.

Niebuhr's style of writing is highly involved and his speech is rapid. He is over the heads of the average college audience, but probably that is a reflection upon modern education rather than upon Reinhold Niebuhr. His leaping intellect often has piercing insights and he sometimes makes sweeping generalizations without tracing out the logical processes involved. This is frequently unfair to a given opponent or a complex movement like liberalism. There is an unfinished character in his creative thought and he often states a bald paradox without needed qualifications. Niebuhr makes enemies and many in the groups he attacks are naturally opposed to him—liberals, modernists, anti-theistic humanists, Marxists, pacifists, religious and economic fundamentalists. But on almost every count, he bears the marks of a prophet, a prophet on the theological right wing and on the social left wing. Like the prophets in opposition to the priests Niebuhr is often occupied with the "secular" side of life. Neither he nor Booker Washington was continually technically religious. When engaged in economic and political matters their whole lives seemed to be motivated by the love of God and man, especially in their concern for the underprivileged.

Niebuhr believes, with Plato, in the importance of the myth. There are some truths which transcend rational understanding and human experience and cannot be philosophically stated. Niebuhr does not mean the term mythical in the sense of imaginary or legendary, but as truth stated in story form. Thus the myth of the Fall, which is neither history nor science, and the parables of Jesus, state truth in the most effective way. Religion is to him not an opiate but the most powerful motivation and dynamic for social action. God is not a source of mystical private comfort, but in him we may find strength to enter the battle for a better order, as well as the peace and power by which to resolve the contradictions and tragedies of human life. Niebuhr is a healthy extrovert, believing in a gospel of individual salvation, but chiefly burdened as the principal representative of the social gospel in America today. His life suggests the epitaph to Sir Christopher Wren in St. Paul's Cathedral: "If you seek his monument look about you." He is a follower of a God who hideth himself. And he embodies Micah's summary of human duty.

In his *Leaves From the Notebook of a Tamed Cynic*, almost a diary of his inner life during his first pastorate in his Detroit church of workers and middle-class folk, one can see him driven step by step in his conscience to the position of socialism and pacifism. He has been compelled to modify both positions. He still accepts the basic thought of Marx's economic theory that the private ownership of the social means of production which results in such gross inequality of wealth and poverty and in mass production but utterly inadequate distribution, will inevitably destroy itself through its own inner contradictions and lead to a socialized planned economy. He still believes in the socialist diagnosis and the socialist objectives. He sees that the insistence of economically privileged classes upon their "free enterprise" after the war is as selfish as each class always is in its own interests and that nothing but a planned economy can give work to all and justice to all.

He would utterly disagree with Marx, however, at the following points: 1. In Marx's view of the universe as organic but not superorganic, where Marx takes the view of atheism and Niebuhr of theism; 2. in Marx's overemphasis upon violence arising partly from the bitter hatred of his own heart, which led almost inevitably to the abuse of power in Soviet tyranny and to the cruelty of three great purges; 3. in Marx's shallow utopian view of human nature, quite blind to human selfishness and sin; 4. in Marx's inadequate political theory which credulously believed that once the means of production were socialized, the state would be superfluous and would "wither away"; and 5. in Marx's rigid Hegelian dialectic which holds that, without God, the world is evolving by an automatic procedure "from lower to higher" to install a reign of justice "with iron necessity." This was not science but religion. Niebuhr shows that Marx, unconscious of wishful thinking, was able to construct a system that contained all his desires and a universe that seemed to be cooperating with him. Marx imagined that he had discovered by strictly scientific processes the laws which made the ultimate victory of the proletariat practically demonstrable. His unspiritual but socially prophetic vision was a secularized version of the oft-repeated apocalyptic vision of a redeemed society, not of the chosen people, but of the chosen proletarian class. He had read his own revolutionary purpose into the structure of the universe and had derived more from Judaism and Christianity than he realized, however much he abhorred all religion as he understood it, or rather misunderstood it.

Niebuhr could no longer support the Socialist party when it

became isolationist and pacifist, but he felt there was more hope of a just social order in the future development of the New Deal. He is under no illusions with regard to the present administration, but he sees clearly that there are manifestations of a smoldering class war even now in Washington. Corresponding to the "two hundred rich families" which, with the Fifth Columnists and appeasers betrayed France, he sees those who are defeatists and monopolists in America today and those who would make any lucrative secret deal with the Axis powers to preserve their own privileges. They doubtless consider themselves patriots just as did Laval, Bonnet and the rich families which sought to appease Hitler. Whatever the motive may have been, the touchstone in France was friendship for Hitler; the touchstone in America is hatred of the President and of the New Deal by the profiteers, the economically privileged and the middle-class dependent upon them for their financial support and their ideas.

Those who have no wider horizon than the comfort and help of personal religion might ask what all this has to do with religion or the discovery of God. Niebuhr, like the prophets of Israel, would reply, "much in every way." He sees that all that pertains either to the saving of the individual soul or the redemption of society has everything to do with religion. Nothing human is foreign to him. He sees that large numbers of Christian people are the chief obstacle to social justice, and that there is more flagrant injustice today in the capitalist "Christian" nations than in the time of Amos twenty-six centuries ago. This is one application of the "immoral society" which applies to the church as well as to the state. But, just as in the days of the prophets, it is the very people who most need his message who most resent it and are completely blind to it. In his effective organization, *Union for Democratic Action,* which unites labor and intellectuals, Niebuhr is working for genuine democracy at home and abroad, which he believes must be realized even during the war and more fully in a just and lasting peace.

Niebuhr believes that the inexorable logic of history has reached its climax in the present World War, for war is only an overt expression of covert tensions and conflicts which exist in every stable and peaceful social situation. The most powerful

state in Europe has sworn to destroy our North Atlantic civilization, and freedom has for the time being almost disappeared
from the European continent, which has become like a vast
concentration camp. Niebuhr strives for a just and lasting peace
but not a prematurely "negotiated peace," which cannot achieve
international brotherhood. The blithe religious perfectionism
of many is blissfully ignorant of the Janus-faced character of all
human decisions. Niebuhr believes in the moral imperative of
love—we must love God, our neighbor, and our enemy—but to
love our enemies does not mean that we must connive at their
injustice.

Niebuhr would agree with Professor Hodgson of Oxford, "the
way to love our enemy is to fight him in the spirit of good-will,
the spirit which in the very act of striking him down recognizes
him as a brother." He agrees with Karl Barth that this war "is
a large-scale, police measure which has become absolutely necessary to repulse anarchism." No war will ever end war and make
peace; but Niebuhr agrees with Augustine, Luther and Schweitzer that a defensive war may be the only way of preserving a
democratic society which alone can make a just and lasting
peace. This can never emerge from Hitler's conquered slave
states, nor from mere appeasement of Hitler. Therefore, Niebuhr
believes this is not a holy war—for no war, no police force, no
state is holy—but it is a just and necessary war.

Although Niebuhr was a pacifist for some years and a leader
in the *Fellowship of Reconciliation*, with some five thousand
other former pacifists in America and Britain, he feels that he
can no longer maintain the pacifist position in reason or in
conscience. He believes, however, that while personal religious
pacifism and the "vocational pacifism" of Elton Trueblood has
permanent validity for those who hold this conviction, pacifism
as a social and political strategy for state and church is seriously
mistaken. He would protect the approximately one in three
hundred in the last draft in Britain and the corresponding
minority in this country who feel that they must take the position of *conscientious objectors*, but he also agrees with the remaining two hundred and ninety-nine out of every three hundred who are equally *conscientious defenders* of their country
and of civilization. Niebuhr sees that we must render to Caesar

the relative duties that pertain to the state, but we must also render to God the absolute obligations due to him.

He believes that if we still need the use of force in our relatively Christian city, state, and nation, we cannot in the outer world of Hitler's barbarism stop Hitler by magic, or maintain law and order by Gandhi's nonviolent perfectionist methods. Indeed he believes that it is sheer illusion to think that at this late date God will work an immediate miracle in history for those absolutists who seek to turn the other cheek and overcome demonic evil by perfectionist love. Niebuhr feels that he is a responsible member of the state as well as of the church, and that necessity is laid upon the Christian conscience to win both the war and the peace. He believes, however, that it would be fatal for the church officially to bless war, identify itself with the state, and become a recruiting station for war. The task of the state is the preservation of order to provide for the general welfare; the task of the church is redemption. The Christian must render his service to both.

The reason we include Niebuhr here among the thirty pathfinders in this volume is not because of his economic and political views but because he has discovered God—in his life, his character, his multiform sacrificial service and in his teaching. He is a simple Christian. He has the same deep sense of human sin and divine grace that we found in Paul, in Augustine and in Luther. With none of the morbid introspection of John Bunyan, he yet has a deep sense of his own exceeding sinfulness. If the marks of the individual Christian are the four cardinal characteristics of humility, faith, purity and love, the writer desires to bear personal testimony, after knowing this man for thirty years, since student days, that Reinhold Niebuhr bears them all. Some who misunderstand him think that Niebuhr is arrogant. He is polemic and sometimes heated or impatient in argument, but this is combined with a deep and genuine personal humility. Like most men he is somewhat sensitive to criticism but he is not hypersensitive. Our desire here is not to justify or defend Niebuhr, but his all-important message on the discovery of God and on personal and social religion which we fear is not being realized by those who need it most.

While one cannot point to spectacular suffering in his life, as in those of some of the medieval saints, he always works far beyond his limited strength and often frail health. He is one of the busiest men in America, in demand upon a hundred platforms and in a hundred pulpits. He is often called to Washington and works tirelessly in a dozen different organizations, yet he has found time to take what is sometimes called the "religious emphasis week" in the three principal universities of Yale, Harvard, and Princeton in recent months, asked by the students themselves to speak to them upon vital, personal religion, with all its inevitable social implications. Indeed it would be difficult to find another who has such a dynamic message today for students and faculty, for intellectuals and for labor, in his life and in his teaching, in character and in service, and who so keeps the balance between the individual and the social aspects of Christianity, between the spiritual and the practical, the devotional and the rational, the Hellenic and the Hebraic, the ancient and the modern.[12] This man has discovered God.

MOHANDAS KARAMCHAND GANDHI, 1869-

Gandhi was born in a little seaport town near Bombay. He is a Gujarati, from an unwarlike peaceful race long pillaged by their warlike neighbors, the Marathas. For three generations the Gandhis, belonging to the shrewd bania caste of traders and moneylenders, had been prime ministers in several small Indian states. Mr. Gandhi says in his *Autobiography: The Story of My Experiments with Truth*:[13]

For me truth is the sovereign principle, the Absolute Truth, the Eternal Principle, that is God. Though the path of relative truth is

[12] Niebuhr's principal books in chronological order are, *Does Civilization Need Religion?* 1927; *Leaves From the Notebook of a Tamed Cynic*, 1929; *The Contribution of Religion to Social Work*, 1932; *Moral Man and Immoral Society*, 1932; *Reflections on the End of an Era*, 1934; *An Interpretation of Christian Ethics*, 1935; *Beyond Tragedy*, 1937; *Christianity and Power Politics*, 1940; *The Nature and Destiny of Man*, the Gifford Lectures published in two volumes, 1941 and 1943, by Charles Scribner's Sons, New York. Niebuhr is editor of *Christianity and Society* and *Christianity and Crisis*, and contributing editor of *The Nation*.

[13] This, and quotations which follow are much abbreviated and sometimes fragmentary selections from the two volumes of Gandhi's *Autobiography*, C. F. Andrews' *Mahatma Gandhi, His Own Story*, and his *Mahatma Gandhi's Ideas*.

straight and narrow, even my Himalayan blunders have seemed trifling, for daily the conviction is growing that He alone is real and all else is unreal.

The outstanding impression my mother left on my memory is that of saintliness. She was deeply religious. She would not think of taking her meals without her daily prayers, and to keep two or three consecutive fasts was nothing to her. As a boy, I was shy and avoided all company; my books and my lessons were my sole companions. It is my painful duty to record here my marriage at the age of thirteen.

His girl wife was of the same age and quite illiterate. Even after his marriage, Gandhi was afraid to sleep in the dark yet was ashamed to confess his fears to his child wife who was bolder than he. It was this timid creature who became, perhaps, the most fearless man of our day, who though "kicked, beaten, and spat upon as a coolie" in South Africa, stood at times almost alone against the weight of the world's greatest Empire. After his course in high school and college, he went to England for three years to complete his education as a barrister. Before going, he made three solemn vows to his mother and kept them faithfully: to live a celibate life, never to touch liquor, and to abstain from meat while in England. Here he was deeply impressed by a study of the Sermon on the Mount and the New Testament. When the Reverend F. B. Meyer asked him to become a Christian, Gandhi replied that he felt that all his spiritual needs could be met by Hinduism, and that in any case he could do more good by remaining a Hindu than by embracing the religion of the conquerors who held India by the sword. Gandhi said later: "Nothing could prevent me from embracing Christianity should I feel the call. I have long since taught myself to follow the inner voice."

Upon his return to India, Gandhi lost his first law case in court through shyness, and after a few years in comparative failure he went to South Africa on a lawsuit. Here he found his fellow Indians suffering cruel injustice and made their cause his own. When he settled his lawsuit out of court, to his own loss, and the grateful Indians were giving him a farewell dinner before his return to India, he laid before them the indignities and injustices suffered by their fellow Indians. They pleaded with him to stay another month and help them. The month was finally extended to twenty strenuous years. Gandhi writes: "The farewell party was turned into a working committee. . . . Thus God laid the foundations of my life in South Africa and sowed the seed of the fight for national self-respect." It was here that Gandhi was captivated by the moral ideal put forward by Tolstoy. He writes: "Tolstoy's *The Kingdom of God is Within You* overwhelmed me. It left an abiding impression on me." He returned again to a study of the Sermon on the Mount and determined to leave all, embrace a life of poverty, and practice rigorous ascetic self-control and entire nonviolence in his own life and in his experimental ascetic ashram. He founded Tolstoy Farm as one of his first experiments with truth.

The majority in the West will never understand Gandhi, just as they have never fully understood the oriental Jesus. Though the greatest pacifist the world has ever seen, in the political arena, Gandhi is not a logically consistent absolutist. He supported Britain in three wars, including his active recruiting in World War I, and was thrice decorated for bravery. He writes:

He who is not qualified to resist war, may take part in war, and yet wholeheartedly try to free himself, his nation and the world from war. So long as I lived under a system of government based on force and voluntarily partook of the many privileges it created for me, I was bound to help that government to the extent of my ability when it was engaged in war, unless I non-cooperated with that government and renounced to the utmost of my capacity the privileges it offered me. [Yet Gandhi and Nehru both came to know in bitter experience the truth of Sir John Seely's admission: Subjection for a long time to a foreign yoke is one of the most potent causes of national deterioration.]

For long years Gandhi supported the British Constitution. Yet as truly as Washington or Jefferson, Gandhi and Nehru both now passionately demand independence for their country.

Occidentals cannot understand Gandhi and think him a hypocrite because he combines the work of the saint with that of the politician. He unites three contradictory characters in one—Gautama Buddha, Francis of Assisi, and the rational revolutionist, Thomas Jefferson. We cannot conceive of Jefferson's working always in the spirit of the gentle St. Francis, nor of Francis, "the Little Brother of the Poor," as a farsighted and powerful statesman. But Gandhi combines them all. He is as wise as a serpent and harmless as a dove. Two men have led two of the great revolutions of the twentieth century—Lenin and Gandhi. The one with clenched fist, standing upon an armored car in Petrograd, called for a revolution of blood and iron, of social justice by compulsion. The other sits cross-legged upon the floor in the posture of Buddha, turning his spinning wheel of destiny. Imprisoned again and again in South Africa and later in India, in forced confinement he read hundreds of the best books, both religious and secular, chiefly in English. When Mr. Gandhi goes to prison he always takes with him four precious books—the *Bhagavad-Gita*, the *New Testament*, something of Tolstoy's, and Ruskin's *Unto This Last*. He also takes a trunkful of new books. Even in prison he continues to be a well-read man.

Just as Plato strove for a synthesis of the best thought of his day, and Augustine sought to unite the truths he found in Hebraism and Hellenism, Gandhi is seeking a synthesis of the truths in Hinduism, Christianity, and Buddhism, in full sympathy with the best in Islam and all other faiths. He says:[14]

I call myself a Sanatani Hindu because I believe in the Vedas, the Upanishads, and all Hindu Scriptures, and therefore in divine incarnation. . . . I do not disbelieve in "idol-worship." I believe that no one truly knows the Scriptures who has not attained perfection in innocence, trust, and self-control and who has not renounced all possession of wealth. I believe, along with every Hindu, in God and His Oneness, in rebirth and salvation. I believe the Bible, the Koran, and the Zend-Avesta to be as much divinely inspired as the Vedas. My belief in the Hindu Scriptures does not require me to accept every word and every verse as divinely inspired. . . . Nothing elates me so much as the music of the *Gita* or *Ramayana*. I know the vice that is going on to-day in all the great Hindu shrines, but I love them in spite of their unspeakable failings. I think that idol-worship is part of human nature. We hanker after symbolism. No Hindu considers an image to be God.

Hinduism is not an exclusive religion. It is not a missionary religion though it has absorbed many tribes in its fold. There is underlying all change a Living Power that is changeless, that holds all together. That informing Power or Spirit is God. He alone is. This power is purely benevolent. God is Life, Truth, Light; He is Love; He is the supreme Good. God must rule the heart and transform it. I cannot account for

[14] Brief quotations from *Mahatma Gandhi's Ideas* by C. F. Andrews, pp. 35-49.

the existence of evil by any rational method. I call God long-suffering and patient precisely because He permits evil in the world. I know that He has no evil in Himself. I shall never know God if I do not wrestle with and against evil, even at the cost of life itself. The purer I try to become the nearer to God I feel myself to be. Meanwhile I pray with Newman:

> Lead, Kindly Light, amid the encircling gloom,
> The night is dark and I am far from home,
> Lead Thou me on.

To me God is Truth and Love. He is the searcher of hearts. He knows us and our hearts better than we do ourselves. God is personal to those who need His personal presence. He is long-suffering. He is patient, but He is also terrible. And withal He is ever-forgiving. He, therefore, who would pray to God must cleanse his heart. Faith is nothing but a living, wide-awake consciousness of God within. He who has achieved that faith wants nothing. . . . He who would be a devotee must serve the suffering and the woebegone, by body, soul, and mind. A prayerful heart is the vehicle, and service makes the heart prayerful. Hinduism as I know it entirely satisfies my soul. There was a time when I was wavering between Hinduism and Christianity. When I recovered my balance of mind I felt that to me salvation was possible only through the Hindu Religion. Yet, it was the New Testament which really awakened me to the rightness and value of Passive Resistance.

I want to identify myself with everything that lives. For me there are no politics devoid of religion. They subserve religion. Politics bereft of religion are a death-trap because they kill the soul. The path to self-purification is hard and steep. To attain to perfect purity, one has to become absolutely passion-free in thought, speech and action. I know that I have not in me yet that triple purity. That is why the world's praise fails to move me. It often stings me. To conquer the subtle passions seems to me to be harder far than the physical conquest of the world by force of arms. I must reduce myself to zero.

Both Christians and Hindus see incarnated in Gandhi their own highest principles and loftiest character. Each, however, would like to have him drop one obnoxious agitation and take one final step of orthodox submission that would make him true to their own faith. Orthodox Hindus would like to have him leave the untouchables alone; while orthodox Christians would like to have him drop his "politics," his agitation for liberty, and be baptized and openly become a Christian. But there are some seven hundred million Christians in several hundred Protestant sects and more than a score of "Catholic" churches who may exhibit the grace of the sacrament of baptism. Let us leave to the handiwork of God this simple unorthodox soul who puts us all to shame.

Edward Thompson, the English poet, thus writes with discerning discrimination, testifying to the moral greatness of Gandhi and, unconsciously, to that of the British as well:[15]

Mr. Gandhi's politics are often inadequate to questions that fall outside a village economy—the defence of India, for example, in a world beset with totalitarian powers. God has been very good to India following a Gandhi by a Nehru who will have courage to carry Gandhi's work into a world that the older man distrusts. Gandhi is busy always *with the individual*, not with large-scale planning and action. Gandhi's weapon of *ahimsa* or "non-violent non-resistance" succeeded in India because used against a government that recognized that the game of insurrection and repression had rules; his enemy had streaks of humanity and liberalism. The government found itself ultimately helpless when line after line of Nationalists stood up fearlessly to be struck down by the *lathis* of the police, while British spectators were overcome with shame, and American journalists hurried off to cable home their indignation.

Gandhi has never been taken in by his own legend; his impishness, his sense of humor brings him constant happiness. Like Socrates, he has a "daemon" and when that daemon has spoken, he is as unmoved by argument as by danger. India, weak and disarmed, had no other weapon than non-violence. Mr. Gandhi has been *"sitting dharna"* at the British Empire's doorstep for close on forty years (as an aggrieved person at the door of an oppressor or enemy, sat fasting until death or redress released him). In April 1919, General Dyer shot down nearly two thousand people in the death-trap of that sunken garden at Amritsar, where the wounded were left all night to crawl and cry out. There followed the infamous debates in both Houses of Parliament and the mean agitation that whipped up a subscription of twenty-six thousand pounds to the Dyer Testimonial Fund. When circumstantial evidence was pressed upon the National Congress committee to show that General Dyer had deliberately "lured" the crowd into the garden so as to slaughter them, Gandhi brushed it aside saying "I do not believe it, and it shall not be set down in the report."

[15] Abbreviated from "Gandhi, a Character Study," in *Mahatma Gandhi*, by Sir S. Radhakrishnan.

At his trial, in 1922, I began to see that Gandhi challenged, not so much the British dominion, as the whole modern world that has mechanized and arrested human life. His cult of the spinning wheel was wise and justified. Gandhi's humanity is one of the profoundest things that history has seen. He has pity and love for every race, and most of all for the poor and oppressed. He is genuinely desireless; he regards all men and women equally, his own son being no more to him than the son of a sweeper. He is without fear or care for self. He is humorous, kindly, obstinate, brave. India was cracked, shattered and patched. For the first time since Buddha she knew a stirring that spread to her remotest places. Gandhi has held up a hope before the outcastes who have begun to dream that they come within the category of human beings. He has definitely shifted the course of a people's way for the future. He is one who has set the stamp of an *idea* on an epoch. When the insanity now ravaging the world has passed away, then my own country, as well as India, will look on this man as one of its greatest and most effective servants and sons.

The writer, who spent ten days with Mr. Gandhi in his home and at the Lahore Nationalist Congress in 1929, desires to add his own personal testimony as to Gandhi's discovery of God:

I differ radically from Mr. Gandhi in some of his political views, and in what seems to me his too individualistic religion which relies almost solely upon the appeal of sainthood, and sees no necessity for social control and a planned economy such as Nehru and Archbishop Temple recognize as essential. I reject Gandhi's asceticism that looks upon sex as unholy and marriage as a necessary evil. I do not agree with his absolute pacifism for I believe it is sheer delusion to think that by turning the other cheek in love to the invading hosts of Japan or the demonic Hitler it would now be an act of political realism, and would miraculously save a country from the moral degradation of the status of a slave state. I differ from Gandhi again, in that I believe in the right and duty of Christian missions to proclaim an evangel of love and share their treasures, as Schweitzer is doing in Africa, and as C. F. Andrews did in India. But I desire to bear witness, in spite of all this, that Gandhi gives evidence, as much as any man in the world today, that he has discovered God. After a long life of wide travel, meeting thousands of religious people, I find him the most impressive personality

I have ever met. And I would say more: he seems to be, in spite of his faults, one of the most Christlike men I have ever known. He incarnates the Hindu's daily prayer:

> Lead me from untruth to truth
> Lead me from darkness to light
> Lead me from death to immortality.

As evidence of Gandhi's discovery of God, I may be permitted to recall certain incidents that occurred when with my wife and Mr. and Mrs. Kirby Page, we saw Gandhi in action: In 1929 we arrived at Mr. Gandhi's settlement, or ashram, on his "day of silence" which lasts from Sunday evening at seven until Monday at the same hour. He feels that he must have one day a week absolutely free for rest, for thought, for meditation, for prayer. During that day he does not open his lips to say even Yes or No. He smiled when he saw us, as he had been expecting our coming, and sent us a kindly little note saying that he would see us when he broke his silence that evening. He appeared at first to be an almost toothless old man, thin, emaciated, with large ears and close-shaven gray head; his body being clad only in a coarse homespun cotton cloth. His physical presence, like that of Socrates or the Apostle Paul, seemed weak and unprepossessing. Yet after the first few moments with him we never noticed those homely features again. We were gazing into the depths of a great soul which seemed to shine out of his whole face. He moved about in the world before us but he seemed to live in God.

That evening we sat with him in the open air by the river bank where he sleeps. For an hour he answered our questions about his experience of God, about prayer and the things of the spirit. We were surprised to learn that once he had doubted everything and had at one time been an atheist. He said he had observed that others had found this experience of vital religion, and he had resolved to make the world's faith in God his own. We saw him daily at his half hour of prayer which begins each morning at four o'clock out under the stars, while it is cold and dark, and again at half past seven each evening. Here we were privileged to join him in a service of worship twice daily. Each day we sat close to him at meals upon the floor with the hundred and fifty inmates of the ashram. Gandhi slipped in last and

sat beside the children. He ate twice each day only a small bowl
of the curds of goats' milk and a bowl of fruit. Yet on this
scanty fare he does the work of several men. Seated next to me
on the other side was a Hindu employer who had already given
away about half a million dollars, or half his wealth, and was
devoting all his time and the balance of his fortune to Gandhi's
crusades. On all sides we saw the remarkable influence of the
Mahatma, or great soul, both in the changed lives in the ashram
itself and throughout India.

On the occasion of one of his former fasts of twenty-one days,
the Hindus and Mohammedans had been killing each other in
riots until it almost broke his heart. Sleepless, in agony of mind,
he finally resolved to do what the Orient alone would understand and what would there be effective. He would fast for
three weeks; he would not touch a morsel of food for twenty-one
days. He had recently had an operation for appendicitis and was
a mere shadow of a man weighing then about ninety pounds.
On the twelfth day of the fast the doctor said that his pulse was
failing and that he would surely die if he did not take food. He
only smiled and said: "Have faith in God. Have you forgotten
the power of prayer?" He was stronger on the twenty-first day
than he had been on the twelfth, having done his full work
every day. When at last he broke his fast he called upon a Hindu
comrade to read his favorite passage of Scripture, he asked his
Mohammedan brother to lead in prayer to the one God and
Father of all; and then requested his Christian friend, C. F.
Andrews, to sing his favorite hymn, "When I Survey the Wondrous Cross." Then he was carried out, too weak to walk.

One evening at the Lahore meeting of the Indian National
Congress, of the Nationalist party his enemy had risen to speak,
endeavoring to win the majority from allegiance to Gandhi to
his own method of violence. Gandhi was to reply to him and
then the vote was to be taken. At half past seven, while his
enemy was still speaking, came his hour for worship. We saw
him slip quietly away from the back of the platform, and followed him to his tent for his unfailing hour of prayer. We tried
to recall any other politician in the world today, or any other
statesman in history, who at the crisis of the debate would count
prayer a really more dynamic, a more practical and efficacious
way of working than taking part in the debate.

We saw him at the meeting in Lahore when some fifteen thousand delegates were gathered in the great tent at the National Congress. He had been sitting quietly out of sight at the back of the platform, always engaged in his hand spinning. The time had arrived when he must present his epoch-making resolution on India's political future. He remained seated, as he is unable to speak standing because of his weak heart, and with the microphone held close to his lips, he quietly moved his resolution, first for sympathy for the viceroy, the present Lord Halifax, because of the attempt which had just been made upon his life, and then for independence for India. There was no oratory; no "give me liberty or give me death." He reminded one more of St. Francis speaking to his beloved community.

On the final day we saw him as he was starting on his way to give a last message to the Congress. Outside the tent a great crowd had gathered in the hope of seeing him as he passed, for, owing to the newspaper, railway, telegraph, radio and modern means of communication, he is undoubtedly more widely known and is followed by more millions during his own lifetime than was any religious leader of the past. Every eye was fixed upon his frail figure, and the upturned faces of his people were lit up with an affection we had never seen for any other man on earth. It was like a shaft of sunlight falling upon the throng. Mothers would hold up their children that they might see him, once in a lifetime, as he passed. Educated men would close their eyes in prayer, or stoop to touch the hem of his garment, or kiss those aged feet, or gather the dust from his sandals and then kiss their hands. The golden heart of the East knew and loved its own.

We saw his face for the last time as he disappeared in the great tent, to take up what then seemed the almost hopeless struggle for India's freedom. He moved as calm as Gautama Buddha, in the unbroken peace of an inward spiritual Nirvana, as loving as St. Francis, and on that battle-scarred old face, which bore the marks of mobs and imprisonment, of fasting, of failure and of heartbreak, we saw a light—"the light that never was on land or sea."

ALBERT SCHWEITZER, 1875-

Albert Schweitzer, Alsatian philosopher, theologian, musician, interpreter of Bach, and now medical missionary in tropical

Africa, is brilliant enough and broad enough, with the stature of a spiritual giant, to give him the place of honor as the last among the living examples of our thesis, "man discovers God." Schweitzer was born in 1875, a son of the evangelical Protestant manse, educated at the village school, the town Gymnasium, and the University of Strassburg. After winning a traveling scholarship for postgraduate study in Paris and Berlin, he was ordained curate at St. Nicholas, as well as lecturer at the university and shortly after he became principal of the theological school at Strassburg.

Schweitzer soon became famous on four counts: 1. His original theological writings on Jesus and Paul immediately gave him a place as one of the most brilliant theologians of our generation. 2. His two volumes on the philosophy of civilization, *The Decay and Restoration of Civilization* and *Civilization and Ethics*, rank him as a philosopher and place him in the forefront of modern social thinkers. 3. As a master organist his Bach recitals are famous in eight European capitals; he is an expert and consultant on organ construction, and he is the author of the most scholarly and understanding interpretation of Johann Sebastian Bach. 4. When he was thirty-four years of age and already famous in Europe, he turned his back upon his reputation and ambition, and took his medical degree that he might serve as a doctor in equatorial Africa. He took this step with the motive of seeking to right a great social wrong, paying, so far as in him lay, the white man's debt to the Negro, and as a Christian by "emptying himself" to render a thank offering for all that he felt to be his undeserved privileges and happiness.[16]

Even as a boy, Schweitzer was a dreamer, with poignant sympathy sharing the pain of the animal world. In manhood, he

[16] For facts concerning Dr. Schweitzer's life, I am indebted to his biography by Magnus Ratter, as well as to his own works which are before me as I write: *The Religious Philosophy of Kant*, not translated, (1899); *The Quest of the Historical Jesus* (1910); *J. S. Bach*, two volumes, (1911); *Paul and His Interpreters*, (1912); *The Mystery of the Kingdom of God*, (1914); *The Decay and Restoration of Civilization* and *Civilization and Ethics*, (1923); *Christianity and the Religions of the World*, (1923); *Memoirs of Childhood and Youth*, (1924); *The Edge of the Primeval Forest*, (1929); *More From the Primeval Forest*, (1931); *The Forest Hospital in Lambarene*, (1931); *The Mysticism of Paul the Apostle*, (1931); *My Life and Thought: an Autobiography*, (1933); *Indian Life and Thought*, (1936); *From My African Notebook*, (1938).

incorporated this sentiment in his system of philosophy which centers in his reverence for life. Schweitzer developed first as a saint and an artist; and only later as thinker, theologian and historian. In his *Memoirs of Childhood and Youth*,[17] he writes:

I was born in the little town of Kaysersberg, in Upper Alsace, in 1875. My father lived there as pastor and teacher of the little evangelical congregation. I was a very sickly child and cried the whole way on going to school for the first time. I never looked for trouble by being aggressive, but as I grew older, I liked measuring my bodily strength with that of others in a friendly tussle. . . . One day I had a wrestle with a bigger and stronger boy and when I got him down, he jerked out "Yes, if I got broth to eat twice a week, as you do, I should be as strong as you are." This (fact of poverty) caused me much suffering. Broth became nauseous to me. I refused to wear an overcoat or to dress differently from the poor boys. I got the stick over this but I stood firm.

When I was eight, my father gave me a New Testament which I read eagerly. [Even at this age Schweitzer was a born higher critic asking his parents why Jesus' family was poor and what they did with the gold and gifts of the three wise men from the East.] I was a quiet and dreamy scholar with a horror of studies and letter writing which lasted for years. A savior appeared in the person of a new master. Experience of his self-disciplined activity had a distinct effect upon me. He became my model. That a deep sense of duty, manifested in even the smallest matters, is the great educative influence has, thanks to him, become with me a firm conviction, in all that I have had to do as an educator. My passion for reading finally became unlimited. Once I have begun a book, I can never put it down. I would rather sit up all night over it.

. . . From my mother I inherited a terribly passionate temper. I played every game with terrible earnestness, and got angry if anyone else did not enter into it with all his might. When I was nine I struck my sister because she was a slack opponent. From that time I began to feel anxious about my passion for play and gradually gave up all games. I have never ventured to touch a playing card. When a student I gave up forever the use of tobacco.

As far back as I can remember I was saddened by the amount of misery I saw in the world around me, especially for the unfortunate animals. In my evening prayers, I used to add silently a prayer that I had composed myself for all living creatures: "O, heavenly Father, protect and bless all things that have breath; guard them from all evil, and

[17] Abbreviated from *Memoirs of Childhood and Youth*, 1924, and *My Life and Thought: an Autobiography*. *The Memoirs of Childhood* were written at the request of his friend, the Zurich psychoanalyst, Dr. O. Pfister.

let them sleep in peace." [After protecting the birds from the other boys who wanted to kill them, Schweitzer says]: From that day onward I took courage to emancipate myself from the fear of men. There slowly grew up within me an unshakable conviction that we have no right to inflict suffering and death on another living creature unless there is some unavoidable necessity for it.

To be prepared for confirmation, I was sent to old Pastor Wennagel who wanted, in submission to faith, all reasoning to be silenced. But I was convinced that the fundamental principles of Christianity have to be proved true by reasoning, and by no other method. And this certainly filled me with joy. During the last weeks of the preparation for confirmation I was so moved by the holiness of the time that I felt almost ill. [As boy and man, Schweitzer was ever both saint and rationalist, Suffering Servant and heretic.] My next great experience was over the question of my right to happiness. Out of the depth of my feeling of happiness there grew up gradually within me an understanding of the saying of Jesus that we must not treat our lives as being for ourselves alone; we must all carry our share of the misery which lies upon the world. When I was twenty-one while still a student I resolved to devote my life till I was thirty to the office of preacher, to science, and to music; I would then take a path of immediate service as man to my fellow men. Finally a chain of circumstances pointed out to me the road which led to the suflerers from leprosy and sleeping sickness in Africa.

Schweitzer's *Quest of the Historical Jesus* fell like a bombshell upon the theological world. After reviewing all the earlier attempts for two hundred years to write a life of Jesus, analyzing them and showing where they were inadequate, Schweitzer proceeds to make his own contribution. His searching quest failed to verify the traditional liberal picture of Christ, or to find the historical Jesus as humanist, ethical teacher and social reformer proclaiming the fatherhood of God and the brotherhood of man. Rational theology had sought to bring the historical Jesus straight to our time as Teacher and Saviour. But as Schweitzer found "He does not stay; he passes by our time and returns to his own." Instead of the traditional picture, Schweitzer found Jesus proclaiming the near approach of the Kingdom of God which was wholly future and to be established by divine intervention. Jesus taught only "a transition ethics," which would be transcended in the Kingdom which was swiftly to come. Schweitzer maintained that while Jesus' outlook was other-worldly and world-negating, our modern view must be world-accepting, yet he held that Jesus' eschatological view does not lessen the significance of his words for our time: "That which is eternal in the words of Jesus is due to the very fact that they are based on an eschatological world-view. They are appropriate, therefore, to any world."

As we have already seen, Schweitzer is unique in that at the early age of twenty-one he made the deliberate resolve to follow the intellectual pursuits of theology, philosophy and music until he was thirty, and then to take a path of immediate sacrificial service to his fellow men. When he reached the age of thirty, he read the magazine of the Paris Evangelical Missionary Society calling for a doctor at Lambaréné on the Ogowe River, in what is now Free French Equatorial Africa. He decided at once that he would go: "The article finished, I quietly began my work. My search was over." After a full medical course, specializing in tropical medicine, on Good Friday, 1913, he set out for Africa without the support of a missionary society, with only some seven thousand dollars of his own money to build a little hospital and to provide for his work for two years, a royalty income of a thousand dollars a year, and the good will of a widening circle of friends who were to support him. On his own resources, Schweitzer traveled to Africa, built his own hospital and rendered heroic sacrificial service in the midst of the Dark Continent. If "a saint is a man that makes goodness attractive" this would place Schweitzer among our mystic saints, as well as among our brilliant thinkers and scientists.

Anyone who will read between the lines of Schweitzer's *On the Edge of the Primeval Forest*, the four books about his experience in his hospital in Africa, and his *My Life and Thought*, will see that he himself was the silent Suffering Servant in the whole mission to Africa. Whether consciously or unconsciously he is reliving the fifty-third chapter of Isaiah in darkest Africa. He writes:

I had read about the physical miseries of the natives in the virgin forests, and the parable of Dives and Lazarus seemed to me to have been spoken directly to us. I resolved when thirty years old to study medicine and put my ideas to the test. I started with my wife, who had qualified as a nurse, for Equatorial Africa because Alsatian missionaries of the Paris Evangelical Mission told me that a doctor was badly needed there, on account of the rapidly spreading sleeping sickness. My work was undenominational and international; for humanitarian work should be done by us as men, not as members of any particular nation or religious body. After a year's residence, fatigue and anemia begin. At the end of two or three years, one becomes incapable of real work and must return to Europe for at least eight months to recruit. I treated and bandaged the sick in the open air before the hospital was built. The heat is intolerable. The poor creatures have rowed themselves two hundred and fifty miles upstream to visit the doctor and can hardly stand from exhaustion.

In the first nine months, two thousand patients were examined and treated for malaria, sleeping sickness, heart disease, rheumatism, pneumonia, tumors and a long catalogue of diseases with their misery and pain:

A poor fellow is brought to me for an operation. I am the only person within hundreds of miles who can help him. When the moaning creature comes, I lay my hand on his forehead and say to him: "Don't be afraid! In an hour's time you shall be put to sleep, and when you wake you won't feel any more pain." Scarcely has he recovered consciousness when he ejaculates, "I've no more pain! I've no more pain!" His hand feels for mine and will not let it go. Then I begin to tell him and the others who are in the room that it is the Lord Jesus who has told the doctor and his wife to come to the Ogowe. The African sun is shining through the coffee bushes but we, black and white, sit side by side and feel that we know by experience the meaning of the words, "And all ye are brethren." Would that my generous friends in Europe could come out here and live through one such hour! And who will make this work possible? The fellowship of those who bear the marks of pain. Those who have learned by experience what physical pain and bodily anguish mean, belong together all the world over: they are united by a secret bond. He who has been delivered from pain and anguish must help to overcome those two enemies and bring to others the deliverance he has himself enjoyed. This is the "Fellowship of Suffering."

Christianity is for the African the light that shines amid the darkness of his fears; it assures him that he is not in the power of the spirits, and that no human being has any sinister power over another, since the will of God really controls everything that goes on in the world. That thought fills my mind when I take part in a service in the mission station. In proportion as the Negro becomes familiar with the higher moral ideas of the religion of Jesus, he finds utterance for something in himself that has hitherto been dumb, and something that has been tightly bound up finds release. The feeling of never being safe from the stupidest piece of theft, however, brings one sometimes almost to despair. My copy of *Bach's Passion Music* into which I had written the organ accompaniment was taken. As the natives say, "It goes for a walk."

Three hospitals had to be built in turn and a hut erected for the treatment of sleeping sickness which had reduced the inhabitants of Uganda from 300,000 to 100,000. In the midst of a journey in the jungle, there suddenly leaped to Schweitzer's mind the theme of his philosophy upon which he had long meditated in the African jungle, which he was to expand in his lectures in Oxford and other centers in Europe.

At sunset as we were making our way through a herd of hippopotamuses, there flashed upon my mind, unforeseen and unsought, the phrase, "Reverence for Life." The iron door had yielded: the path in the thicket had become visible. Now I had found my way to the idea in which world- and life-affirmation and ethics are contained side by side! Now I knew that the world-view of ethical world- and life-affirmation, together with its ideals of civilization, is founded in thought.

The World War I from 1916 to 1918 was for Schweitzer the Crucifixion Chorus in Bach's *Mass in B Minor*. After four years in tropical Africa with his wife ill, his money and health gone, in debt for his hospital, at a day's notice because of war hysteria, Schweitzer was arrested and brought to prison in France. He was barely able to save his surgical instruments and the manuscript of his philosophy on *Civilization and Ethics*. He continued to think out and write his philosophy in the African jungle and in prison in France. He wrote from his prison experiences of the need of forgiveness: "It was part of the madness of the world. We must forget that time of hatred and fear." He felt that the war was raging as a result of the downfall of civilization. Lack of proper food, African malaria, anemia, and prison confinement led to his serious illness and to the necessity of two dangerous operations. Easter, 1920, however, brought Schweitzer spiritual renewal and resurrection. Bach's trumpets were sounding in his soul again. He traveled and lectured in England and

Sweden, gave organ recitals in Spain and over Europe, and wrote another book. Europe had received him with open arms and still offered him a distinguished career; yet he heroically decided, like Livingstone, to return again to Africa even though he had to go alone without his sick wife.

In 1924, Schweitzer returned to Lambaréné with a European helper. In 1925, a third doctor came and a second nurse to serve in his enlarged hospital. During the present war, the Free French speak highly of the excellent work being done by Schweitzer, especially the scientific work of his institute. Both Africans and Europeans working in the timber mills and mines of the region share in the benefits of the hospital. The Free French high commissioner, General Dr. Sice, has made a substantial monthly grant to the institution, and General de Gaulle has sent the following message to Dr. Schweitzer: "I know your merits and your reputation. I thank you for giving your services as you do to aid French science. I shall be pleased to see you when I make my next voyage to Africa."

We can trace Schweitzer's intellectual Pilgrim's Progress in his *Civilization and Ethics* where he makes a survey of more than thirty ethical thinkers from Socrates to William James. Though not always orthodox, Schweitzer is always Christian. He wrestles with God as did Luther. He accepts the antinomy that in the natural world God is revealed as a mysterious creative force, but in ourselves we experience God as Personality, as ethical Will.

It so happens that Albert Schweitzer is the last of the witnesses—thirty-four in all—called in support of our thesis that man discovers God. In a unique way he is a representative man. The Hebraist and Hellenist are as well balanced in him as are the mystic and the rationalist. He is at once like Plato, an idealist, like Aristotle, a realistic scientist, and, though in some respects like the sensitive "pessimist" Jeremiah, he more closely resembles the great anonymous Prophet of the Exile, as a Suffering Servant of humanity. He refused to go to Africa as German, French, Alsatian, or Protestant evangelical, but only as "man"— an untitled son of man. He is a sympathetic scholar of the New Testament. But he is such a prophetic critic that his one passion is truth and his enemies are error and superstition. He is orthodox to the extent that he is a humble Christian, minister, and missionary, but he is so frankly "heretical" that he declined to submit to a theological cross-examination by the fundamentalist committee of the Paris Missionary Society which had just rejected a previous candidate because he did not believe that the author of the Fourth Gospel was John the son of Zebedee.

Schweitzer was glad to meet every member of the committee individually with regard to his personal religious experience, and to submit to the most searching examination on tropical medicine, for he was going to Africa not to talk but to act, and silently to heal the sick in what Livingstone called "the Dark Continent, the open sore of the world." Yet preaching to his patients was sheer joy when he was trusted enough to take the religious services. He passionately sought and admired the good in all men and systems—for with Paul, Schweitzer believed that "all things are yours"—in the Stoics and Spinoza, in Schopenhauer and even Nietzsche, in the embittered Reimarus and the tolerant Harnack, and in all races, religions and systems of philosophy. Yet he seemed to have an especial affinity for the Chinese, the Hindus of India, and his little brothers in Africa.

In their pathways to God, he was equally in sympathy with the mystics, the reformers, and the scientists; and in quite a unique way, he has always kept the balance between science, art and religion throughout his life. During the early months of his preparation for Africa, he was an intense student of the science of medicine and surgery; at the same time he completed new editions of his writings on Bach and his *Quest of the Historical Jesus*; he gave one or two organ recitals in France and in Germany; he could not yet tear himself away from preaching in his own pulpit, and had not yet resigned as a theological professor and principal of his college in Strassburg. During a single month, while in prison in World War I, Schweitzer acted as a physician for his fellow prisoners, wrote his philosophy of *Civilization and Ethics*, and practiced on the table and floor in lieu of a musical instrument to prepare for his organ recitals in the eight European cities from Madrid to Stockholm, which were again clamoring for him as the great interpreter of Bach.

The armchair critic can easily point out that neither he nor his contemporary higher critic, William Rainey Harper, whom he resembled in many ways, should have attempted so much—

that they should not have overworked from sixteen to eighteen hours a day, should not have labored to be scholars, writers, lecturers, administrators, musicians, citizens, patriots and Christian missionaries all at once. But neither of them could help it. Each had in him—as did every one of our pathfinders in greater or less degree—that spark of the divine that compelled him to attempt the impossible, that stimulated his avid interminable search for truth, that, ever forgetting the things that lay behind, was straining toward the infinite that lay before, as eternal adventurers in the endless discovery of the inexhaustible God.

And let us note again how Schweitzer brings forth from his treasures things new and old, how he keeps the balance between rigorism and humanism, world-denial and world-affirmation, pessimism and optimism. The critic, safe in his easy optimism, may carp at Schweitzer as a "pessimist" when this man of sorrows admits:

> Only at quite rare moments have I felt really glad to be alive. I could not but feel with a sympathy full of regret all the pain that I saw around me, not only that of men but that of the whole creation. From this community of suffering I have never tried to withdraw myself. It seemed to me a matter of course that we should all take our share of the burden of pain which lies upon the world. That a thinker like Leibnitz could reach the miserable conclusion that this world is the best that was possible I have never been able to understand.[18]

We give heed to Socrates before he drinks the hemlock, to Jesus in the Garden and to Schweitzer as he thus concludes his philosophy of life in the Epilogue of his *Autobiography*:[19]

> Two perceptions cast their shadow over my existence. One is that the world is inexplicably mysterious and full of suffering; the other is that I have been born into a period of the spiritual decadence of mankind. With the spirit of the age I am in complete disagreement because it is filled with disdain for thinking. The spirit of the age never lets man come to himself. He is forced into skepticism about his own thinking. He has no longer any spiritual self-confidence. I acknowledge myself to be one who places all his confidence in rational thinking. Renunciation of thinking is a declaration of spiritual bankruptcy, in the

---

[18] *Albert Schweitzer: My Life and Thought*, p. 280.

[19] Abbreviated excerpts from *My Life and Thought*, pp. 254-282, Lambaréné, March 7, 1931.

expectation that men will end by accepting as truth what is forced upon them by authority.

Here Schweitzer shows the spirit of Luther and of Niemoeller.

The city of truth cannot be built on the swampy ground of skepticism. Mysticism is a form of elemental thinking, because it enables the man to put himself into spiritual relation with the world.

In Reverence for Life there is a renewal of elemental thinking. By placing myself in the service of that which lives I reach an activity exerted upon the world which has meaning and purpose. Everything which exists is a manifestation of the Will-to-Live. The ethic of the Reverence for Life is the ethic of Love widened into universality. It is the ethic of Jesus, now recognized as a necessity of thought. I rejoice in the new remedies for sleeping sickness. But every time I have under the microscope the germs which cause the disease, I cannot but reflect that I have to sacrifice this life in order to save life. Man is able to preserve his own life only at the cost of other life. Any profound world view brings men into a spiritual relation with the Infinite. Reverence for Life is ethical mysticism. It has therefore a religious character. Through the active ethic of love it is related to Christianity. I know that I myself owe it to thinking that I was able to retain my faith in the religion of Christianity. The essential element in Christianity as it was preached by Jesus is that it is only through love that we can attain to communion with God. We experience God in our lives as Will-to-Love. Love is the spiritual beam of light which reaches us from the Infinite. In the knowledge of spiritual existence in God through love, man possesses the one thing needful. "Love never faileth." What Christianity needs is to be filled to overflowing with the spirit of Jesus. Christianity during these nineteen centuries is merely a beginning, not the full-grown Christianity springing from the spirit of Jesus. I am devoted to Christianity in deep affection.

No explanation of evil in the world could ever satisfy me, but I never let myself get lost in broodings over it. Because I have confidence in the power of truth and of the spirit, I believe in the future of mankind. In my own life anxiety, trouble and sorrow have been allotted to me in abundant measure. But I have had blessings too: that I am allowed to work in the service of mercy; that my work has been successful; that I receive from other people affection and kindness in abundance; that I have a well-balanced temperament which varies little; and an energy which exerts itself with calmness and deliberation. I feel it deeply that I can work as a free man when the lack of freedom is the lot of so many. With calmness and humility I look forward to the future. Whether we be workers or sufferers, it is our duty to conserve our powers, as being men who have won their way through to the peace that passeth all understanding.

We cannot do better than end with his own great words at the close of his *Quest of the Historical Jesus* which voice both his unsolved problems and his indomitable faith:

The names by which men expressed their recognition of him as such, Messiah, Son of Man, Son of God, have become for us historical parables. We can find no designation which expresses what he is for us. He comes to us as One unknown, without a name, as of old, by the lakeside, he came to those men who knew him not. He speaks to us the same words: "Follow thou me!" and sets us to the tasks which he has to fulfill for our time. He commands. And to those who obey him, whether they be wise or simple, he will reveal himself in the toils, the conflicts, the sufferings, which they shall pass through in his fellowship, and, as an ineffable mystery, they shall learn in their own experience who he is.

In concluding this chapter on "The Modern Discovery of God," we make only one contention that each of these men, though poles apart in all but this one thing, discovered God, and that this discovery was the distinctive and formative element in his life. Tolstoy was the greatest genius, though in character the most unlovely of them all. His discovery of God in his initial religious experience was the redeeming feature of his life, though he never carried it to its completion and though his life was always marred by his legalistic and egocentric philosophy. He began to study and to follow Jesus who calls men to the true God-centered life; but he never abandoned his self-centered existence.

President Harper was spiritually only a minor prophet but the application of science to religion is such a necessity for educated men today that we believe he has a place among our witnesses. One has only to read of Isaac Newton, for instance, with his almost medieval religious ideas, to realize the importance of historical criticism in our own discovery of God. Science does not discover God, nor enable a man to lead a whole life, nor enter the Kingdom of God as a little child. But though its sphere is limited, science is a revelation of God and no man dare despise it who would see life steadily or hope to be guided toward all truth, infinite and exhaustless though it may be.

Booker Washington may at first sight have seemed a strange intrusion in this chapter; but if he represents the forgotten man, an excluded, segregated economically enslaved race, he may be used of God as a Moses, not only to lead his own people out of bondage, but to deliver a message to the blind and proud master race which enslaves them. Almost anyone will profess his willingness to love the Negro at a distance, so long as he "keeps his place." But are we prepared to love him as man, as brother, created spiritually free and equal? Are we prepared to give him God's place?

We may think what we like of Reinhold Niebuhr, but what shall we do with his message of social justice, suffering from the sickness of our acquisitive society? Do we recognize the besetting sin of our age and economic order? It is to be feared that there are those who, all unconsciously, do not want to understand Niebuhr's message. Just as there are those who do not want to discover God, unless he "keep his place" in the distant heavens, without interfering with men's self-centered lives or knocking at the door of each individual heart.

We may or may not understand or like the inclusion of Gandhi also in this chapter. But has this nonviolent apostle of peace and freedom no message for our imperialistic warring world and for our proud Anglo-Saxon race? We may or may not understand or appreciate Albert Schweitzer and his ministry of healing in Africa. But as we also face the unsolved problem of evil has this symbolic "Suffering Servant" of humanity no message for most of us who know so little of vicarious sacrifice in our own experience?

We could hardly have chosen six men who differed more widely than those we have studied in this chapter, but can we deny that each in his own way had discovered God, and that each, whether by way of warning or example, may have some possible significance for us in our own growing discovery of God?

CHAPTER X

OUR DISCOVERY OF GOD

WE MUST now bring our study to a close, endeavoring to gather up from many lines of thought some of the principal lessons from the more than thirty lives of representative men whom we have studied. In the first chapter we found from the analogy of human relations that a personal friendship is not made possible by a rational demonstration of the existence and character of the friend, but only by the co-ordinate activities of self-revelation and answering trust, or of self-communication and discovery. If there is a God, adequate to the whole universe and to humanity's need, he must have revealed himself, whether in nature or in history, in the prophets or in Christ, if we are to discover him in experience.

Reminding ourselves again of Luther's word, "God is in heaven and thou upon earth," we must not scorn the dim or broken light that we have, for it is quite enough to show the way for practical living. We found in the first chapter that though the refracted divine revelation is only perceived "little by little," and ever imperfectly, there is gradually built up within the man who discovers this self-revealing God a central core of experience which becomes a touchstone to test further truth or, to change the figure, a frame of reference by which to try all alleged revelation. Once we are convinced of the character of God as righteous love, nothing that contradicts that central moral certainty can be considered revelation. All immorality, all superstition, all unworthy conceptions of God must be progressively eliminated from a pure ethical monotheism.

We must frankly recognize that our readers are of two classes, those who move in the sphere of what has been traditionally called natural religion, and those who accept what is termed revealed religion. The first place chief emphasis upon reason, the second upon faith. Natural theology is the scientific study of religion. The believer in natural religion thinks that a rational analysis of life will help him to arrive at the meaning of life.

243

The believer in revealed religion is convinced that beyond the utmost reach of human reason the great mysteries and antinomies of life remain forever unsolved. He holds that God is not and cannot be adequately revealed in nature and history, but that, while the divine is revealed in a measure in all life and in all religions, there is a special self-disclosure of God through the prophets, culminating in Jesus Christ, who is the fundamental and final disclosure of the divine nature. He believes that in him alone the final enigma and antinomy of life between justice and love, between "wrath" and mercy, is solved.

We repudiate any distinction of spheres as belonging to natural or revealed religion; e.g. the sphere of the first was traditionally supposed to be Kant's God, freedom and immortality, and that of the second such truths as the incarnation, the atonement and the Trinity. The distinction is not in the subject matter of the two but in the method followed, whether it be reason or faith. There is thus a correlation between natural religion and reason and between divine revelation and faith. One discovers God progressively revealed in nature and history; the other apprehends revelation by faith. The believer in natural religion may hold that nature and history are an adequate revelation of God, but the believer in revealed religion thinks that nature and history require revelation to complete them.

The writer frankly and unequivocally takes the position of revealed religion. He goes the whole way with modern science; he gladly accepts the method of historical criticism. As he sees all light that reaches man's cloudy earth refracted and colored in his prisms and lenses, so he sees all humanity, all revelation in the Bible and even the human life of Jesus subject to historical relativism, e.g. as in the apparent expectation of Jesus of his early return. Yet nonetheless, he sees in Jesus Christ the fundamental and final revelation of God, so incarnate in humanity that we can expect no revelation that can ever invalidate him. Once Christ is apprehended we have the full, essential inner core of revelation, the final moral certainty of ethical monotheism. We then have the clue to the meaning of nature and history. We could agree with Victor Hugo in *Les Misérables* that at Waterloo a whole European system crumbled away. Napoleon could not win the Battle of Waterloo, not because of

Wellington or Blücher, but because of God. Napoleon had been denounced in the infinite, as doubtless another has been in our own day. His fall had become morally necessary. "He embarrassed God."

So in Christ we have a philosophy of history. We fear no chaos, no world war, no downfall of an economic or political order. All creation is redeemed. The divinely ordained end is certain. Beyond all human error, sin, tragedy and betrayal, we hold a sure and certain hope. We have received a Kingdom that cannot be shaken. At this point the writer is in full agreement with Paul, Augustine and Luther; and with the moderns, Reinhold Niebuhr and William Temple.[1] We believe in the full Personality of the ultimate Reality which we call God. This personal God can be adequately revealed only in and through persons, though this revelation is refracted or distorted by essential defects in these persons.

There is a vain quest for certainty and a natural craving for authority by fallible man. Every fundamentalist would agree with Pope Leo XIII when he states that we have this in the Scriptures: "All the books . . . are written wholly and entirely . . . at the dictation of the Holy Ghost . . . It is impossible that God Himself, the supreme Truth, can utter that which is not true."[2] The Roman Catholic is driven by logic to the further belief in an infallible church and in an infallible spokesman to interpret this faith once for all delivered.

We admit that all human belief rests at first on authority. Before we can verify it we must believe our parents that six times six equals thirty-six. We must accept from them loyalty to truth, abhorrence of falsehood, parental obedience and belief in God. Later we must authenticate all these in experience when we have time to work out and verify or amend them. As the result of that process the writer finds no infallible authority in the church or in the Bible. All have erred and the Bible is quite human in its many mistakes. God empowers men to do his will

[1] Our debt to William Temple's *Nature, Man and God*, pp. 3-27, 301-325, is evident and acknowledged, and in the section that follows on Christ as the keystone of the arch of history, we are indebted to his *Mens Creatrix*, pp. 93-128, 255-260.

[2] *Dictante Spiritu Sancto.*

through the enlightenment of their natural faculties and affections. All existence is a medium of divine revelation.

This revelation was manifested primarily in historic events and in the illumination of the minds of the prophets to interpret them. God does not reveal abstract truth in oracles. He reveals himself. He reveals himself in persons and finally in a Person. Therefore the writer believes in no creed, no dogmas, no book and no church as infallible. He believes only in the self-revealing God, uttering himself in his Word as Creator and providential ruler, finally incarnate in history, and even entering the sinful individual heart by the Spirit, God's immanent presence in man. He knows nothing of the Trinity as a dogma if it professes to know the inner being of God; he only desires humbly to realize this threefold experience of the one God in human life, as Father, Son and Holy Spirit.

In accepting the spheres both of science and religion, we recognize a wholesome tension between the scientific and the religious habit of mind. Like Schweitzer, we do not profess to be able to solve the problem of evil, but we believe that God accepts the occurrence of evil as a consequence of the principle of the creation of free and responsible men. Man has no freedom as over against God, but can find complete human freedom in glad submission to God. The presence of evil can even enhance the excellence of what on the whole is good; e.g. the crucifixion of Christ seemingly supremely bad if taken in isolation, becomes supremely good if taken as the pivotal center of the whole scheme of things. We cannot explain evil away but we can fight it away; we can overcome it by good as we enter into God's plan of vicarious redemption for man. We can believe in a good God and an ultimately good Kingdom of God only because God is overcoming and reducing evil, just as, in principle as far as in him lies, Albert Schweitzer is doing this in tropical Africa. "The existence of God is fully credible only if evil is being transmuted into good." That cannot be fully realized unless God the Supreme Good finally becomes the apparent good to every man: i.e. until every man discovers God. We take the present world, not as a sphere for immediate happiness in the best of all possible worlds, but as a sphere for character building, a sphere of moral discipline and freedom where man's supreme need and his only satisfaction and completion are found in his discovery of God.

We found that progress in our discovery of the divine through the prophets led us at last to the full and final revelation of God in Christ. Neither in the preparatory prophets nor in their consummation in Jesus of Nazareth are we disturbed by the human imperfection of the record, nor by the historic relativity and limitation of every life we study, for some of us see the light ever shining and the invisible God himself revealed in the "image" or "portrait" of his truly human Son. Without Christ a final keystone is lacking in our converging human experience. Whatever our approach to truth—in science, art, morality, philosophy, or religion—we rise toward some hoped-for goal, or end, or summit; some final principle which we seek to unify all life and give it ultimate meaning and value.[3]

To ultimate questions of why, whence, whither, confessedly the sciences can give no answer. Science cannot create, finally explain, nor satisfy the deepest hungers of humanity. Science can harness power from the cataract or the lightning, it can build or destroy a material civilization. It can flash its messages round the world—yet it has no message today for a frustrated humanity. It cannot create culture, or brotherhood, or human happiness, or final hope. Human reason can show that the world is coherent, that it forms a single system, but it fails to find the actual principle of unity which holds the world together and which makes it a cosmos instead of a chaos. The crown of the edifice of science and reason, if there be such, would be in a loving, omnipotent Will. But science never finds God in its test tubes, nor within the range of its microscope or telescope, nor in the conscious or subconscious of psychology. It rears a mighty palace of truth but finds no keystone for its completing arch. It begins to build its vaulting tower to heaven, but it still stands incomplete, a conflicting Babel.

Similarly the goal of art is not reached. Science disturbs, art seeks repose. We enjoy a picture, a poem, a cathedral, a symphony, but it does not prompt us to any action, or policy, or reform. The aesthetic emotions and the loftiest feelings of love and devotion are recalcitrant to any logical or philosophical treatment. They yield a mystical experience that seeks at the summit the immediate apprehension of an absolutely satisfying object in "the moment eternal." But the moment does not last. . . . Art, like science, confessedly falls short of the goal of

[3] We add here a portion of several paragraphs from *Maker of Men*, pp. 130-136.

life and even of its own goal. It points toward an ideal experience of the contemplating soul of some image truly adequate as an expression of the whole world's ruling principle. It seeks the absolute and ultimate in Beauty, but it does not of itself give us God, or life, or lasting satisfaction. The keystone of its lofty arch of beauty and promise is still lacking.

Similarly the goal of ethics is not reached. The troubled conscience stands in awe before the starry heavens above and the moral law within. Ethics shows that the highest moral good for man consists in a perfectly integrated character and in a life of love and fellowship with one's fellow men. Ethics tells man what to do but leaves him impotent. Agonizing after good works or moral perfection only drives one toward shipwreck upon the supernatural. Duty-doing never by the utmost of human capacity reaches the possession of God. The warring world today is the consummation of man's selfishness, sin, and moral impotence. Ethics suggests a Will which is perfectly self-determined, and yet is active altogether in love, and such a Will, if it controls the universe, is the very principle of unity sought by science, art, and morality; for only if there be such a Will is the universe fully rational, yielding ultimate Truth, Beauty, and Goodness. But ethics, everywhere under the aegis of relativity, can only fitfully disturb man's conscience. It cannot empower him. Its mounting arches have found no keystone of completion.

So philosophy of itself can only show at most that God must exist if the world is completely reasonable, and that he is the ground of the possibility of all certainty. But of itself it can never give certainty in anything, nor refute ultimate skepticism. It reaches noble heights in Socrates, but in the end "it knows that it knows nothing." Philosophy of itself finds no goal nor satisfying end, some twenty-five centuries after its beginning. Therefore science, art, morals, and philosophy seem to require for their own completion, and for their unity with one another, the existence of an adequate God which none of them can prove or reveal.

All the great religions also reach out toward the belief in a single ruling power, toward a God both of righteousness and love, transcendent and immanent, creator and redeemer, unseen yet incarnate, a plenary God, adequate to the whole universe, to humanity's suffering and hope, and to each man's need. But is this goal ever fully reached save in the God and Father of our Lord Jesus Christ? Socrates and Buddha tell men to look to themselves, but in the end each awakened man cries: "O wretched man that I am, who shall deliver me?" Jesus does not mock men by telling them to save themselves. He calls them to follow him that he may make them like himself. He is himself the Way to the

Father's heart and the Father's home for every wandering prodigal or lonely soul. As Augustine found, the human soul can only find rest and completion in a God of absolute power and of absolute love. All these mounting arches of science, art, ethics, philosophy, and the ethnic religions rise in converging lines of hope, but each by itself is incomplete. Of themselves they never reach their meeting point. There is always lacking a completing keystone as the crown and summit.

Is this completion not found in "the stone which the builders rejected"? . . . Is he not both cornerstone and keystone, both alpha and omega? To man's self-sufficient reason, to his proud science and its glittering achievements, to his skillful arts, to his Stoic morality and pharisaic self-righteousness, to his proud philosophy, to his most costly treasures in his personal, tribal, and national faiths, which one and all fall short of completion and lasting satisfaction, is not Christ himself the possible answer—the only possible answer? To whom else shall we go?

We may start as did the first four disciples in Galilee, who were asked nothing about themselves—no tests, no profession, no promises, no creed. A multitude across the centuries, a great throng that no man can number, have through Christ discovered God. We see not yet all things in this sorry world subject to him—but we see Jesus crowned with glory and honor. The logic of life, the lesson of the years, the quest of the centuries, the search of science, art, morality, philosophy and religion, all look toward one final keystone and completion of our groping thought and broken lives. Without this completion, life falls in chaos.

Thus Christ becomes the inevitable touchstone and keystone of religion. Natural religion leads inevitably to him as a mystery, while revealed religion finds in him the ultimate solution of our problems. You cannot understand nature without man. You cannot understand man without God. You cannot fully comprehend God without Christ. You cannot find the meaning of Christ without the cross. "You cannot understand Christianity without seeing man controlling nature and worshipping and obeying the God whom he meets in Jesus Christ as love on the cross and judgment on the throne. Christianity involved the great divide as well as the great invitation. You can only understand the love upon the cross as you see it in the light of the judgment on the throne. You can only understand the judgment on the throne as you see it in the light of the love upon the cross."

You must not only see life steadily but you must see Christianity steadily and make it *whole*; its rigorism and its theistic humanism, its whole gospel individual and social, for the making of a new man and a new society, its human discovery and its divine revelation.

Though ourselves grounded in the divine revelation and human discovery of ethical monotheism, we can understand the view of the nontheistic humanist who clings to his "religion without revelation," and craves the threadbare aesthetic comfort of a religion without God. But we do not envy this humanist. At times he may be as lonely as was Paul Elmer More before he believed in the incarnation. The humanist looks on all men as his brothers but they have no father. He sees one human family but it is an orphaned world, for the brothers cannot say "Our Father." There is no divine creation, revelation, redemption or destiny for man.

The frankly atheistic Communist regards all religion, that of the theist and the humanist alike, as "the opium of the people." Stalin persecuted Christian believers as truly as did Nero or Domitian. Marx would defend the tolerance of his dialectic philosophy and Stalin his broad constitution providing for the four freedoms—on paper. But he puts us to shame in his insistence upon economic justice though he knows little of liberty.

If "the gentle reader" can forgive a seemingly harsh statement, Marx, Lenin and Stalin all felt essentially the same burning social message that Amos proclaimed in his demand for social justice. As fiercely as Amos denounced the robbery of the poor in Samaria, they condemned the impersonal wholesale robbery of the poor by our heartless economic system today, with its resulting slums, and periodic unemployment. They flamed in burning moral indignation at the all too large proportion of a people impoverished in body, mind and spirit, whether in prerevolutionary Russia or France or in "God's own country," America. What a world we live in! How passing strange that these "atheists" felt apparently as deeply as did Amos the blasphemous sin of the robbery of the poor, at a time when orthodox Christians, whether in Czarist Russia or plutocratic America, were the chief supporters of an economic order of special privilege for the rich and terrible privation for the poor, whether the poor were Russian workers or American Negroes or southern share-croppers.

What a spectacle for men and for angels! Here are "wicked atheists," whatever their misguided methods of cruelty, passionately concerned for the poor and for all races alike. And here are "good Christians" hating a President and his New Deal because he tried to recover at least a fraction of the rights of social justice for the ill-fed, ill-clad, ill-housed and for the Negro, that Amos demanded long ago. And who is my neighbor, who is my brother in this mixed world of moral contradictions? Is it the Christian, the atheist, the humanist; the rich, the poor, the white, the Negro? Whoever will do the will of God, whoever will do to the least of these, Christ's brethren—hungry, thirsty, stranger, naked, sick, and in prison—what Jesus himself did, he is my brother.

This is what the Dean of Canterbury has been trying to say. In Canterbury Cathedral and Westminster Abbey, he calmly declared that in this war for humanity, Soviet Russia is strong militarily because she is strong morally. He believes that she is strong morally because she has recognized racial brotherhood and has collectivized or socialized all the means of production on which man's livelihood depends in order to achieve what we call justice, and to end forever the blasphemous poverty, slums and periodic unemployment which characterize the Anglo-Saxon Christian nations. These nations of course always shun the word capitalism and euphemistically define their economy as one of free enterprise, rugged individualism, or the American plan.

It is said that, together with Fifth Columnists and appeasers, "two hundred rich families betrayed France." The Dean of Canterbury believes that, so far as their betrayal of their country was concerned, it is irrelevant whether these betrayers were devout Catholics, Protestants, humanists or atheists; irrelevant whether the crucifiers of Christ were deeply religious Pharisees, a cynical agnostic Pilate, or a shouting mob of common people; irrelevant whether rich Tories in England and monopolistic millionaires in America who would rather preserve their special privileges than save their country or humanity, are orthodox Christians, humanists or atheists. He believes that selfish isolationism for any individual or class or nation is doomed. The dean does not for one moment say that vital religion does not matter; for dynamic religion which is both individual and social makes all the difference in the world as it did for Jeremiah or for Jesus. But God's salvation is not intended for the selfish individual soul for a future heaven of bliss but for the saving of society in the love of God and man.

OUR CONCLUSIONS

THE adventurers and discoverers studied in this volume were men of like passions with us, who knew doubt and sorrow and heartbreak; men who had sinned and suffered and failed. But they were men who won through to victory, each in his own way. Spanning nearly thirty centuries of history, from all continents and intellectual climates, from Asia, Europe, Africa and America, men of ancient and modern times, Christians and non-Christians, rationalists and mystics, saints and scientists, prophets and poets—no two were alike, yet all were one in a common discovery. Each had found God, and each reinforced our thesis that man discovers God. Each found something; no one discovered all. Truth was incarnated in some degree in what each man was, in what he did, in what he said.

Let us think again of these men. There was the "divine Plato," who amazed us both in what he found of God and in what he failed to find; Philo of Alexandria, Plotinus, and the modern Platonists and humanists. There were the rugged prophets of Israel: Amos, Hosea, Micah, Jeremiah, and the great Unknown of the Exile; there were the great discoverers of the New Testament who have become household words and intimates of unnumbered millions: Matthew, Mark, Luke, John—and Paul, born out of due time, yet who turned the world upside down. We recall St. Augustine and his lofty synthesis of Hebraic and Hellenic thought and life; the great saints among the mystics who are the permanent possession and glory of our failing humanity: the gentle Francis, and the humble, anonymous Imitator of Christ, the beloved Brother Lawrence in his kitchen, and Pascal with his scintillating thoughts, George Fox broken in prison but with his inner light undimmed. These mystics were typical of a nameless multitude in the forests and ashramas of India, past and present, in a thousand monasteries, medieval and modern, and in practical service in distant mission fields in Asia, Africa and the islands of the sea, Catholic, Protestant, and non-Christian, whose Socratic prayer was answered, "Make us beautiful within."

In our spiritual heritage we claim alike the pagan philosophers and Jewish prophets, the Catholic saints and Protestant reformers: Martin Luther, titanic alike in his faults and failings, in his fearless courage and his spiritual genius; John Bunyan, our beloved fellow traveler in our own halting Pilgrim's Progress in life's journey; John Wesley with his spiritual sanity as he helped to change the moral tone of English society; and Jonathan Edwards, our American saint, philosopher and evangelist, last and greatest of the Puritans.

We recall as part of our own enriched spiritual heritage the scientists' discovery of God: the great Newton, mathematical genius; the devout Pasteur, servant of humanity; the simple believer Michael Pupin; and our contemporary, Arthur Compton, Nobel physicist and fearless Christian layman—each in his way a fallible saint, each bearing his courageous spiritual witness in a scientific and skeptical age. We claim that man discovers God in this age of sophisticated modernism as well as in ancient ages of faith. If Tolstoy's bondage to literalism left him frustrated in philosophic anarchy, he is nevertheless a warning to us and at least he made a real beginning in his discovery of God. To William Rainey Harper many of us look with loyal affection as to a modern minor prophet whose priceless liberating scientific method of historical criticism helped to strike from our age the heavy shackles of superstition, and forever dispelled from some of us unworthy views of a Moloch-like bloodthirsty God of cruelty.

We recalled the life of Booker Washington who discovered God for himself and for his people. We selected him in order to stimulate our belief in the brotherhood of man and also to remove a serious hindrance to our own further discovery of God in our almost totalitarian practice in America of a master race and a segregated, despoiled and economically enslaved race. We turned then to Reinhold Niebuhr, a modern representative of the gospel of sin and grace, misunderstood as a prophet in his own country and age as were his predecessors. It is our hope that he may help us to recover the message of Amos: "Woe unto them who are at ease in Zion, and self-confident, who oppress the weak, who crush the needy. But let justice roll down like waters and righteousness like a perennial stream." And the more terrible message of Jesus "Blessed are ye poor . . . but woe unto you that are rich. You tithe mint and anise and cummin and omit the weightier matters of justice and mercy and faithfulness."

We studied next the life of Gandhi as a strange anachronism, a son of Gautama Buddha, a gentle St. Francis and, however non-violent, a rational revolutionist like Thomas Jefferson—all three in one. We rejoiced to find such Christlikeness so far from the orthodox ecclesiastical fold in this man typical of a great multitude of non-Christians who have discovered God and who put many of the orthodox to shame. Finally we observed Albert Schweitzer, theologian, musician, thinker and sacrificial servant, a Christlike humble physician in the forests of darkest Africa. French-German, rational mystic, philosopher saint, he remains to us something of an enigma.

Save the most bigoted fundamentalist, can anyone deny that these adventurers all discovered God, and that each·in his own way bears witness to man's discovery of God? Do not these men bear cumulative testimony to a religious reality which encounters man and is reflected in their experience? Do they not show the typical and normal response of human nature to this objective spiritual stimulus? Is there any adequate way of accounting for these men—and a vast multitude like them—in their character, their teaching and their service to humanity, save by the reality of God?

If we recall the evidence of the discovery of God gathered from the characters in this book some of us may be able to draw a few general conclusions from this study. These witnesses are all the more valuable because of the wide variation in their theological and philosophical backgrounds, in their widely separated centuries, and in their differing characters and training. There were, nevertheless, certain experiences and characteristics that nearly all had in common. However they varied in expression, every one recognized that he was a sinner, that he was utterly unworthy, that he was guilty before God, and that he was completely unable adequately to change, or save, or satisfy himself. Every one without exception, however, came to believe in God as his only hope. Each earnestly sought God, hungered and thirsted for righteousness and could have said in the universal spiritual language of the Psalmist: "As the hart panteth after the water brooks, so panteth my soul after thee, O God. My soul thirsteth for God, for the living God."

In their discovery of God, most of them experienced a spiritual awakening, or period of moral crisis, or conversion. Whether this was sudden or gradual, almost every one entered the straight and narrow gate to the new life by the dual process of what is usually called repentance and faith. Not that these men were orthodox or conventional, for as discoverers and pathfinders most of them were not so, and we have no desire to force them into a standard pattern of experience. Nevertheless, whether consciously or unconsciously, and whether in these terms or not, most of them had some negative experience corresponding to the repudiation of the old sinful self and its cardinal vices of pride, unbelief, lust, and selfishness. These four cardinal sins or their equivalent—several or all of them—were found in our adventurers and are in every normal man.

Conviction was normally followed by repentance and repentance by faith, for faith alone could apprehend and appropriate the grace of God. We can trace this normal process from the earliest prophets to the last repentant sinner amid all the varieties of religious experience. Whether it was a Protestant instantaneous conversion, or the long, arduous ascent of the mystic's ladder through the three stages often called the Purgative, Illuminative and Unitive way, nearly all normal men who find God pass through the negative and positive aspects of repentance and faith.

All of our adventurers should also help us to draw one more conclusion, that, however they differed, all of these men when they came to know God as Father sought to become more worthy sons; they utilized certain "means of grace," fulfilled certain conditions of growth, that they might be conformed to the type of character they sought. Whether Plato, in the hoped-for final realization of the vision of the Ideas of his abstract values and patterns, or Paul and Wesley who believed they would be finally conformed to the likeness of Christ, *all paid the price of certain conditions of growth.*

The fivefold means used by the Christians, at least, were: 1. The study of the truth which most of them believed they found in the Word of God, whatever they conceived this to be. 2. They matriculated and became serious students in the school of prayer, arduous and joyous. 3. Without exception all devoted themselves to strenuous service for their fellow men, most of them following their Master as he went about doing good. 4. Most of them found necessary the means of grace in the church and its sacraments, or in the group of the beloved community, from Plato in his Orphism, Philo in his Mystery, St. Paul and St. Francis in the Church Catholic conceived ideally as the body of Christ, and even George Fox in his sacrament of silence, in the inner light and group mysticism of the Friends. 5. All who followed to the end learned a final lesson in suffering and the daily discipline of life, which most of them found complete only in the experience of the Suffering Servant, or in the cross of Christ. Each had to learn in his own experience what Jesus meant when he said: "If anyone wishes to follow me, let him deny himself, take up his cross, and so follow me. Whosoever loseth his life for my sake will save it." This principle of sacrifice is evident in the Hindu Gandhi with his years of rigorous discipline, his hours of prayer, his weekly day of silence, his periods of fasting and his resulting radiant character. It is equally clear in the Christian Albert Schweitzer in the jungles of Free French Africa.

We are impressed not so much by the wide variety in expression and theology of our adventurers as by the remarkable unanimity and almost identity of experience in a few essential points: sin and grace; repentance and faith; conversion and progress; the means of growth in the equivalent of the Word of God as the food of truth, prayer as the believer's vital breath, sacrificial service, the beloved community and its rites, or sacraments, or prophetic preaching, and finally the discipline of suffering. The road may be rough, there may be many or few who find it early, but the way opened up by these pathfinders lies clear before any who wish to follow it.

To realize what this way means for us we must recall our adventurers again. Plato and Plotinus presumably found as much of God by the method of natural religion, i.e. by human reason and by mystic or intuitive experience, as it is possible for man alone to find. If we follow this method, we may expect at best the same results, though we are neither as wise nor as good as was Plato. The prophets of Israel found the assurance, the dynamic and comfort of a God of righteousness and love, a God of nature and history, but with the problems of evil and of human suffering left unsolved. As recorded in the New Testament the early Christian, articulate first in the Apostle Paul, found the solution and the end of man's long search and of human discovery in the God and Father of Jesus Christ. If Jesus was the revelation of God's nature of holy love, and if in the life and death of Jesus we see not a human catastrophe but a divine act and self-manifestation, then man's last problem is solved.

Once for all in Christ man discovers the self-revealing God. And how does he find this experience? He finds it just as our Christian adventurers did. He begins like the first four disciples by the lakeside in Galilee to follow this still partly unknown mysterious man who bids men "Come and follow me." They make a progressive or increasing discovery in their halting experience until they are ready for Christ's final challenge:

My son give me thy heart. Surrender thy life to the self-manifesting God who is thy Creator, thy crucified Redeemer, thy Helper, the Spirit of God longing to possess thee and mold thee into his image. For thou wert created in the image of God. Perhaps thou didst not know or care that thou hadst a heavenly Father or that thou art thyself a prodigal, either feeding on fleshly husks or still farther estranged by pharisaic pride. Still, whoever thou art, and wherever thou art, give me thy heart.

Spiritually there are two kinds of men: those who are living the self-centered and those who are seeking to live the God-centered life. The element of perversion or estrangement from God in any life is due to self-centeredness. Life can never be fully integrated or satisfied about the self as a center. It can only be fully meaningful or complete when it becomes God-centered. For God is the real center of the real world as truly as the sun is the center of our solar system. A false Ptolemaic theory does not make the earth the center, and a self-centered existence does not and cannot realize the ends of life. Not only in the time of Augustine, but eternally, "Thou hast made us for thyself and the soul is restless until it finds rest in thee." That is another way of saying, "Man cannot be saved, nor either individual or society attain to completion, except by the total elimination of self-centeredness."

It is not selfhood but self-centeredness that is evil. It may take the form of selfishness, pride, or lust, but this is the essence of sin. Just as Augustine had to turn from his lust and pride and self-centeredness to God, so must we. Just as Paul, or Luther, or Wesley, or Schweitzer turned from the sinful self to God when they discovered he was manifest in Christ, so must we. It was wholly irrelevant whether one was a Pharisee or a publican, of the type of the elder or the younger brother in the parable of the prodigal son, each had to cry "Father I have sinned"; each had to return to the Father's heart and home. While that heart is open for all men of all religions and of no religion, there is One who can say "I am the Way and the Truth and the Life." And there is no other way but God's way; Gandhi as well as Schweitzer has found it.

One may agonize long and kick against the pricks as did Saul of Tarsus, one may labor in gloom for years as did John Bunyan, one may fail for more than a decade to enter as a little child as did Luther or Wesley; or one may wait until the eventide of life humbly to bow and enter the straight and narrow way like the Princeton Platonist, Paul Elmer More. Or one may pass through the portal which men miscall death and enter the great Beyond without ever having repented or believed, without having entered the experience of sonship or the way of life. But whither shall one flee from God's presence? Though I take the wings of the morning and dwell in the uttermost part of the earth or sea even there shall God follow and find me. Though I ascend into heaven I shall find that God is there; though I make my bed in hell—"Thou art there"; for however long or short it may be, self-centeredness is hell, and hell is simply the absence of God. As Milton's Satan confesses "myself am hell." How long does it last? Whether it be a moment or a millennium it lasts just as long as self is life's center, whether man counts himself "good" or bad. And here is the eternal, the amazing good news—life offered as a gift to simple faith. Early or late the day will come when each will find that under heaven, or in heaven itself, there is no other way but God's way.

Now the chief point in all that we are saying, and in all the costly experience that our adventurers have undergone during the centuries, is this: that we have such an One and such a way. If we have offered any evidence in this volume where we have tried to trace the long pilgrimage of these adventurers and discoverers across the years, the object has been that each should be induced to enter upon this way; that each may become himself an adventurer in the endless discovery of God; that each may realize that *now* is the accepted time, for it is the only time of which we are sure; and finally that each may know in his own experience the eternal truth that man discovers God.

Those who have really discovered God do not ask for more light, or higher spiritual truth than we find in Jesus. This is man's moral and spiritual summit in the God and Father of our Lord Jesus Christ. Nineteen centuries have added nothing to this summit where man discovers God, and nineteen millenniums cannot negate it nor detract from it. We are never satisfied with ourselves, nor with our past discovery or attainment. Man's science, art, morality, philosophy, religion, and his books sacred and secular are all imperfect and incomplete. Every one of our adventurers and pathfinders was consciously so; but no one of them lived his life in vain. Each had discovered something of God and if God be infinite and the spiritual universe is, as we believe, as vast and various as is the material universe, doubtless each has won the glory of going on and still to be, in the great Beyond.

If we have offered any evidence that man discovers God, the object has been to induce *each to become himself an adventurer in the increasing discovery of God*. All of our pathfinders join in testifying to one supreme experience. All join the great cloud of witnesses—Plato, Philo of Alexandria, Plotinus and the Neoplatonists; Amos, Hosea, Micah, Jeremiah, the Prophet of the Exile; Matthew, Mark, Luke, John and Paul; St. Augustine, Francis of Assisi and the Imitator of Christ, Brother Lawrence, Pascal and George Fox; Martin Luther, John Bunyan, John Wesley and Jonathan Edwards; Sir Isaac Newton, Louis Pasteur,

Michael Pupin and Arthur Compton; Count Tolstoy, William Rainey Harper, Booker Washington, Reinhold Niebuhr, Mohandas Gandhi and Albert Schweitzer—all join the great cloud of witnesses, from the Church Militant and the Church Triumphant, with those from the East and from the West who enter the Kingdom of God, testifying with one voice: man discovers God—"men who by faith conquered kingdoms, administered justice, obtained promises, escaped the edge of the sword, from weakness won to strength. They all won their record for faith. . . . Therefore, with all this host of witnesses encircling us, we must strip off every handicap, strip off sin with its clinging folds, to run our appointed course steadily, our eyes fixed upon Jesus as the pioneer and the perfection of faith—upon Jesus who, in order to reach his own appointed joy, steadily endured the cross, thinking nothing of its shame, and is now *seated at the right hand of the throne of God.*"

INDEX

Absolute, 11, 21, 31, 191
Aesop's Fables, 199
Africa, 83, 235
Agnosticism, 23
Alexandrian Jews, 24, 25
Allegory, 27, 28
Alternation, 3
Ambrose, 74, 82
American Revolution, 151, 197
Amos, xi, 11, 37, 38-41
Anabaptist movement, 138
Andrews, C. F., 221, 224
Angelico, Fra, 94
Anthropomorphism, 25, 59
Aquinas, Thomas, 63, 161
Arianism, 151
Aristotle, 8, 15, 28, 34, 38, 57, 67, 75, 161
Arminianism, 106, 150, 156
Armstrong, General S. C., 203
Arnold, Matthew, 29
Arnold of Rugby, 194
Asbury, Francis, 143
Assyria, 36, 37, 42, 43
Athanasian Creed, 65
Atlanta Exposition, 204
Augustine, St., 4, 23, 63, 72-84, 94

Baalim, 36, 42
Babylon, 49, 50, 51
Bach, J. S., 8, 236, 238
Bacon, Roger, 88, 163
Baillie, John, 211
Bainton, Roland, xiv
Baptist, 119, 134, 196
Barth, Karl, 36, 157
Beaufort, M., 100
Bedford, 117, 134
Beecher, Henry Ward, 173
Benedictine abbeys, 87
Bennett, John, 213
Bernard, 85, 92, 94
Bernardo, 88

Bethel, 39, 40, 42
Bethlehem, 44
Bible, 12, 40, 95, 148, 193, 196
Bibliolatry, 56
Binitarian view of God, 69
Boehme, Jacob, 86, 164
Book of Martyrs, 139
Boston Common, 154
Brahe, Tycho, 163
Breasted, Thomas, 181
Briggs, Professor, 193
Bristol, 148
Browning, Robert, 1, 29
Buck, Pearl, 208, 209
Buddha, 67, 187, 223, 230
Buddhism, 17, 187
Bullock, Governor, 204
Bunyan, John, 116, 117, 134-141
Burnet, Bishop, 164

Caligula, 24
Calvin, John, 13, 63, 69, 105, 126, 138
Calvinism, 1, 125, 150, 157
Cambridge Platonists, 29, 85
Canterbury, Archbishop of, 187, 227
Canterbury, Dean of, 251
Canticle of the Sun, 90, 91
Cardinal virtues, 30, 60
Carlyle, Thomas, 29, 117
Carmelite Order, 101
Carnegie, Andrew, 204
Carthage, 73, 81
Carver, George W., 206
Channing, William Ellery, 157
Charles the Second, 134
Chatauqua College of Liberal Arts, 194
Chateaubriand, 105
Chicago, 194, 198
Christianity, 44, 51, 196, 208
Church, 12, 13
Cicero, 73, 82, 105
City of God, 24, 72